Catastrophe & Cultu

**Publication of the Advanced Seminar Series
is made possible by generous support from
The Brown Foundation, Inc., of Houston, Texas.**

**School of American Research
Advanced Seminar Series**

Douglas W. Schwartz
General Editor

Catastrophe & Culture

Contributors

Gregory V. Button, *Independent researcher and consultant*

Christopher L. Dyer
Department of Marine Affairs, University of Rhode Island

Virginia García-Acosta, *Centro de Investigaciones Estudios Superiores en Antropología Social (CIESAS) Mexico, D.F.*

Susanna M. Hoffman, *Independent Researcher*

J. Terrence McCabe, *Department of Anthropology, University of Colorado*

Michael E. Moseley, *Department of Anthropology, University of Florida*

Anthony Oliver-Smith, *Department of Anthropology, University of Florida*

Robert Paine
Department of Anthropology, Memorial University of Newfoundland

S. Ravi Rajan
Department of Environmental Studies, University of California, Santa Cruz

Sharon Stephens
Departments of Anthropology and Social Work, University of Michigan

Catastrophe & Culture

The Anthropology of Disaster

*Edited by Susanna M. Hoffman
and Anthony Oliver-Smith*

School of American Research Press
Santa Fe

School of American Research Press

Post Office Box 2188
Santa Fe, New Mexico 87504-2188
sarpress.sarweb.com

Acting Director: Cynthia Welch
Copy Editor: Jo Ann Baldinger
Series Design: Context, Inc.
Indexer: Jan Wright
Printer: Cushing-Malloy, Inc.

Library of Congress Cataloging-in-Publication Data:
Catastrophe & culture : the anthropology of disaster / edited by Susanna M. Hoffman and
Anthony Oliver-Smith.
    p. cm. — (School of American Research advanced seminar series)
    Includes bibliographical references and index.
    ISBN 1-930618-14-X (alk. paper) — ISBN 1-930618-15-8 (pbk. : alk. paper)
    1. Disasters—Social aspects—Congresses. 2. Disasters—Research—Congresses.
3. Social structure—Congresses. 4. Ethnology—Congresses. I. Title: Catastrophe and culture.
II. Hoffman, Susanna. III. Oliver-Smith, Anthony. IV. Series.

HV553 .C275 2002
363.34—dc21   2001054174

This book was printed on paper that is FSC certified.

Cover illustration: © Corbis, 2001

In memory of Sharon Stephens

Contents

Figures and Tables

Acknowledgments

To be invited to a hostel, fed every meal, and bedded in comfort while enjoying a week of free-reined discussion with colleagues on a topic of mutual interest is a gift of almost indescribable value. We wish to thank the cooks, the cleaners, and every candlestick maker who made our stay at the School of American Research possible so that we could hammer out the heavy subject of disaster. Above all, we wish to express our gratitude to Douglas Schwartz, then president of the School of American Research, who saw the critical pertinence of our subject and the need for a synthesis. Our gratitude goes as well to Duane Anderson for his gracious assistance and tour guidance, Cecile Stein, who coordinated our seminar, and Joan O'Donnell, former director of SAR Press, who directed this volume to publication, with the able aid of the press's acting director and production manager, Cynthia Welch, and copy editor Jo Ann Baldinger. Each and every individual at the School of American Research made the term "enabler" into encomium.

In addition, we want to thank our fellow participants in the seminar for their hefty work, their vital essays, and their salient discussion. We offer our appreciation, too, to the significant others in the life of every participant, who held down the home fronts and kept them from disaster while we sat so nicely coddled. Very sadly, one of our valued colleagues in the project, Sharon Stephens, passed away less than a year after the seminar, and it is to her memory that we dedicate this book. We would like to express our deep sorrow to her family and thank them for allowing us to publish her contribution.

Catastrophe & Culture

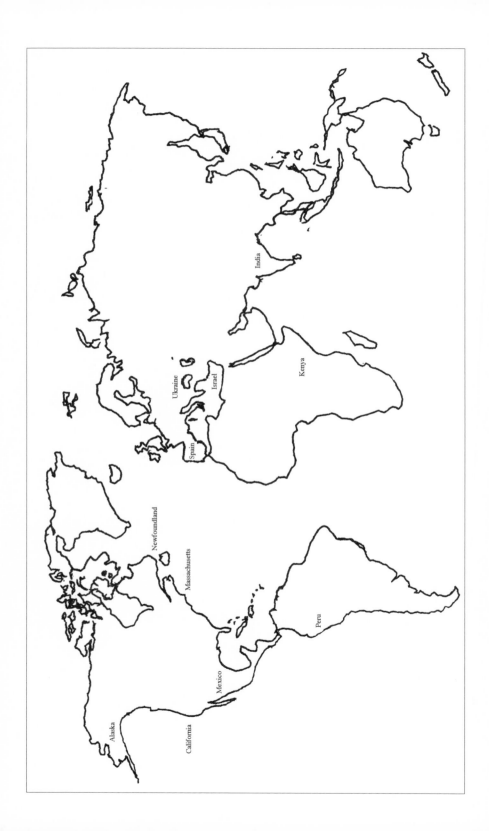

1

Introduction

Why Anthropologists Should Study Disasters

Anthony Oliver-Smith and Susanna M. Hoffman

Disasters do not just happen. In the vast majority of cases, they are not "bolts from the blue" but take place through the conjuncture of two factors: a human population and a potentially destructive agent that is part of a total ecological system, including all natural, modified, and constructed features. Both of these elements are embedded in natural and social systems that unfold as processes over time. As such, they render disasters also as processual phenomena rather than events that are isolated and temporally demarcated in exact time frames.

The conjunction of a human population and a potentially destructive agent does not inevitably produce a disaster. A disaster becomes unavoidable in the context of a historically produced pattern of "vulnerability," evidenced in the location, infrastructure, sociopolitical organization, production and distribution systems, and ideology of a society. A society's pattern of vulnerability is a core element of a disaster. It conditions the behavior of individuals and organizations throughout the full unfolding of a disaster far more profoundly than will the physical force of the destructive agent.

It is only through the pattern of events and processes that emerge in this "conditioned" conjuncture of a community and hazard that what we call a disaster takes place. Although the multidimensionality and multiple subjectivities involved make formally defining disaster highly problematic, for purposes of this introduction, we venture such a step here by stating that a disaster is

> a process/event combining a potentially destructive agent/ force from the natural, modified, or built environment and a population in a socially and economically produced condition of vulnerability, resulting in a perceived disruption of the customary relative satisfactions of individual and social needs for physical survival, social order, and meaning.

Since the definition of disaster cannot be entirely separated from the concomitant matter of hazard, we describe *hazard* as

> the forces, conditions, or technologies that carry a potential for social, infrastructural, or environmental damage. A hazard can be a hurricane, earthquake, or avalanche; it can also be a nuclear facility or a socioeconomic practice, such as using pesticides. The issue of hazard further incorporates the way a society perceives the danger or dangers, either environmental and/or technological, that it faces and the ways it allows the danger to enter its calculation of risk.

Although human beings and groups clearly play major roles in the emergence and evolution of both hazards and disasters, we have excluded those processes that result from human intentionality. Things that humans do deliberately with a knowledge of and expectation of an effect are not disasters. Thus, the nuclear bombing of Hiroshima and Nagasaki and the destruction and impoverishment that result from large development projects such as the Narmada dam complex in India fall outside our purview here. However, the similarity of outcomes in these examples illustrates the definitional complexities that disasters present.

Anthropologists have studied disasters since their postwar emergence as a research field, but only quite recently have disasters actually become a focus for anthropological research. After World War II, research on human behavior during bombardment evolved into the social scientific study of natural and technological disasters, and anthropologists were among the earliest contributors. Generally these early studies occurred because anthropologists were examining other issues in places that had experienced disasters (Belshaw 1951; Schneider 1957; Firth 1959; Schwimmer 1969). Only one anthropologist, Anthony F. C. Wallace (1956a, 1956b, 1956c, 1957), actually carried out research in which the primary focus was the human structuring of the disaster experience. As the field of disaster research began to expand, anthropological participation remained low, as did understanding of what the study of disasters could add to anthropological inquiry. Despite W. Lloyd Warner's (1947) advice that there was much to be learned about society and culture "when all hell breaks loose," a particularist and functionalist emphasis on the construction of cultural profiles based on the ethnography of "normal, daily" life precluded addressing the issues of disruption and change that disasters represented.

With the reemergence of interest in sociocultural change, multilinear evolution, and cultural ecology in the 1960s, and the interest in political ecology and discourse analysis that arose in the 1980s, the issue of disaster has become increasingly salient to the concerns of anthropologists. Anthropologists are learning that they have an important contribution to make to the study of disasters and that disasters in turn have great expository relevance to the inquiries of their field (Hoffman and Oliver-Smith 1999; Oliver-Smith 1996). Disasters, both natural and technological, are becoming more frequent and more serious as communities become more vulnerable. They are impacting ever-larger numbers of people around the world. The increasing vulnerability of communities, and the consequent intensity of disaster repercussions in regions where anthropologists have traditionally studied, challenge the field to come to grips with the practical problems that disasters present. At the same time the alarming increase of disasters and their aftermaths have clearly demonstrated how much light catastrophes can shed on the content of anthropological purview.

When hazards threaten and disasters occur, they both reveal and become an expression of the complex interactions of physical, biological, and sociocultural systems. Hazards and disasters not only manifest the interconnections of these three factors but also expose their operations in the material and cultural worlds. Disasters present conjunctural opportunities for documenting linkages among such features as intensification of production, population increase, environmental degradation, and diminished adaptability and also provide opportunities to delve into human social realms and cultures. In the face or threat of disruption, as people attempt to prepare, construct, recover, or reconstruct, how they adjust to the actual or potential calamity either recants or reinvents their cultural system. Disaster exposes the way in which people construct or "frame" their peril (including the denial of it), the way they perceive their environment and their subsistence, and the ways they invent explanation, constitute their morality, and project their continuity and promise into the future. Few contexts provide a social science with more opportunity for theoretical synthesis of its various concerns than does the study of disaster provide anthropology. Within disaster research, anthropology finds an opportunity to amalgamate past and current cultural, ecological, and political-economic investigations, along with archaeological, historical, demographic, and certain biological and medical concerns.

The possibility that the study of disasters could lead to reducing the theoretical and methodological gaps that presently separate the ecological, political-economic, and cultural perspectives in anthropology was one major motivation for the advanced seminar that we organized for the School of American Research in October of 1997. As a whole, our group recognized both how particularly anthropology lends itself to the study of hazard and disaster and how crucially calamity lends itself to the exposition of anthropological topics. As events and processes, hazards and disasters are totalizing phenomena, subsuming culture, society, and environment together. Anthropology as a discipline embraces in its substantive platform the physical, biological, and social aspects of human existence. It includes developmental and comparative perspectives. As part of its approach, it poses specifics against larger wholes and examines issues of social change and evolution (Torry 1979b). With the holistic perspective that is the hallmark of the field, anthropology provides a theoretical framework that can encompass the entire scope of disaster causation and impact, including even analysis of the essentially novel conditions that have emerged in human-environment relations in the latter half of the twentieth century. As anthropology entails a comprehensive format shared by no other social science, it can—and well should—take a place at the center of disaster theory, research, and practice.

The critical need for synthesis in our understanding of disasters arises from the fact that human communities and their behaviors are not simply located in environments. The development of a society is also the development of its environment, and the resulting relations emerge from the multiple continual processes of exchange through the porous boundaries between them (Ingold 1992). Yet we are increasingly compromising this linkage. Human interventions have brought about a reduction of functional diversity in human communities along with increased spatial homogeneity, thus compromising our ability to adapt and react (Holling 1994). In the framework of global change, disasters play the role of the canary in the mine for all humankind. A synthesis of disaster knowledge can also contribute significantly to efforts to aid disaster victims and prevent disaster from occurring to at-risk populations. While our purpose in the seminar was explicitly theoretical, it is both appropriate and necessary that this theoretical project be linked to policy and practice.

DISASTER RESEARCH AND ANTHROPOLOGICAL THEORY

So varied are the theoretical issues that can be explored in the context of hazards and disasters, we can only touch on the broad themes here. We frame these issues from the perspective implicit in our definition of disaster, namely that disasters challenge society and represent forces to which the society must adapt along a number of fronts, ecologically, socially, and ideologically. In disasters, every feature of a society and its relations with the total environment may be impacted. Coherence and contradiction, cooperation and conflict, hegemony and resistance, as they are expressed through the operation of physical, biological, and social systems and behavioral practices, become manifest. Due to the numerous issues implicated, the definition of disaster itself remains a complex matter that continually merits further exploration.

At the baseline, adaptation has been one of the central concepts in anthropology since the field's emergence in the nineteenth century first focused on human biological and cultural evolution. In order to survive and to ensure maintenance, demographic replacement, and social reproduction, human beings interact with nature through a set of material practices that are socially constituted and culturally meaningful (Patterson 1994:223). These material practices include food production, shelter, and, at the most fundamental level, defense. All are accomplished through social arrangements; all modify the natural and social world in ways that enable to some degree the persistence of the society through time. The premises upon which humans make basic productive decisions are multiple. They emerge from direct environmental stimuli, social organizational forms, and ideological mandates. Disasters provide but one, albeit possibly the most dramatic and revealing, moment in which this process of adaptation to an environment is both manifested and tested in immediately observable ways.

One of the fundamental features to which individuals and communities must respond is the natural environment where they dwell. In general, most hazards are systemic elements of certain environments. Droughts have been occurring in the Sahelian region of Africa for millennia; hurricanes occur with reasonable predictability on the Atlantic and Gulf coasts of the United States; earthquakes are endemic to the western coast of the Americas, the entire Mediterranean, and much of Asia. These environmental processes are not novelties where they occur, but periodic regularities. Any account of human adaptation and cultural change and evolution, therefore, must refer to hazards as normal features of specific environments.

When hazards become activated, the degree to which they bring about a disaster in a society is an index of adaptation or maladaptation to the environment. Many societies in their native practices, before colonization, globalization, and other interferences, had knowledge and strategies to deal with the nature of their physical platform, to the extent that a disaster, at least up to certain extremes, might not even constitute a "disaster" to them, but simply part of their lifeways and experience (Schneider 1957). For example, Sahelian nomads for centuries adapted to the periodic droughts of their region through interethnic cooperative linkages with sedentary farmers and by altering migration routes (Lovejoy and Baier 1976). In contemporary conditions, these strategies often have been disrupted by such things as governmental policies, economic development, population increase, or nation-state boundaries, such that maladaptation, conditioned by the outer world, now hovers near (see McCabe, this volume).

Hand in hand with adaptation, the role of hazards and disasters in mobilizing forces of cultural change is vastly understudied. Much of the sociological research conducted not terribly long ago considered that disasters rarely played a significant part in the evolution of a society (Sjoberg 1962). The time depth supplied by anthropology's archaeological and historical perspectives, however, has increasingly made evident how causal disasters have been in bringing about cultural transformation. There is much to be learned about cultural and societal modification from the calamities a people endure. Not only do societies undertake immediate adaptations after impact, but these can also set in motion forces with long-term implications for the evolution of each society (Hoffman 1999).

The frequency with which a hazard is activated and produces a disaster brings forth consideration of the temporal factor in culture change. As Holling (1994) has noted, the time frames in which natural processes unfold vary considerably from those in which human decision making takes place, thus permitting considerable trial and error in societal adaptation to the environment. While many hazards display their presence quite constantly, others, despite their systemic environmental quality, may not occur with great frequency, allowing the possibility of maladaptive responses over time. If these maladaptive responses become institutionalized, they may lead to increases in societal vulnerability that in due course may bring about calamity and social collapse. Consequently, hazards and disasters, and how societies fare with them over long periods of time, are potential indices of not only appropriate environmental adaptations, but ideological ones as well. These cultural adaptations include innovation and persistence in memory, cultural history, worldview, symbolism, social structural flexibility, religion, and the cautionary nature of folklore and folk tales.

Disasters unmask the nature of a society's social structure, including the ties and resilience of kinship and other alliances. They instigate unity and the cohesion of social units as well as conflict along the lines of segmentary opposition. The distribution of power within a society reveals itself not only in the differential vulnerability of groups, but in the allocation of resources in reconstruction as well. Disasters provide a unique view of a society's capacities for resistance or resilience in the face of disruption. The basic social organizational forms and behavioral tenets of a society are exhibited and tested under conditions of stress. By exposing the capacities of social organization and ethos to cope with immediate forms of duress due to impact and emergency and with the sustainability of these efforts over long-term periods of reconstruction, disasters facilitate the study of human sociability. Patterns of consensus, competition and conflict, tensions between genders, classes, castes, age groups, occupations, all come into focus in disaster situations and provide the opportunity for the expansion of ways to scrutinize generally accepted wisdom regarding social and cultural differentiation.

Socially expressed questions regarding human needs, resource access and distribution, property relations, and altruism and self-interest are other prime issues that disasters elicit for substantive and theoretical exploration. Technological disasters such as oil spills and the like have constituted whole new challenges to resilience and sustainability, presenting cultures with conditions and devastation the victims could in no way preconceive or prepare for. In these situations, sometimes the research outcomes suggest cultural crisis or disintegration.

Disasters divulge matters of time and space use. They bring to the fore the power of place attachment. They undrape canons and law, customs and practices, the novel from the entrenched tradition. In this manner disasters often reveal the deeper social grammar of a people that lies behind their day-to-day behavior. Disasters also display and articulate the linkages between the local community and larger structures. The substance and expression of normal relations between community, region, state, and nation are measured as formal and informal agreements and alliances are called upon to mobilize resources and support in stressful conditions. The forms of expression that such linkages take under conditions of impending threat, impact, relief, and recovery expose their substance and viability in ways not evident under normal conditions. Under certain circumstances, the performance of state-level organizations in the disaster process also becomes a catalyst for readjusting the character of relations and interaction between local communities and the structures of the larger society.

Disasters offer a lens through which to view the relationship between the ideological and the material. Cultural perceptions of environmental hazards, dramatic events, and mortality tell much about ideologies of human-earthly and human-supernatural relations. How concepts of uncertainty, peril, safety, fortune, and fate are constructed and perceived constitutes basic features of worldview. Such cultural constructions, and the ways they are enacted, are often, then, posed against the realities experienced in disaster preparation, impact, and recovery. Not only are the nature and operation of mental constructions revealed, but at times novel forms and interpretations also emerge. Concepts of social and cosmic justice and the nature of existence as well come to the fore.

People formulate meanings for what has occurred, and in the formulation process another aspect of social process comes to light. Very often various interpretations of events are produced, bringing up control of definition and "story," along with tales of praise and vilification. "Ownership" of a disaster, that is, the right to claim that it occurred, who its victims were, and the "true account" of events, origin, consequences, and responsibilities, often erupts as a very contested form of discourse in all stages of a disaster. Such definitions even extend to risk—whether risk is recognized, and, particularly in our global age, who gets to outline the amounts and limits of risk. In the negotiation of these, disasters lay bare ideological unity or tensions within the community and its constituents, and between the community and outside entities.

Ceremonies and rituals arise, old, wholly new, or with new matter in old form. Myths and legends spring up, and their efficacy becomes manifest. Along with cultural change, researchers can witness cultural conservation and its mechanisms. Within disaster scenarios, nostalgia, cultural rigidity, and even cultural mummification arise. Deeply pervasive custom as opposed to mutable surface detail is made plain. The drift of uprooted populations to new environments or of sectors of populations to marginal and hazardous places and positions goes far in explaining how people ultimately immigrate or divide. In both traditional and novel manners, language and linguistic usages emerge to express events, name the peoples and parties involved, and manage the allegiances and contestations, so that, on top of all else, disaster brings to light sociolinguistic application and invention.

Disasters, in short, intertwine anthropology's platforms of assay so that the research is returned to the fourfold essence of the discipline. Disasters link the physicality of humans in their survival needs and behavioral capacities as these interplay within environments to the sociocultural orders and milieus humans create, the processual depth of sociocultural orders as revealed through archaeology and history, and the many texts of human life, including the spiritual, symbolic, and sociolinguistic.

THE PROBLEMS OF DISASTER RESEARCH AND ANTHROPOLOGICAL METHODOLOGY

While the long-term development and many-leveled aspects of disaster make anthropology particularly relevant to its study, these same aspects bring back to anthropology particular conundrums. Whether rapid or slow in onset, disasters and the vulnerability leading to them unfold over time, often considerable amounts of time. Likewise the socioculturally conditioned responses to them transpire both relationally and historically. Disasters have pasts, presents, and futures, whether they arise from events that people consider to be sudden, such as earthquakes, or those, such as droughts or toxic exposures, that occur unperceived over long periods only to be recognized well after their initial manifestations. Eminently social, disasters are worked out in complex interactions and discourses in which the needs and interests of many involved individuals, groups, and organizations are articulated and negotiated over the often extended duration of the entire phenomenon.

While much important data about disasters can be gathered by synchronic slices based on questionnaires, surveys, and "crash" emergency overviews, the actual processes by which people and communities respond to risk, threat, vulnerability, impact, and recovery are best understood through on-site ethnographic research. The value of ethnographic research is particularly evident during the process of reconstruction, when people must traverse the difficult path between restoration and change. This process of negotiation between what has been lost and what is to be reconstituted generally involves tensions among diverse interest groups and values. Methods that privilege narrative and observation, with researchers present and in dialogue with participants to gather local knowledge and information, are far more appropriate for exploring the process of adjustment and recovery than are more synchronic forms of research (Oliver-Smith 1979).

Disasters, no matter how large, are experienced first at the local level. Even an enormous disaster affecting great areas and legions of people, while it may result from a single climatological, geological, or technological phenomenon, ultimately comes down to a compendium of local but related disasters experienced throughout the region. Not all communities experience a disaster in the same way or to the same degree; each undergoes a catastrophe in the context of its own profile of vulnerability. The same disaster agent will show great variation in patterns of destruction as well as interpretation of cause, effect, and responsibility. Such variation challenges more global, macro approaches. By the same token, it is necessary to understand the total phenomenon, both physically and socially. Disasters, therefore, compel us to pair multisite ethnography with quantitative methods capable of accessing greater levels of aggregation.

Just as the spatial dimensions of some disasters present challenges to anthropological research, temporal dimensions can prove equally problematical. Disasters rarely conform to personal, academic, or funding agency schedules. Most anthropological research is planned out considerably ahead of actual entry in the field. Proposal preparation and review is a lengthy process, typically locked into a schedule of deadlines that is not responsive to such contingencies as a disaster. Some research funding organizations have programs that are designed to support rapid response or perishable data research, but they generally fund very short-term, event-focused kinds of research as opposed to the more important processual aspects of disasters that require longer-term commitments of ethnographic methods.

Researchers rarely enjoy the flexibility necessary to supplant personal and professional commitments that have been in place for some time in order to undertake long-term research on a rapid-onset disaster. Even less available is the prescience to carry out the necessary pre-disaster vulnerability analysis that allows a fuller understanding of impact and recovery. On the other hand, communities and regions around the world know where certain kinds of disasters occur with some regularity, and many undertake forms of vulnerability analysis in their preparedness and mitigation strategies. Anthropologists in these situations can complement community strategies with in-depth analyses of local-level vulnerability, particularly where both intersect with chronic or systemic hazards. Moreover, many of us return periodically to the areas where we conduct our anthropological research, yet another advantage for comprehending the long-term unfolding of a disaster and utilizing the extended story of disaster for our expositions and theorems.

FROM THEORY AND METHOD TO PRACTICE— AND AN OBLIGATION

The practice of disaster relief and reconstruction is an exceptionally complex task, made even more so by the urgent needs of those affected. Anthropologists involved in disaster research carry the responsibility of the field's fifth, and often un-embraced arena, applied anthropology. We cannot forget that we are part of the communities we study, as well as part of the global community, and have a responsibility to mitigate the suffering of others to whatever degree we can. We also play a role in protecting the environments upon which we all depend. As a result of the nature of our inquiry, anthropologists can provide valuable sociocultural information and perspectives that can contribute to improving the outcomes of disaster mitigation, management, and reconstruction. Furthermore, since disaster victims often come from the most vulnerable sectors of society, we assume a special charge of being a voice for people and places that cannot always be heard.

As a consequence of the nature of disasters and the problems involved in their examination, considerable disaster research is actually undertaken in the context of assistance. This circumstance, and the very real aspects of death and destruction that vulnerability and calamity encompass, bring to the foreground two further matters in the anthropological study of disaster: (1) what anthropology can do for disaster management as well as research, particularly regarding the moral issue of aid; and (2) the ever-present specter to the more academic side of anthropology, the connection between theory and practice. While not always recognized, both issues are extraordinarily important in the study of disaster and the use of disaster as a study context.

To begin with the latter, theory and practice should ideally be closely connected. When policy and practice are not based on a solid understanding of human behavior in general and cultural behavior specifically, the probabilities of success of both are limited. Conversely, policy and its application can serve as an important proving ground for the relevance and predictive ability of theory. If policies and practices do not coordinate and do not produce successful results, it is the programs and their applications, not the people, that are at fault; but it is always the people who suffer.

One of the common sources of the policy-practice defect is its construction on culturally bound assumptions. In disaster contexts, aid often gets delivered in inappropriate forms and according to unsuited principles. Anthropology can provide the nuanced understanding that may more sensitively discern applicable relief. Through their primary methodology and research, anthropologists can obtain and provide a more holistic perspective of the societies they study and thus are in a significantly better position to inform the structure of aid as well as to project the possible distribution of effects of a disaster throughout a social system. An awareness of the sociocultural configurations of a society can be an important factor in avoiding the major problems that follow disasters. These include not only problems of waste and inapt assistance, but also the severe social conflict, anomie, substance abuse, and other socially derived difficulties that often plague groups in the aftermath of severe calamity. In addition, many of the benefits and potentials that emerge in the oft-witnessed post-impact solidarity and other forms of social capital that occur after a disaster might not be lost if a culturally knowledgeable mediator were available to work with communities and agencies. Unfortunately, in-depth sociocultural data are rarely asked for and more rarely appreciated. This situation remains a challenge for anthropologists concerned with improving outcomes in disaster relief and reconstruction.

The uneven record of disaster preparedness, relief, and reconstruction consequent to both natural and technological disasters on every continent of the globe over the last three decades can in some measure be attributed to a lack of understanding of the local contexts in which disasters are experienced. It is rarely understood that the form and results of disaster management are preconditioned by the structure of the local society and its articulation to national and international orders (Maskrey 1996). When a preconceived, uniform model that does not take into account provincial vulnerabilities and capabilities is applied in a calamity's aftermath, it frequently produces inappropriate relief and reconstruction aid that bear real and damaging repercussions for affected populations. As a result, local people and groups must turn their efforts toward affecting the performance of outside institutions and/or, ultimately, attending to officially unrecognized reconstruction projects to assist their recovery themselves. Failure to understand regional realities almost inevitably results in poor articulation among the various national and local governmental and nongovernmental organizations and institutions involved in disaster management. The result is relief and reconstruction that are in the best case ineffective, in the worst, insulting and damaging.

A moral issue thus arises when an anthropologist takes on a disaster study. Anthropologists have the training and perspective necessary to provide the relevant database for more effective delivery of disaster aid and also to contribute importantly to the planning and operationalizing of such aid in the field. One of the most problematic dimensions of disaster assistance is that, like the disaster itself, the task carries with it a multiplicity of perspectives. The disaster victim does not interpret disaster assistance in the same way the aid agency does. Questions of need versus loss, of relative deprivation, of internal competition, of change versus continuity all come into play in disaster assistance and often bring out contention between survivors and those that have come to assist them. Far too much room for misinterpretation and misunderstanding of intentions exists on both sides of a disaster scenario to allow for a simple ad hoc approach in the relationship between aid agency and a disaster-stricken community. Anthropology has a long history of analyzing the values and structure of action of institutions. By understanding the orientations and how such orientations reverberate upon relationships with individuals and groups, anthropologists can work toward a better "fit" between agencies and communities in terms of formulating appropriate goals, methods, and outcomes. Anthropologically trained personnel can contribute to a reorientation of dominant disaster management models, making them more decentralized, more capable of integrating local resources of organization, material, and technology, and better able to address the multiple realities and rationalities involved in catastrophes.

CATASTROPHE AND CULTURE

The goal of this volume is to explore the potentials of disaster for anthropological research, while not ignoring the concomitant responsibility of exploring the potentials of anthropology for the field of disaster. In a previous work we attempted a benchmark work on the topics involved in the anthropological study of disaster (Oliver-Smith and Hoffman 1999). Here the major hope is to find areas of complement and synthesis in the ecological, political-economic, and cultural approaches in anthropology, along with perspectives from archaeology and history. The papers that follow illustrate a number of paths for achieving this aim. They demonstrate the value of disaster in illuminating issues in anthropology while showing the great utility of anthropological perspectives in revealing dimensions of disaster. Each carries import in this age of increasing vulnerability to hazards.

To begin the volume, Anthony Oliver-Smith offers a brief discussion of the complexity and multidimensionality that challenge disaster research as well as a brief overview of the development of the field. He highlights in particular the emergence of the concept of vulnerability as key in opening possibilities for theoretical advancement in both anthropology and disaster studies, as vulnerability draws attention to the intersections of society, culture, and nature that become expressed in the disaster process. In order to explore the potentialities in this intersection, Oliver-Smith probes the implications of the dominant cultural construction of the relationship between society and nature for generating conditions of vulnerability. This discussion is followed by an exploration of the process through which the cultural, economic, and political forms and conditions that generate vulnerability and disasters are inscribed in the environment. Finally, the epistemological difficulties inherent in the relationship between cultural interpretation and the material world of risk, threat, and impact of disasters are examined.

Virginia García-Acosta offers, defines, and clarifies the relevance of the historical perspective in the anthropology of disaster. She shows how historical analysis untangles the many threads of social cultural actions, decisions, and structure that go into creating vulnerabilities.

Economics, social structure, and ideology all come into play. Certain social processual steps, commonly ignored, cause the encounter between hazard and population. García-Acosta also demonstrates that disasters are self-revelatory: they expose the very history, often hidden, that leads to their own making. Disasters palpably show that history is not only the past, but the present as well. Examining long-term records, she finds that disasters, particularly droughts and consequent agricultural and food crises, have long been chronic aspects of the Mexican environment. Through disaster, history gives a critique of social reality. In searching history, part of her effort is the imperative to discover current vulnerable populations and take steps to protect them.

While the contexts considered in the anthropological study of disaster generally are limited to natural and technological disasters, excluding equally devastating but more purposefully contrived events such as war, refugees, and holocaust, Robert Paine's analysis of the cultural management of risk was too pertinent for our seminar to leave out. His article explores how cultures control the "flow" of danger into their recognition of risk. In particular, his chapter examines the "no risk" scenario, that is, the various ways certain groups and cultures repress the acknowledgment of hazard. Paine contrasts a separatist group in which danger is embraced and "invited" with an occupational group where facing unknown perils in a situation of limited resources prevents the probe for dangers, and then turns as his main example of a "no risk" policy to Zionism and the state of Israel. He outlines two differing approaches to "no risk," the religious and the secular, and examines the mechanisms used to transmit the ethos of "no risk" in what he calls a "full risk" situation. Paine's study contains broad implications for the entire field of disaster research. He refers to people who return to hazardous environments after a catastrophe, touching on place attachment and ideology. He brings up the cultural construction of normalcy that often contradicts the assessment of outsiders and aid agencies. Arguing that risk policies are a matter of adaptation, Paine finds that adaptation is not just physical, but also hinges on the perception of adaptation. He raises the question of temporality, of how certain cultural policies can last, and invokes cultural transmission and sociolinguistics.

Sharon Stephens's paper again takes on the subject of risk, an invisible calculation of risk affecting us all. Stephens analyzes a series of lectures and discussions about the science of radiological protection that took place at an international course on radiological protection in Cambridge, England, in 1995. At the core of the article is the determination by a group of "experts" of what constitutes acceptable radioactive risk, not for a single culture but for the entire world. The discussions followed the nuclear incident at Chernobyl and its concomitant fallout. Involved is the negotiation and control of perception, ideology, and denial, along with the hegemony of "scientists" who separate themselves as a community of "the knowledgeable" apart from the "irrational and ignorant" public. Stephens demonstrates that it is not scientific "facts" but assumptions that are packed into expert assessments, and that "facts" themselves are tools created for particular cultural and political purposes. The group of experts is significantly uniform in gender, race, class, culture, and regional origin. The concerns brought up by lay attendees regarding such matters as the nuclear risk to children, women, and indigenous people are both feminized and discounted by the experts. Stephens further demonstrates an extremely pertinent point about hazards and twenty-first-century conditions and globalization: a disaster in one place, particularly a technological one, can have profound and far-reaching effects across all peoples and cultures of the world.

Susanna Hoffman next takes the discussion into the nonmaterial level in an examination of disaster symbolism. People experiencing or expecting calamity everywhere have belief systems filled with symbolic expressions dealing with their situation. While disaster symbolism often overlaps environmental symbols, it moves to representations beyond. Basing her study on the 1991 Oakland firestorm and other material, Hoffman explores disasters that are seen to arise from nature. When natural disasters occur, particularly in societies that divide nature from culture, people often first attempt to "re-culturize" the natural happening. If the symbols they use to represent nature involve embodiment, frequently they separate out disasters from the more benign side of nature and "disembody" the disasters. The disaster becomes a "monster," either in the guise of a formless terror or the frightful second side of an otherwise kind god. The monster has many implications involving cultural and political control. Disaster symbolism also commonly involves cyclical schemes with grand and implied apocalypses and revivals. Hoffman then turns to the symbolic implications involved in technological disasters as opposed to natural ones. As technological disasters arise from the wrong ideological realm (culture, not nature) and always stand outside of cyclical time schemes, they present particular problems. They defy detachment and leave behind the stigma of lasting scorched earth. They also provoke particular rituals. Symbols give disaster context, content, emotion, and meaning. They implement cultural and personal survival as well as effecting cultural modification or conservation.

Gregory Button pursues a similar but more political-economic line in his exploration of the various forms of cultural framing that are employed by different parties in the representation of technological disasters. Focusing primarily on the Woburn contamination case that resulted in a concentration of childhood leukemia and other ailments in a neighborhood north of Boston, Button reveals that the choice of frames by various parties produces discourses that place or elide responsibility for the contamination. He is particularly concerned with mainstream media's habit of relying on government and other official sources for their interpretation of events while ignoring the voices of victims of the disaster who have alternative constructions of what has transpired. Button contrasts the representation of the Woburn tragedy in Jonathan Harr's best-selling book *A Civil Action* with the accounts of community members. He reveals the hegemonic ideological aspects in Harr's account that underplay the role of local people and organizations in their own defense, displace responsibility, and reinforce a political-economic system that produces man-made disasters.

Christopher Dyer's look at the *Exxon Valdez* oil spill continues the expansion of anthropology's need to look at the articulation of small village to nation-state and international community. Practically no situation so dramatically exposes this articulation as does disaster. Dyer examines the effect of the oil spill on several communities, all dependent on the local ecology for subsistence. With these examples he develops the concept of "punctuated entropy." Dealing with the "punctuation" of ecological blows, Dyer demonstrates how cultures can drift into adaptive entropy and collapse. Without the framework of anthropology, Dyer feels the multileveled examination required is impossible.

His five-year study points to the involvement of physical, environmental, and sociocultural realms that interweave for all human groups. Adaptation in interplay with political economy comes to the front. Dyer follows how disasters both expose and impact social structure, reproduction and child rearing, economics and subsistence, political functioning, and such nonmaterial qualities as the traditions of communities. Again, the definition of peril and who controls the definition are implicated.

Michael Moseley similarly develops an adaptational perspective in exploring, through archaeology, the economic and demographic ramifications of long-term drought and concurrent natural disasters in the Andes. In particular, he aims to expose the implications for major cultural change in the linkages between protracted disaster, such as drought, concomitant increased vulnerability, and the concurrence of sudden-onset disasters such as earthquakes. Moseley maintains that protracted drought bears similarity to autoimmune deficiency disease in that both depress human response capabilities. While a society may be able to rebound from the onset of a single severe sudden-onset disaster, if such an event occurs during a protracted drought, recovery from such convergent disaster processes may be virtually impossible, thus opening the door for widespread cultural change.

The response capabilities of people facing drought also draw the attention of Terry McCabe, whose eighteen years of fieldwork among the Turkana pastoralists of northwestern Kenya provide the basis for examining the social organizational strategies for adapting to disaster. The Turkana are well acquainted with droughts. They know that they will occur, although not predictably, and that their survival depends on the effectiveness of their coping strategies. Indeed, one of the salient features of McCabe's discussion is the Turkana's understanding of drought as an integral part of the ecological system in which they participate. Consequently, their response to the onset of drought is deeply ingrained in their system and evokes a number of carefully considered and time-tested strategies in both economics and social organization. Like Moseley and Dyer, McCabe cogently addresses the negative impacts of poorly designed policies; in this case, famine relief, development, and conservation programs on traditional systems of resource use.

Finally, Ravi Rajan addresses the forms and processes by which the changing character of socially produced threat and risk in a globalized world challenge the competency of institutions and societies to protect the public from disaster. Rajan's contribution explores the responses of civil society to the Bhopal gas disaster of 1984. His analysis focuses on the mobilizing rationales and concrete actions undertaken by the disaster relief, medical, and political-legal sectors in their efforts to aid the victims of this terrible industrial disaster. The degree of incompleteness and ineffectiveness that characterized these responses demonstrates for Rajan serious lacks of both expertise for confronting these novel forms of disasters and political structures necessary for producing adequate responses. In conclusion, Rajan points to the important catalytic role that anthropology, with its contextual and culture-specific ethnographic approach, can play in the analysis of the problem of missing expertise for revealing why "even the best conceived policies and programs tend to unravel on the ground."

2

Theorizing Disasters

Nature, Power, and Culture

Anthony Oliver-Smith

Disasters have become a metaphor for many processes and events currently unfolding in the contemporary world. In scholarly and popular literature, the word "disaster" is frequently associated with a wide array of contemporary problems. Its use lends both relevance and urgency to the title of an article or book, particularly those dealing with social or environmental problems. Although the concept of disaster is often appropriately linked to undeniably important issues in these works, however, apart from a few notable exceptions, the disaster emanating from the problem discussed is rarely dealt with in any detail or depth. Part of the problem is that disaster is often considered an event rather than a process. But in focusing on an environmental or social problem, many of these books and articles are actually dealing with one dimension of the processual aspect of disaster—the social and technological construction of conditions of vulnerability.

Another reason why the discussion of disasters is often so cursory is that, despite the fact that "disasters are good to think," as Stephen Kroll-Smith (1998) notes, they are also difficult to think, because of their multidimensionality. Disasters are all-encompassing occurrences, sweeping across every aspect of human life, impacting environmental, social, economic, political, and biological conditions. Disaster research literature has been fragmented along disciplinary lines, with each field focusing on its own domain of interest, such as organizational behavior (sociology), the "hazardness" of a place (geography), or risk assessment policies and practices (political science). Common definitions have been hard to come by, prompting concern for the scholarly integrity of the field (Quarantelli 1985, 1998). Given its holistic perspective, anthropology is perhaps uniquely suited to tackle the theoretical challenges that disasters present.

Considering the diffractive use of the term and the multidimensionality of its expression, it has become ever more challenging to develop theory that has application or relevance to the expanding concerns disasters encompass. As the increasing occurrence of interactions of natural and technological hazards has made many disasters more complex, the theoretical challenge in turn becomes more complex. Also needed is a means to address the multidimensionality of the problem. Disasters exist as complex material events and, at the same time, as a multiplicity of interwoven, often conflicting, social constructions. Both materially and socially constructed effects of disasters are channeled and distributed variously within the society according to political, social, and economic practices and institutions.

Disasters come into existence in both the material and the social worlds and, perhaps, in some hybrid space between them. When we have a way of theorizing that hybridity, fundamental as it is to human life, disaster researchers will have achieved a great deal not only in our own work, but for the social sciences and humanities as well. It is to that theoretical challenge and to the implications of disaster research for anthropological theory that I wish to direct my attention in this chapter. Disasters offer a unique context in which to pursue such a theoretical breakthrough. Conversely, I wish to demonstrate as well what anthropology can offer to the field of disaster research and management.

Disasters occur at the intersection of nature and culture and illustrate, often dramatically, the mutuality of each in the constitution of the other. My initial goal is to explore the multidimensionality of disasters in terms of that mutuality. From that exploration I hope to address issues that might lead to the eventual formation of a coherent theoretical framework for disaster causation that encompasses both natural and social scientific perspectives. And finally, I hope to contribute to a more general theoretical discussion about how we understand environments as both socially constructed and biological/physical spaces. Disasters seem to be especially apt as contexts and processes that illuminate these complex relationships, particularly in the ways they challenge societies materially, socially, and ideologically.

THE MULTIDIMENSIONALITY OF DISASTER

Disasters are multidimensional because they are both physical and social event/processes. For heuristic purposes, I want to refer to the broad array of "objective" natural and technological phenomena that produce or trigger disasters and create a wide variety of physical impacts. The term "disaster" includes event/processes that range from slow-onset phenomena, such as droughts and toxic exposures, to rapid-onset events, such as earthquakes and nuclear accidents. In Kenneth Hewitt's (1997:26) view, disaster agents include natural hazards (atmospheric, hydrological, geological, and biological), technological hazards (dangerous materials, destructive processes, mechanical, and productive), and social hazards (war, terrorism, civil conflict, and the use of hazardous materials, processes, and technologies). While certain social hazards (war, terrorism, etc.) produce many of the features common to disasters (see Paine, this volume), I wish to limit my discussion to natural and technological hazards. The array of disaster impacts from natural and technological hazards, ranging from rapid destruction and death from earthquakes to effects that go unperceived or unexperienced in the physical sense often for many years, as in the case of toxic exposures, also encompasses wide variation. The variability of physical manifestations alone challenges our capacity to encompass the array of phenomena that generate and occur in disasters within a single theoretical framework.

Disasters are also both socially constructed and experienced differently by different groups and individuals, generating multiple interpretations of an event/process. A single disaster can fragment into different and conflicting sets of circumstances and interpretations according to the experience and identity of those affected. Disasters force researchers to confront the many and shifting faces of socially imagined realities. Disasters disclose in their unfolding the linkages and the interpenetrations of natural forces or agents, power structures and social arrangements, and cultural values and belief systems. The many socially constructed facets of disasters form the basis for the idea that disasters disclose fundamental features of society and culture, laying bare crucial relationships and core values in the intensity of impact and the stress of recovery and reconstruction.

Indeed, disasters focus in uncommon intensity the widest possible variety of intersecting and interpenetrating processes and events of social, environmental, cultural, political, physical, and technological natures. As disasters develop and occur, all dimensions of a social structural formation and the totality of its relations with the environment become involved, affected, and focused. In disasters are expressed continuity and contradiction, cooperation and conflict, power and resistance. All are articulated through the operation of physical, biological, and social systems and their interactions among populations, institutions, and practices. There are few contexts in which the mutual constitutionality of the physical and the social are so starkly displayed as in a disaster.

In this fashion, different interpretations of disasters emerge for specific purposes or goals of various disaster projects. Those who focus on behavior approach disaster differently than those examining societal-environment interactions. Agencies involved in disaster management or reconstruction establish operational definitions that serve to activate and demarcate their involvement in events and processes. Although the multidimensionality of disasters presents a complex challenge to researchers, it also provides researchers an important opportunity to ask synthetic questions. Mining this rich vein that disasters bring into intense focus is the real challenge presented to theory as well as practice, and it is little wonder that researchers noting the disastrous nature of crucial problems prefer only to mention their potentiality rather than to engage in in-depth discussions. As disaster researchers, we need to tackle this multidimensionality and probe the multiple linkages and relationships they reveal for sociocultural theory and, by the same token, establish what anthropology can offer to the study of disaster.

CHANGING PERSPECTIVES IN DISASTER RESEARCH

There is no question that great strides have been made in conceptualizing disasters since the emergence of the field half a century ago, when it focused primarily on individual and group behavior in disaster. The most important departure from the hazard/event/behavior focus that had characterized the field since the 1950s was the refinement of the concept of vulnerability, which looks at those aspects of society that reduce or exacerbate the impact of a hazard. Earlier perspectives had allowed for a certain "passive" form of generation of vulnerability to hazards and disasters largely resulting from what were considered inappropriate human actions, such as building on flood plains and fault lines, driven by irrationality, ignorance, and misjudgment. In the 1970s, however, anthropologists and cultural geographers working in the developing world found that mainstream disaster studies brought little of value to the task of analyzing disasters in third-world contexts. These researchers criticized the essentially passive role prior investigators had assigned to society in risk etiology and the scant attention paid to local, national, and international factors in creating or exacerbating both risk and impact. Anthropologists concerned with advancing the field of cultural ecology urged researchers to focus on hazards from an ecological and social organizational perspective (Vayda and McKay 1975). Researchers from and in the third world called for a rethinking of disasters from a political-economic perspective, based on the high correlation between disaster proneness, chronic malnutrition, low income, and famine potential, which led to the conclusion that the root causes of disasters lay more in society than in nature.

The most explicit formulation of the new approach was outlined in Hewitt's *Interpretations of Calamity* (1983). Rejecting the dominant view that disaster is basically the collapse of the productive functions of the social order, Hewitt posited that most natural disasters are more explainable in terms of the "normal" order of things, that is, the conditions of inequality and subordination in a society rather than the accidental geophysical features of a place. This perspective shifted the focus away from the disaster event and toward the "on-going societal and man-environment relations that prefigure [disaster]"(Hewitt 1983:24–27).

This more acute version of the vulnerability concept linked general political economic conditions to very particular environmental forces to understand how basic conditions such as poverty or racism could produce susceptibilities to very specific environmental hazards. Vulnerability thus integrated not only political-economic forces but environmental forces as well, defined in terms of both biophysical and socially constructed risk. The working definition provided by Blaikie et al. (1994:9) is currently among the most utilized:

> By vulnerability we mean the characteristics of a person or group in terms of their capacity to anticipate, cope with, resist, and recover from the impact of a natural hazard. It involves a combination of factors that determine the degree to which someone's life and livelihood is put at risk by a discrete and identifiable event in nature or in society.

Vulnerability is generated through a chain of root causes embedded in ideological, social, and economic systems, the dynamic pressures of a demographic, socioeconomic, or ecological nature, and specific sets of unsafe conditions that, when combined with a natural hazard, produce a disaster (Blaikie et al. 1994). This more complex understanding of vulnerability enables researchers to conceptualize how social systems generate the conditions that place people, often differentiated along axes of class, race, ethnicity, gender, or age, at different levels of risk from the same hazard and of suffering from the same event. By incorporating specific political, economic, and social variables in combination with specific environmental features, the cause of disasters is situated in the interface of society and environment. In that sense, in addition to serving metaphorical purposes, disasters also function metonymically. The linguist Jacobsen (1956) distinguishes between metaphor and metonym. Though both concepts are figures of equivalence, they are generated by different processes—metaphor according to similarity between things otherwise different, metonym according to continuity or associations between part and whole, cause and effect, thing and attribute. Thus, Hurricane Mitch is a metonym for the actual disaster, which encompasses all the technological and social constructions of vulnerability that brought about such devastation in Honduran society and environment.

Vulnerability expresses the multidimensionality of disasters by focusing attention on the totality of relationships in a given social situation and the formation of a condition that, in combination with environmental forces, produces a disaster. Wilches-Chaux identifies eleven different forms of vulnerability—natural, physical, economic, social, political, technical, ideological, cultural, educational, ecological, and institutional vulnerability (1989:3:20-41). The model Piers Blaikie et al. (1994:29–30) present subsumes these different forms into causal chains. Blaikie et al. situate ideologies of political and economic systems as they affect the allocation and distribution of resources in a society in the chain of explanation and identify these ideologies as among the root causes of disaster. The linkages of ideologies to specific dynamic processes and unsafe conditions, they readily admit, become less definite and difficult to pinpoint in the causation of specific events. The sociocultural forms through which linkages are established and maintained remain to be explored in depth. These linkages become further complicated in the context of increasing globalization of natural and social systems and their mutual interaction. Basically, the concept of vulnerability needs to be unpacked, not necessarily in terms of its variety of forms, as Gustavo Wilches-Chaux has already ably done, but theoretically for its ecological, political-economic, and sociocultural implications. Unpacking vulnerability requires that a number of crucial theoretical tasks be undertaken to disclose the deep sociocultural and political economic underpinnings of events that are usually understood as environmental disturbances.

If, as vulnerability theorists maintain, disasters are more a product of a society than of a specific nature, certain questions concerning the conjuncture of culture, society, and nature arise. What are the general outlines of how the social production of disaster takes place? A second question should address how the cultural, political, and economic forms and conditions that characterize vulnerability are inscribed in an environment. And a third question should explore the relationship between cultural interpretation and the material world of risk, threat, and impact of disasters. Finally, how do we theorize the linkages among the three issues?

CONSTRUCTIONS OF NATURE AND SOCIETY

The first theoretical task involves the analysis of the implications of the cultural construction of nature-society relations for the production of the conditions of vulnerability and the occurrence of disaster.

Vulnerability, while linking cultural and social structures and the environment in causal chains, leaves implicit a fundamental feature of that causation, namely the relationship between society and nature, which is one of the basic pillars of any ideological system. Anthropologists have documented that society-nature relationships are expressed cross-culturally in a wide variety of forms.

Due to its historical hegemony and continued expansion, the model of society-nature relations dominant in the West merits special attention. This model places human beings and nature in opposition to each other. It was not always so. Although the opposition can be traced to classical Greece and Rome, in the medieval period nature was commonly conceived as in partnership with humanity (Harvey 1996). Human beings were seen as part of nature, part of God's creation, whose goal was to know both nature and God (Williams 1980:73). Many of these essentially more integrative or conservationist attitudes have endured in Western culture to the present, but a more utilitarian perspective toward the natural world also became more evident and eventually dominant in the seventeenth and eighteenth centuries (Redmond 1999:21).

This ideological shift reflected both changes taking place in local practices and the emergence of a nascent global system. Scientific and philosophical discourses of the time began to see humans as ontologically distinct from nature. Indeed, nature provided a contrasting category against which human identity could be defined as cultural rather than natural in the work of Hobbes, Locke, and Rousseau. It is important to note here that a category of humans, now recognized by the term "the other," was characterized by its association with the phrase "in a state of nature." Now, as then, certain people get relegated into the "nature" category as the need arises. The nature/culture dichotomy thus becomes important in terms of vulnerability in that those put into the nature category are frequently the most vulnerable to disasters such as epidemics, genocide, forced displacement, and so forth.

Descartes also conceived of nature as "other," detached and external to humans and the world of thought, thus reifying nature as a thing devoid of meaning in itself (Harvey 1996:134). From this position of separation or detachment, Western human-natural relations have been constructed in terms largely of subject-object (Bird-David 1993:121).

Nature has been constructed as a fund of resources that human beings have not only a right to dip into, but also a right to alter and otherwise dominate in any way they deem fit. Moreover, the enlightenment ideal of human emancipation and self-realization were closely linked to the idea of control and use (Harvey 1996:121–22). Locke, responding to changing systems of production and property relations in seventeenth-century England, emphasized the natural individual rights of life and liberty. He asserted that God had given the earth to humanity and that since each individual was the embodiment of all humanity, each had the right to the fruits of his or her own labor in the natural world (Locke 1965:327–28). Locke's assertion is only one of the clearest expressions of the linkage between an unfettered exploitation of nature and the self-realization of human beings. Indeed, it was considered that one of the tyrannies from which humankind would be emancipated was that of nature. This doctrine of natural liberty would soon become the cornerstone of Adam Smith's thought linking self-realization and societal benefit to the specific institution of the market.

The belief in social domination further specified that nature would also benefit from human action. Western ideology frequently summons up images of nature replete with savagery and violence. Tennyson's image of "Nature, red in tooth and claw" was nourished by Christian theology that saw nature as fallen and evil. From the disaster perspective, such a vision also implicitly juxtaposed the violence and disorder of nature with the order of human culture and civilization. This has led to a construction of hazards as disorder, as interruptions or violations of order, by a natural world that is at odds with a human world. Its bounty or its savagery notwithstanding, nature is seen as plastic, ultimately dominable or malleable to the purposes of humankind.

The "plasticity myth," as Murphy (1994) has termed it, is based on the idea that the relationship between humans and their environments can be reconstructed at will by the application of human reason, which imposes order on a disorderly, but essentially malleable, nature, to bring it into line with human purposes. Following the separation of humans and nature, human rationality is not subject to the limitations of nature, because the exercise of our rationality over nature has both subjugated nature and emancipated humans. Thus, humans are "capable of manipulating, domesticating, remolding, reconstructing, and harvesting nature" (Murphy 1994:5). The subjugation of disorderly nature to human rationality is epitomized in the regimentation imposed on forests by German forestry in the eighteenth century. The clearing of other species of lesser commercial value, the weeding, the orderly files of trees, all led to the reduction of diversity of insect, mammal, and bird populations, rendering the forest more vulnerable to storm felling, fire, and pests (Scott 1998:20). Nonetheless, in both the market and the command economy, the enthusiastic application of human rationality, motivated by individual or collective productionist goals, is the primary means by which nature will be dominated and human beings emancipated.

Even much of the current criticism of ecological degradation is based on the conception that society must learn to care for and safeguard nature. Other critical perspectives construe the human world as out of step with some supposed natural order, with solutions to be found in bringing the human world back to harmony with natural order. Although it is hard to disagree with the spirit of these positions, they are still flawed in that they are constructed from a fundamentally dualistic perspective in which society exists as a collection of human constructs and relations, and the environment is "out there," waiting to be acted upon in the cause of sustaining human life. The problem is couched in terms of human beings developing the proper ways to act upon or in concert with the environment. The relationship is still expressed in dualistic terms of two separate entities in some kind of interaction, whether healthy or distorted. In the case of disasters, such a conceptualization may lead to policies and practices that address symptoms but not causes, condemning us to repeat constantly the exercise as both causes and symptoms evolve with our attempts to address them. Furthermore, the inherent dualism in such a construct leads down a blind alley, or perhaps down two parallel alleys, as far as advancing human ecological theory goes.

THE HAZARDS OF DOMINATION

There is now good evidence that many catastrophes traditionally attributed to natural causes were more than likely generated, at least in part, by human practices, both collectively and cumulatively. The rise and fall of many ancient civilizations, from the Mediterranean to

Mexico, were closely linked to long-term patterns of human exploitation and misuse of the environment resulting in agricultural and societal collapse. Recent archaeological research clearly shows that human
environmental impacts, some with extreme consequences, are far from
exclusively modern (Redman 1999). The lessons that might have been
learned from prehistory and history, however, were obscured by the
rapid expansion of the Western system and its seeming capacity to dominate nature (Weiskel and Grey 1992:15–16). Indeed, the entire field of
disaster research, anthropological and otherwise, could benefit significantly from a historically informed approach to the analysis of vulnerability (Redman 1999; Tainter 1988; see García-Acosta, this volume).

There is increasing evidence that many disasters today are intimately connected to current conditions of environmental degradation
(Varley 1994; Fernandez 1996). In effect, social and material practices
in combination with natural processes frequently evolve into novel
forms of hazards and potential and actual disasters. The degradation of
the environment, in some cases driven by the quest for profit and in
others created inadvertently by those subsumed disadvantageously in
that quest, now accounts for conditions of accentuated vulnerability to
both natural and technological hazards around the world. Much has
been written of late about the inappropriate forms of natural resource
exploitation engendered by Western conceptions of the nature-society
relationship. However, the actual nature of the problem is not always
agreed upon. Green Movement critics have castigated the Western economic system for its inability to come to terms with the natural limits of
environments, continually exceeding them in a relentless pursuit of
economic profit. Ecological anthropologists and other social scientists
contend that the relationship between humans and their environment
is bound up with relationships among humans themselves through the
double nexus of production. They argue that environmental destruction is ultimately not a question of exceeding natural limits but is
socially constructed, an expression of systems of production and social
exploitation (Collins 1992:179). To what extent does this debate have
relevance for furthering our understanding of disasters? Do disasters
instruct us in environmental limits? Or do they rather inform us only of
specific instances of conditions of vulnerability created and imposed by
human social arrangements structured in and by the production

process? How can the study of disasters clarify the question of environmental versus socially defined limits?

There are limits, although variably elastic ones, in natural systems (Holling 1974, 1994), but they can only be experienced by human beings in social systems in culturally constructed relations with nature. Ecological crises and disasters (if not identical) are produced by the dialectical interaction of social and natural features. Socially constructed production systems that impoverish the essential and absolute level of resources sustaining an environment will create environmental crises and perhaps disasters, impacting a human population. An earthquake as a feature of nature may represent a universal and timeless challenge to human welfare, but it becomes a disaster only in the context of a specific society and a characteristic pattern of vulnerability. Although environmental limitations or challenges are natural features, they are experienced only as the result of human social, economic, and cultural arrangements. The inadequacy of purely ecosystemic approaches for understanding major environmental disasters such as the Sahelian drought of the 1970s convinced many of the necessity of analyzing environmental problems in the framework of large-scale political and economic systems (Vayda and McKay 1974; Lees and Bates 1990:264). McCabe (this volume) provides an excellent example of this type of analysis in his discussion of Turkana adaptation to drought and the intervention of national and international aid agencies. A finer-grained understanding of both environmental conditions and disasters must be based on an approach that can include the dialectical interaction of the agencies of nature and society, recognizing that the environment is a socially mediated force and context experienced by people both positively and negatively, just as society expresses itself environmentally.

To explore how socially produced vulnerabilities are expressed environmentally, the links between the increase and expansion of disasters and the dominant ideas, institutions, and practices of the contemporary world must be established. It is necessary to recall that, along with the detachment of nature and society achieved by eighteenth-century philosophy and political economy, the fortunes of humanity were specifically linked to a set of material practices largely structured by market exchange. The market, its ego-centered ideology rapidly transforming itself into the discipline of economics, thus became constructed as the principal vehicle for individual self-realization and societal welfare. Thus, individuals were not only free but virtually obliged to better themselves with the means that God had provided, namely the natural world. With the reduction of nature to the status of means to the goal of human welfare and the rapid expansion of market exchange driven by a productionist ethic, both the ideological justification and the institutional means were available for a relatively unfettered mastery over and unrestrained exploitation of the natural world. Furthermore, the mutually reinforcing pairing of ideology and science (economics) produced a set of institutionalized material practices through which human beings engaged the object of their domination for their new purposes of emancipation and self-realization.

The material practices were oriented by a form of value obtainable only through the institution of the market. The quest for this surplus value is unending and limitless both by definition and by necessity, due to competition in the market. Since the creation of value at least starts in the appropriation from nature, capitalist economies require the justification supplied by concepts of domination over nature and the plasticity of nature, enabling the elevation of exchange value over any values that might be ascribed to nature. The result of embracing the rationality of essentially short-term gain has been unprecedented extremes of material wealth and poverty, unprecedented levels of environmental destruction, and the rapid amplification of socially constructed vulnerability.

Socialist economies as well have been deeply affected by both the myth of plasticity and the productionist ethos. Although the dialectical relationship between humans and nature was a central feature in Marx's thought, he was also deeply impressed with the powers of human rationality expressed in capitalism to mobilize the forces of production to bring nature under control (Murphy 1994). Socialist economic policies, though hardly a faithful enactment of the little that Marx actually said about what socialism would be like, have participated in the attempt to subjugate nature through the implementation of collective labor with their own expressions of the goals of human emancipation and self-realization. In effect, both capitalist enterprise and socialist state have proceeded under the premise that nature is plastic, capable of domination by human reason. In so doing, both rendered pollution, depletion of resources, and other forms of environmental change subordinate to production goals (Murphy 1994:5).

The material practices of engaging the natural world, and their supporting cultural value systems, are enacted and expressed in and through social relations that are themselves inscribed in the natural world. Material practices transform the natural world. They produce ecological conditions and environments that not only enable survival on a day-to-day basis but also are conducive to continued social reproduction, therefore inscribing particular systems of social relations in the environment (Harvey 1996:183). This process of inscription reflects materially those contradictions that are inherent in both the social system and the relationship between the society and the environment (Cronon 1983:13–14, as cited in Harvey 1996:27). Thus, contradictions in social relations are expressed through material practices as contradictions within the environment (Harvey 1996:185). Disasters are perhaps the most graphic expression of those contradictions.

Since human environments are socially constructed, the positive and negative effects of these practices are distributed as a reflection of systems of social relations. Therefore, the instantiation in nature of certain forms of social relations creates effects that are specific to them. Social, political, and economic power relations are inscribed through material practices (construction, urban planning, transportation) in the modified and built environments, and one of the many ways they are refracted back into daily living is in the form of conditions of vulnerability. In general, environmental security is a premium enjoyed predominately by the beneficiaries of the social relations of production and distribution, but there is not always a perfect relationship. Cultural values can distort the relationship, convincing the wealthy that it is safe to live on hurricane coasts and on fault lines with spectacular views. Even then, superior engineering, generally only available to the well off, reduces that vulnerability significantly. Insurance also buffers loss and induces people to occupy risky places. But both the wealthy and the poor are implicated in the construction of vulnerability. The wealthy, through the excessive consumption of market-accessed resources such as secure land and water, withdraw large quantities of them from use by the general population. Moreover, in the continued reproduction of their wealth, they are frequently involved in despoiling public goods such as the air and the oceans, thus engendering further vulnerabilities for the general population (Murphy 1994). The majority poor, through their desperate and sometimes inappropriate use or overuse of the few resources available to them, both degrade their environments and place themselves in harm's way, largely through the lack of reasonable alternatives for daily survival.

CULTURAL CONSTRUCTIONS OF CALAMITY

In many ways, any theoretical inquiry into the nature of hazards and disasters inevitably thrusts us into the tangle of ontological and epistemological questions that deal with the nature of cultural versus material realities. This brings us full-circle back to the nature-culture debate, which replicates many of the issues of the materialist-culturalist debate (Biersack 1999). Some scholars in disaster research suggest that disasters are entirely sociocultural constructions—that is, the presence or activation and impact of a hazard are not necessary for a disaster to take place. All that is necessary for a disaster to have occurred is the public perception that either a hazard threat exists or an impact has taken place. This position is based on the social-psychological principle that if something is defined as real, whether it is a disaster or, for example, witchcraft, its "reality" is established by its social consequences (Quarantelli 1985:48). In this sense, whether or not one believes in witchcraft, the fate of the hanged victims of Salem is hardly up for debate. Even where a threat or impact is socially recognized, constructions of the disaster vary widely according to social identity and circumstance. Kroll-Smith interviewed a nineteen-year-old man from a small Wyoming town that was experiencing the expansion and contraction of methane plumes in its subsurface. Asked what his family thought about this, he said,

> My dad says this is a disaster. He goes on and on about his business losing money and the government not doing much to help...Mom? She thinks it's a disaster, but not like Dad does. She thinks we could all end up dead or something if one of those plumes explodes...[And you?] I don't know. It seems to me like a flood or earthquake like in San Francisco is a disaster...I did say yesterday or some time that if my fiancée moved

because of the gases, it would be a big disaster. I don't have a car
right now. (Kroll-Smith 1998:165)

Even each individual in this particular family was constructing the concept and perception of a disaster from a different framework of reference, varying from economic losses to physical danger and death and,
rhetorically speaking one would imagine, to the potential uprooting of
a significant other.

In disasters the linkages between concrete material circumstances
and ideological structures may be directly observed as people attempt
to come to terms, to construct meanings and logics that enable individuals and groups to understand what has happened to them and to
develop strategies to gain some degree of control over what is transpir-
ing. The extreme conditions created by disaster occurrence frequently
challenge people's worldviews with profound existential questions for
which meanings consistent with circumstances must be elaborated. All
the social characteristics that significantly structure people in a society
will play a role in the way those meanings and explanations are constructed, giving broad disclosure to the internal variance of a community and underscoring the difficulty of reaching an absolute or
objective determination of the nature of the disaster. Hoffman's (this
volume) exploration of the differential construction and experience of
different groups in the Oakland firestorm illustrates the enormous variability of interpretation generated in disaster. The perception of risk,
vulnerability, and even impact is clearly mediated through linguistic
and cultural grids. There is no question that the range of interpretation
of threat or impact of disaster is extremely wide and largely a function
of social and cultural characteristics of individuals, primarily related to
degrees of integration and group power relations (Douglas and
Wildavsky 1982; Hoffman, this volume).

For a time cultural theory sought to extend this entirely valid conclusion reached at one level of social analysis to empower the phenomenon of language at a much higher level. Language not only became a
shaper of perception but, as the essential ground in which social life
was embedded, acquired determinate power over all social relations. In
this approach language was hegemonic and nonreferential, to the
extent that the world was reduced to a text from which only relativist

understandings could be drawn (Palmer 1990:3). More recently, there has been significant criticism of pure, idealist semiotics (Gottdiener 1995) and a call for greater attention to exosemiotic domains such as economic development and political conflict (Biersack 1999). This "reformed" semiotics explores the sign within social context and links it to the historical, political, and economic domains of the world.

Hazards and disasters, constituted as they are in the society-environment nexus, offer a context in which to pursue these more synthetic understandings of the mental and the material. On the one hand, to say that disasters are social constructs to be read does not dis-embed them from the materiality of the world. Indeed, the physical reality of disaster explicitly challenges theoretical currents that hold that nature is a purely social construction at the ontological level (Woolgar 1988; Tester 1991, as cited in Gandy 1996). The physical existence of disasters establishes an agency of nature that exists independently of human perception. However, human beings are deeply implicated in the construction of the forms and scale in which that agency expresses itself. The impact of these hazards, when they are perceived and cognized, rapidly confirms this agency, but just as rapidly constructs a social text around it that may either reduce or accentuate the impact. We may "read" the disaster as a social text as it unfolds in its particular context, but the natural forces that created it, or even hazard processes set in motion by technology, exist as independent, exosemiotic agents operating according to physical processes that are ultimately prediscursive, "outside" the text, no matter how many texts may be constructed about them after the fact.

Even where, for the sake of argument, the disaster is purely in the perception of the community, its construction is in reference to the physical operation of the material world. The flight and evacuation behavior precipitated by a false rumor of a dam break above a town was not seen to be distinguishable from the behavior of the people who fled the actual break of the Teton Dam; both were viewed as disasters (Quarantelli 1985:47). The people in the first town responded to a rumor, generated a social text about a disaster, and based their behavior, flight, and evacuation on that text. But the hazard processes they were referencing to construct their text were ultimately independent of their interpretation. That the dam existed was certainly part of a social text, as well as a material object. If the dam had broken, it would have been because of certain physical processes, "outside the text," indeed, even in opposition to the text, so to speak, and certain physical results, equally outside and opposed to the text, would have taken place, subsequently to be included in a text. This particular case perhaps speaks to the need to draw a distinction between a disaster and a more general category called "crisis," some of which may occur in purely cultural frames and others, like disasters, in a domain that blends both the material and the cultural. Disasters, because of their material expression, their emergence from human-environment mutuality, and their cultural construction, belong to that class of phenomena that are "neither purely object (nature) nor subject (social discourse)...which lie between the opposite epistemological poles, frozen into the dichotomy between the natural and social sciences" (Gandy 1996:35). They are less frozen into a dichotomy than expressive of the fact that the reality that emerges from the conjuncture of nature and culture is anthropocentric, and thus both material and symbolic. That reality is based on an ecology, as Biersack (1999:11) says, of "incommensurabilities, predicated on the fact that human life lies 'betwixt and between,' neither nature nor culture, but precisely both."

Thus, in a directly physical sense as well as in a symbolic sense, disasters emerge out of contradictions in the mutual construction of societies and environments. And, as Henri Lefebvre (1991; quoted in Harvey 1996:87) notes, "[S]pace was produced before being read; nor was it produced in order to be read and grasped, but rather in order to be lived by people with bodies and lives." Undoubtedly, our cultural life is deeply implicated in the construction of our material life and vice versa, but life does have to be produced before it can be read. Our values and orientations regarding shelter, nourishment, security, and relationships both reflect and affect the material practices and systems of social relations through which they are produced and condition our relative vulnerability within an environment that is mutually constituted by nature and society. Cultural readings can neither eradicate nor create the existence of a natural hazard. If a cultural reading apprehends the existence of a hazard, it may or may not alter practice in such a way as to either reduce or exaggerate the risk of disaster. History is littered with the rubble of societies that could not culturally come to terms with either natural hazards or the forces they themselves partially instituted in their environments through the material practices of production. Natural hazards do not exist primarily as social constructions, nor are they in some essential fashion merely the product of social discourse, which will cease to exist if we stop discoursing about them (Radder 1992). Hazards and disasters demonstrate the exosemiotic agency of nature, but, on the other hand, it is a nature that is mutually implicated in its construction with society through material practices and ideological discourses.

DISASTERS AND THE REENVISIONING OF NATURE AND CULTURE

The interpenetration of forces and conditions posed by the concepts of vulnerability and disasters links disaster research to current efforts in anthropology and related fields to rethink the relationship between culture and nature. The opposition between the two has played a key role in the development of anthropology and other social sciences, enabling the demarcation of culture, as opposed to nature, as the focus of the proper study of humankind (Horigan 1988). Furthermore, the separation between culture and nature also permits a separation between observer (of nature) and observed (nature itself), which is the basis of, for example, the science of biology (Soule 1995:148).

As mentioned earlier, alternative views of the relationship between nature and culture have begun to create more synthetic approaches that can address the mutuality of the two (Biersack 1999). Some prefer to develop approaches that stress a kind of critical realism, emphasizing a balance between the social construction of nature and the natural construction of the social and cultural (Stonich 1993), while others pursue a more anti-essentialist stance, emphasizing the social construction of nature (Ingold 1992; Escobar 1999). These and other approaches are part of an effort to seek a fuller recognition of the role human beings have taken in shaping as well as being shaped by nature by conceptualizing a "bio-cultural synthesis"(Goodman and Leatherman 1998). The "new materialism," as Biersack (1999:11) dubs it, addresses the challenge of bringing nature into the cultural realm without "effacing nature's autonomy from the cultural realm."

The integration of ecological and social theory, however, does not mean the "culturizing" of the environment and nature to the point that they disappear in a haystack of discourses. Like those who "ecologize" culture, those who would "culturize" ecology risk obscuring as much as they illuminate, particularly in terms of the role of disasters in human-environment relations. Disaster researchers are all too well aware that the natural forces present in any environment have enormous power to affect society, but it is society that actualizes the potential of a hazard. This perspective strives to recognize that the objective circumstances that disasters occur in and the material needs they evoke are sociohistorical products.

Those features of an environment that represent dangers or losses, if they are perceived as such, are also organized into an environment in the human context, through choice. That is, some societies recognize risk, take steps to mitigate or not as the case may be, and choose to take their chances. Many natural hazards are not sufficiently frequent or do not produce consistently frequent disasters, such that they may frequently not be perceived as threats, and therefore often are not integrated into human environments. Paine (this volume) notes that risks can be culturally negated if realistic assessments amount to overwhelming threat. However, even when risks are perceived and experienced, some elements of a society still may not be in a position to take the necessary steps to mitigate or prevent the occurrence of a disaster. Such a situation is the essence of vulnerability.

Vulnerability is a concept that allows us to bring nature in from "out there" and facilitates reconceptualizing nature-society relations from a duality to a mutuality. As Ingold (1992) asserts, environmental history and human history are inseparable, each implicated in the processual life of the other, each contributing to the resilience and vulnerability of the other. Disasters are among those phenomena whose analysis requires that the barrier between human activity and ecosystemic activity be collapsed, transforming a relation of difference into a relation of mutuality of the natural and social worlds. If disasters cannot be defined exclusively in natural or social science terms, they may perhaps be seen more productively as a mode of disclosure of how the interpenetration and mutuality of nature and society, with all the consistencies and contradictions, are worked out (Robben 1989).

However, for disasters to be employed in this fashion, environmental features and ecological processes such as earthquakes, hurricanes, floods, and soil erosion must be recognized as features of social life; and social and cultural elements, such as commodities, land markets, and money flows, must be seen as functioning ecologically (Harvey 1996:392). Disaster researchers are uniquely situated to advance this understanding of the nature-culture relationship and, at the same time, employ it to reorient their own research agendas toward more processual and political-ecological explorations. In the most direct sense, this mutual construction of human beings and environments provides a theoretical basis for asserting that we construct our own disasters insofar as disasters occur in the environments that we produce.

GLOBALIZATION, VULNERABILITY, AND DISASTERS

A number of current trends would appear to indicate that an increase in impact and scope of hazards and resulting disasters, already complex and multidimensional, is taking place through combined effects of economic, social, demographic, ideological, and technological factors that are compounding their complexity many times over. Recent research indicates that greater numbers of people are more vulnerable to natural hazards than ever before, due in part to increases in population, but more so to their location in dangerous areas (Quarantelli 1985). In addition, we have created new forms of disaster agents. Technology always has the capacity to malfunction, often with catastrophic effects, but the second half of the twentieth century has seen the creation of completely new technologies, whose mere implementation, regardless of potential or actual malfunction, has had profound environmental and, in some cases, catastrophic impacts. Many of these new technologies, ranging from toxic chemicals to nuclear power plants, have added to the list of hazards that now threaten communities, not necessarily with material destruction, but with altogether novel biologically derived hazards, creating new forms of injury (Quarantelli 1991; see Stephens, Button, and Rajan, this volume). Human technological interventions, while in many cases providing more security, have in other instances added many degrees of complexity to existing natural threats. Furthermore, natural disasters have been shown to trigger subsequent technological disasters.

The implications of such a situation have been manifested in the technological catastrophes of the past two decades, including *Exxon-Valdez*, Bhopal, and Chernobyl, to name only a few of the most prominent. This period has also seen the effects of the domination of nature ethos in the expanded vulnerability to impacts of natural disasters in Hurricanes Hugo, Gilbert, David, Andrew, and Mitch, the earthquakes of Loma Prieta, Mexico City, India, and Colombia, and the droughts of Ethiopia, Senegal, and Sudan, again to name only the headline events. However, the linkage of any particular approach to the economic problem to the construction of vulnerability requires ignoring the distressing environmental record of both capitalist and socialist economies as well as the role many ancient societies played in their own destruction by so-called natural calamities (Weiskel and Grey 1992).

The general culpability of complex human systems notwithstanding, the world is now a global system organized for the vast majority by capitalist markets. There are serious implications of capitalist expansion to global contexts for levels of vulnerability. Markets gained preeminence with the rise of private property and developed to enable the exchange of private goods, but not to regulate the use of private goods. Nor do they work especially well with public goods, and in general they have not been successful in protecting the atmosphere, the seas, rivers, or, in many cases, the land (Murphy 1994:58). The continued expansion of human activities in the world, now almost exclusively a function of the market, is straining both the limits of human adaptive capabilities and of the resilience of nature. The impacts of human-induced environmental change on air, land, and water are slowly exceeding the elasticity of natural systems until they trigger rapid alterations that impact the health of populations, the renewability of resources, and the well-being of local communities (Holling 1994).

Furthermore, the globalization of trade and migration has led to an increasing globalization of biophysical phenomena, intensifying linkages and creating problems across scales in space through reductions in heterogeneity. For example, cargo ships, taking on ballast water in one ecosystem and releasing it in another, are thereby introducing novel species, often with no predators or reproductive controls, and contributing to the creation of one global ecosystem with ecologically unpredictable results (Murphy 1994:18). Temporal scales have also been altered. Natural systems possess a certain level of resilience, allowing for incomplete knowledge, mistakes, and recovery. However, natural resilience also provides a certain lag time during which greed or ignorance can escape responsibility. Increased levels of exploitation are reducing the natural elasticity of systems, shortening the lag time for response before irreversible damage takes place (Holling 1994:93). Both Dyer and Moseley (this volume) explore the serious implications for continuity, change, and survival of community and culture in situations in which resilience of culture and environment is reduced by disasters.

Today many local problems, including disasters, may have their root causes and triggering agents, and possibly their solutions, on the other side of the globe. Through this globalization process problems have become basically nonlinear in causation and discontinuous in both space and time, rendering them inherently unpredictable and substantially less amenable to traditional methods of observation of change and adaptation. Human-induced changes have moved societies and natural systems into essentially unknown terrain, with evolutionary implications for elements of both. As has been argued, societies and nature have always been in a process of coevolution in local, relatively discrete contexts. Now people, economies, and nature are in a process of coevolution on a global scale, each influencing the others in unfamiliar ways and at scales that challenge our traditional understandings of structure and organization, with serious implications for the adaptive capacities of people and societies (Holling 1994:79–81). These findings underscore the changing nature of disasters, emphasizing that they are rooted in the coevolutionary relationship of human societies and natural systems. The challenge is to specify the regional and global linkages that generate destructive forces within our societies and environments. In a sense, disasters are now sentinel events of processes that are intensifying on a planetary scale. The interpretation of the messages brought by these sentinels remains a crucial issue.

CONCLUSION: ANTHROPOLOGY AND DISASTER RESEARCH

As the world becomes increasingly integrated by expanding global systems of communication and commerce, technological or environmental changes in one locale may trigger radical events or change processes resulting in disasters half a world away. Although legal responsibility for such calamity may be difficult to establish, the increase in technological disasters, and in particular those with lasting toxic impact, has an undeniable human agency and is seen by some to endanger faith in human institutions, placing in doubt or calling into question the validity of culture itself, if culture in some sense can be seen as a kind of implicit guarantee of limited predictability in life. Button's and Rajan's discussions (this volume) of the difficulties in assigning responsibility in Woburn and Bhopal, even where cause and effect were proximate, highlights this problem. Horlick-Jones (1995) suggests that modern disasters can even be thought of today as "outrage and betrayal" because they indicate a failure of institutions to live up to their intended mission. It is arguable that the expanded conditions and experiences of vulnerability constitute a significant component of these anxieties. Indeed, although somewhat reminiscent of Anthony F. C. Wallace's (1956a,b, 1957) focus in his landmark work linking the issues of disaster, cultural crisis, and response, Erickson (1994) has called the trauma engendered by such events and processes "a new species of trouble."

The new kind of trouble of which Erickson writes so eloquently seems emblematic of the challenges Roy Rappaport (1992) urged anthropologists to confront in their research and their lives when he spoke of "the anthropology of trouble." Rappaport echoes Vayda and McCay (1975), who called on ecological anthropologists to explore life-threatening hazards that people actually have to deal with rather than ecological issues that may not be locally problematic. The current increase and expansion of disasters and their profound effects upon individuals and communities, particularly in the context of globalization processes, however, are currently undertheorized and require an analytical approach that encompasses all the factors leading to their occurrence. Furthermore, there is a general tendency to confuse symptoms ("troubles") with causes, particularly when human agency is involved. In grappling with the problematics of disasters, anthropologists, working in the holistic framework that is the hallmark of the discipline, can clarify the important distinction between symptoms, the disaster events and processes themselves, and their underlying and largely systemic causes. The holistic perspective is uniquely capable of capturing the multidimensionality of disasters and in doing so can enlarge anthropological theory as well as contribute to disaster mitigation and reconstruction.

Note

I would like to thank all the participants in the seminar for their valuable comments, especially the late Sharon Stephens, whose insight and suggestions contributed greatly to the improvement of this effort. I also very much appreciate the cogent commentary and important suggestions provided by Laura Ogden of the Department of Environmental Studies at Florida International University.

3

Historical Disaster Research

Virginia García-Acosta

Anthropology and history are intrinsically related. One is based on fieldwork, the other on documentary research, and both have theoretical frames. Each, with a different intensity and at a different moment in time, has become part of disaster research. Although sociological studies have dominated disaster research over the last decades, social and cultural anthropological disaster research has made important contributions and shown great progress. Anthropologists have pointed, in particular, to the complex interaction between the physical, biological, and sociocultural aspects of disaster (Oliver-Smith 1995). Historical research on disasters, based to a great extent on an anthropological perspective, has made important contributions to the field of disaster research by obtaining information from documents written in the past. This has occurred in spite of the fact that dominant schools of thought from sociology have preached an ahistorical and even antihistorical vision of disasters.

This chapter offers a historical perspective of present-day anthropological approaches to the study of disasters. It demonstrates the continuing need to use history in the field by showing that history has not yet been surmounted and is still, in a strict sense, part of our present (Palerm 1980). I try to show that one can achieve and apprehend disasters as processes by using historical documents as ethnographic sources of information and posing specific questions, as an anthropologist does when conducting fieldwork with informants.

The need to distinguish between natural phenomena and disasters is an inevitable starting point in both contemporary and historical research. Disasters are processes resulting from preexisting critical conditions in which certain natural hazards play a role. The magnitude and severity of accumulated social and economic vulnerabilities, associated with the presence of a severe natural hazard, result in real disasters, which are processes and, as such, inescapable subjects to be studied from a historical perspective.

People and communities all over the world have historically formulated cultural constructions to confront real and potential disasters. They are not, and have not been, passive actors in the face of disasters, either in their responses or in formulating the concept of disaster itself. Such cultural constructions are part of everyday life and as such need to be understood, considered, and explained. They prevail in the case of almost all natural hazards, but particularly in the case of droughts in past and present agricultural or pastoral societies.

Disaster research in a historical perspective has shown that hazards may act as triggers, in the sense of leading to important social and cultural changes. Hazards can also play the role of revealers or disclosers of the facets underlying certain moments or periods. The study of disasters, in fact, constitutes the thread on which one can weave several histories. Historical disaster research, based on the theoretical perspectives of the anthropology of disaster, makes possible a synthesis of theoretical and methodological considerations, starting from an analysis of past primary sources and historical records of disasters: official documents, personal letters, narratives, and so forth. It has demonstrated that if disasters have become more frequent over time, it is not because there are more natural hazards, but rather that throughout time our communities and societies have become more vulnerable.

In linking anthropology and history in terms of disaster research, this chapter particularly emphasizes the Mexican situation. I begin with a brief examination of the basic contributions Mexican historiography has made to this field; later I focus on certain topics that the historical perspective within Mexican disaster research has shown to be central to this new field of study.

MEXICAN HISTORIOGRAPHY BEFORE AND AFTER 1985

The main contributions to Mexican historiography can be divided into two main periods, whose boundaries are set by the terrible 1985 Mexican earthquake. Before this turning point there was no specific literature dealing with what can be generically termed "disaster studies" in the historical Mexican perspective. Rather, there were two types of writings. The first is informative or descriptive material, such as compilations of hazards occurrence, chronicles, accounts, reports, or monographs of various "disasters" that severely affected Mexican societies of the past. Generally speaking, such accounts are not very analytical, but they do report large amounts of data that can be converted into primary sources of information for more in-depth analysis. Many of them were published during the last quarter of the nineteenth and the beginning of the twentieth centuries and refer mainly to earthquakes and volcanic eruptions, along with meteorological changes.

The second type of written materials are analytical studies and consist of a number of essays that could be considered as background information for historical research on disasters. These studies are generally research-based and might be called social studies of historical disasters, even though none of their authors identified them as such. The vast majority were written by historians, many of whom were directly or indirectly influenced by prevailing trends in the social sciences. All of these deal with more general subjects and issues generally derived from French economic history and historiographic tradition on which they base their analysis. These works do not actually form a clear line of research on the history of disasters, however.

A historical approach to certain economic topics, such as agricultural production, salaries, and particularly the prices of basic agricultural products, leads to the analysis of certain critical moments. Many of these, such as the lack of rain that brought on droughts, are associated with natural hazards (Chávez Orozco 1953; Chevalier 1976; Gibson 1967). These studies, in turn, lead to the analysis of what is characterized as *agricultural crisis,* which in agriculture-based societies implies a generalized crisis because of its effect on the entire society. The historical approach to agricultural crisis was used for the first time to study corn price movements in eighteenth-century Mexico (Florescano 1969). Economic effects were the primary concern of these treatises, but some authors also analyzed the social and political effects of these crises, such as unemployment, migration, epidemics, banditry, and conflicts between factions (Florescano 1969, 1980; Pastor 1981).

Although these studies emphasized the effects of agricultural crises, which can be characterized as part of a disaster and were seen as the direct result of meteorological disruptions that led to extended droughts, some, following the French tradition of *longue-durée* studies, accepted that social, economic, political, religious, or ideological structures and relations traverse long periods of time during which they are modified by many other disruptions. Thus, it was accepted that it was absolutely necessary to study the socioeconomic and political contexts in which crises arise:

> The meteorological factor, even dominant, is not the only one influencing the regularity of economic cycles in antique societies. The structure of land property, of production, of the market, the regional situation, its communications and transports, sellers' power, buyers' situation and other many factors intensify or diminish, limit or expand the violence of these cycles. (Florescano 1969:111–112)

It is undeniable that in agriculture-based societies an extended drought, frosts, or snowfalls can lead to terrible effects, depending on the intensity and duration of each one, two factors that have to be seriously considered (see Moseley, this volume). But it is also clear that the major effects of these events, such as hunger and death, were the result of other associated factors directly related to vulnerability. Access to land, water or trade control, and chronic malnutrition made the poorest people easy prey to disease and epidemics, which in turn led to the highest rates of mortality in colonial Mexico.

Only two studies published before the 1985 events could be considered direct precursors to classic studies on the historical analysis of disasters. They were carried out by Richard E. Boyer (1975) and

Herman W. Konrad (1985). Boyer's book is a case study of the 1629 flood in Mexico City. The author not only looks at the natural phenomenon itself—the heavy rains and subsequent flooding that kept the city inundated for five years—but also makes a thorough analysis of the socioeconomic, cultural, and political contexts before and after the flood and describes the vulnerable conditions that led to the disaster. For Boyer these particular conditions, and not the heavy rains, caused the terrible flood.

Konrad's short but very stimulating essay views hurricanes as one of the environmental variables that influence structural change in ongoing developmental processes, specifically among the pre-Hispanic Quintana Roo Mayas. He believes that hurricanes are a problem that has been overlooked by specialists in that area and culture. Konrad notes that some factors have been identified as agents stimulating shifts, such as demography, disease, ideology, trade, warfare, migration, subsistence, and ecology. To these he adds what he calls "phenomena related to climate (wind, rain, floods), geological disturbances (volcanoes, earthquakes), and natural fires...which a society plays no role in causing" (Konrad 1985:326).

Konrad considers hurricanes to be trigger mechanisms that led to adaptive strategies. He analyzes these adaptive strategies by associating them with settlement patterns (location, choice, and types of settlement on the Caribbean coast); subsistence patterns (backyard garden production, emphasis on root crops, and more intensive systems of production involving hydraulics, terracing, and ridged fields); migration and demographic stability (movement of people, temporary or permanent evacuation of affected areas); warfare (as a result of an increase in conflicts with neighbors or taking tactical advantage of a neighbor's weakness); and trade (reliance on or opening up of new sea or land routes). This study demonstrates, as William Torry, Anthony Oliver-Smith, Michael Moseley, and other anthropologists have stated, that only when disaster research is linked to a specific social and cultural context can it really show the disaster process.

EXPLORING A NEW FIELD OF STUDY

After 1985 a real and systematic interest in historical studies on disasters became apparent in Mexico. The huge dimensions of the 1985

53

earthquake demonstrated that knowledge concerning the history of such phenomena in Mexico was scarce and precarious. Efforts were made to compile more information, and these attempts gradually turned into a field of study in its own right, one that involved the analysis and explanation of history based on the occurrence of destructive natural phenomena.

An initial task was to retrieve the history of earthquakes in Mexico in order to produce an exhaustive inventory. The abundance of information required an extensive analysis of the collected data, which resulted in two outcomes. One was the formulation of descriptive inventories going back to pre-Hispanic times. Unlike those written by seismologists, which as a general rule only include the date, time, and place an earthquake occurred, these inventories contain a vast and varied body of information about every event and cover 450 years of Mexican seismological history (García-Acosta and Suárez 1996, and previous versions: Rojas, Pérez and García-Acosta 1987; García-Acosta et al. 1988). The other was an increasing number of historical studies of one or more earthquakes, which contain diverse analyses and approach the earthquakes as social phenomena. These studies have led to the development of chronologies, local analyses, case studies, social effects and reactions, changes in seismic recording proceedings, and religious conceptions.

Previous studies of crisis and droughts concerning food and price history, especially in agricultural societies, combined with the new disaster studies, in turn stimulated further research on other kinds of disasters. Following the methodology already outlined for earthquake research, an inventory has been drawn up of agricultural disasters in the history of Mexico, with special emphasis on droughts (García-Acosta, Pérez, and Molina, forthcoming; Escobar, forthcoming), yielding a huge amount of data. Several essays have already been written on the topic with increasingly intensive use of theoretical approaches compatible with historical analysis; later I will discuss some of these works.

Research of this kind requires theoretical frameworks that allow for a deeper understanding of the processes deriving from information available on the history of Mexican earthquakes and agricultural disasters (Escobar 1997; García-Acosta 1993). The different theories developed by social sciences in the area of disasters were practically unknown in Mexico until the beginning of the 1990s. The introduction of these perspectives constituted a noteworthy step forward, as well as an inexhaustible source of creative hypotheses. New outlooks and approaches to the study of contemporary disasters in combination with historical studies make possible a new line of thinking, that is, the study of disasters in an historical perspective. Nevertheless, a definite analytic framework for this field is still needed.

Working basically with Mexican historical data, some researchers participated in the foundation in 1992 of the Network for Social Studies in Prevention of Disasters in Latin America (LA RED), an international and multidisciplinary cooperation network. The study of disasters in a historical perspective was one of the priorities on LA RED's agenda and allowed this interest to extend beyond Mexican borders (LA RED 1993). The type of research initiated in Mexico is currently being developed in other Latin American countries. By now, several seminal studies arising from this novel research approach have been published throughout the continent, including twenty disaster studies in twelve different Latin American countries, covering the pre-Hispanic era to the first half of the twentieth century (García-Acosta 1996, 1997). Based on local or foreign archive documents, old books and newspapers, and even archaeological data, sudden-impact events (earthquakes, volcanic eruptions, floods, tsunamis) and slow-impact ones (droughts, epidemics, plagues) are treated in ways that not only address a specific event or analyze what some authors characterize as "critical lapses of time" but also take notice of the context and time period in which the event occurred.

Much has been learned from this interesting effort, in which mainly anthropologists (including ethnohistorians and archaeologists) and historians have participated. First, disaster seen in a historical perspective within a space and time continuum is becoming consolidated throughout the Latin American region. Second, theories and methodologies coming from anthropological research, many of which form part of the so-called alternative trends of thought for the social study of disasters, are quickly gaining currency. I refer particularly to a holistic, evolutionist, and comparative perspective (Torry 1979a) leading to the study of social processes and to the consideration of hazards as part of the context of communities rather than as external elements. Disasters are thus viewed as the result of an encounter between hazards and people who are vulnerable not just physically but also economically, socially, politically, and culturally.

Third, it is recognized that the contributions of social sciences to the study of disasters generally originate after a large-scale disaster (Lavell 1993), and that the recent series of contributions based on a historical approach emerged in Mexico and was extended to Latin America precisely as a consequence of the disaster associated with the 1985 Mexican earthquake. That event served as a trigger in the evolution of this specific school of thought and filled a wide gap in a neglected area of social sciences.[1] As the French historian Fernand Braudel once said, "The great catastrophes...are always food for thought" (Braudel 1986:21).

But a question arises. Accepting that to understand, capture, and analyze disasters it is absolutely necessary to be familiar with the disaster context, and accepting that disasters are social processes that need to be studied in the time and space dimensions only historical perspective provides, one may ask whether it is really possible to apply models built on contemporary realities to societies of the past. Are anthropology's theories and methodologies, traditionally devoted to describing and analyzing other cultures, useful for studying disasters from temporally removed societies?

Within social research on disasters there are different research lines, perspectives, and orientations. Each reality, contemporary or historical, may show differences that force researchers to restructure and modify their approaches. Social praxis has shown that it is necessary to ponder models time and time again before we can propose theories that will allow a better approach and understanding of what happens in social realities.

KEY ISSUES IN THE HISTORICAL STUDY OF DISASTERS

The ideas that follow stem from a series of reflections derived, on the one hand, from proposals that, in my opinion, are the most revealing within the whole pool of suggestions coming from social scientists, especially anthropologists, and, on the other hand, from the enormous amount of documentary material, mainly on Mexican disasters, that has been gathered during the last twelve years. With these reflections I hope to advance the understanding and knowledge of what historical disaster research consists of. When necessary, I will provide examples from Mexican case studies.

Hazards and Disaster Process as Triggers and Revealers

As a starting point, the difference between hazards and disasters must be made clear. Although general definitions often use them synonymously, *hazard* refers to the agent and *disaster* to the process in which the agent and specific physical, social, and economic factors participate:

> What really constitutes a disaster, then, is the combination of a destructive agent from the natural and/or man-made environment and a group of human beings living in a specific local socio-cultural context in addition to regional, national and international spheres as well. (Oliver-Smith 1986b:8)

The idea originally set forth by Charles Fritz (1961), that the study of disasters provides the social scientist with advantages that cannot be compared to studies under "normal" conditions, continues to have appeal. If we accept that some societies live under permanent conditions of imbalance and that their "normal" state is generally characterized by huge social and economic inequalities, then it is true that if a given hazard appears and turns into a disaster, a whole series of circumstances, alliances, and relations arise. These might be unnoticed at other times or perhaps become magnified in the face of the process that the hazard unleashes. Disaster events and circumstances, in fact, provide the social scientist with a particular way of looking at things and allow the synchronic observation of a specific socioeconomic formation.

I have mentioned in other writings that empirical experience based either on fieldwork or historic documents allows researchers to confirm that the presence of certain hazards and the resulting disasters merely detonate a preexisting critical situation (García-Acosta 1992). In turn disasters worsen the socioeconomic situation of the affected population, even leading at times to direct confrontations with the state. The disclosures that the hazard and the disaster process provide of preexisting critical conditions allow us to consider them as catalysts, revealing circumstances that previously were somewhat hidden.

Michael Watts (1983) cites Marc Bloch's observation that just as the progress of a disease shows the physician how the body works, in the same way a social crisis allows us to peek into the nature of the affected society. It is in this sense that an analysis of the process of disaster allows us to carry out a critique of social reality. Therefore, as Wolf Dombrowsky (1987) points out, a social theory of disasters constitutes a critical theory per se. Disasters thus elicit behaviors that reveal certain relationships, rules of conduct, or social functions that might otherwise be hidden.

Hazardous agents play a determinant role as disaster starters, but they are not the sole cause. Disasters are made up of multifaceted components, derived from the socioeconomic, political, cultural, and environmental causes of the affected society.[2] Disasters should be understood as processes unto themselves, rather than merely events that trigger processes.

The quality of hazards and disaster processes as revealers or fuses becomes apparent in two ways. Of particular usefulness for the study of disasters from a historical perspective is the fact that when hazards occur and provoke disasters they lead to a huge amount of written documents in archives, journals, and libraries. These documents may be official or private, legal or novelistic, written from an objective or an alarmist point of view. In any case, they provide an incredible amount of invaluable material for studying not only the disaster itself but also the community, region, or nation under study.[3]

Hazards and disaster processes also reveal the conceptions, alliances, relationships, social order and disorder, structure, and organization of a certain community, region, or society in a more focused way. The information now available on earthquakes and droughts that have occurred in Mexico over centuries has allowed us to study in an evolutionary mode several topics from the most diverse perspectives: urbanization and its effects, political control and alliances among different sectors, mythical and religious conceptions, the role of tributes from the Indians, and the production and consumption of certain foods.

Even if various considerations can be studied synchronically, the fact that we have systematic and continuous information over almost five centuries allows us to provide follow-up and to detect changes and continuities. We can consider circumstances in their diachronic dimension, which allows us also to work with the Braudelian *longue-durée* and to study diachronic disasters. Reliance on long-term records places natural hazards and disasters in an evolutionary perspective (see Moseley, this volume). In this sense, as noted above, the study of any disaster constitutes the thread on which one can weave several histories.

Two examples coming from the Mexican data show how hazards and the disaster process act as triggers diachronically and synchronically and reveal much more than just when, where, and how earthquakes impacted Mexican society over 450 years.

A comparison of colonial earthquake records with those of the nineteenth century shows the growing secularization of Mexican society. Religious responses, ranging from the conception of quakes as acts of God to massive processions after disasters and large numbers of prayers dedicated to Saint Joseph or the Virgin of Remedies as patrons against earthquakes, began to subside as in the nineteenth century. Natural and scientific conceptions related to the origin of earthquakes and other natural phenomena became increasingly important, so much so that scientific theories made great strides by the beginning of the twentieth century. This kind of data allows us to analyze some aspects diachronically, but through them one can also discover, synchronically, how the Catholic Church dominated nearly all aspects of colonial life. When an earthquake took place, the municipal authorities requested that a census of the damage be undertaken under the supervision of experts (*alarifes*, experts in architecture). The experts went up and down streets, especially in Mexico City, and checked every building, noting in detail the type of damage that had occurred, the exact location of the building, and, above all, the name of the owner of the property, who was responsible for the reconstruction procedures ordered by the experts. This information allows us to map out the damage house by house and street by street (García-Acosta, forthcoming; Molina 1990). It also reveals the enormous amount of real estate that was in the hands of various religious bodies, how much property each group had, where each piece was located, what the property was worth at that particular moment, how much it received in rent, and so forth. In other words, information on each earthquake shows the control of urban property by the regular and secular clergy during the colonial period.

The Sociocultural Context

Any disaster research should emphasize and analyze the sociocultural context within which the disaster comes about. The historical evolution of a society accounts for specific situations that are associated with greater or lesser risks. These situations should be considered in local as well as regional and national terms and should include both the "before" and "after" of a given disaster. In this sense regional studies have shown several methodological virtues, not merely documenting aggregate cases but rather helping to differentiate micro-aspects and relating them to a larger framework of analysis. For Mexico this is of particular importance, given the country's large area and broad geographic and climatic variety, which has led to simultaneous events of serious flooding and protracted droughts throughout Mexican history (Lagos and Escobar 1996).

By considering the socioeconomic and cultural contexts in which a certain hazard and disaster develop, we can see that disasters, as processes themselves, form part of broader social processes from which stem the inevitable historical analysis, since history is "the discipline of process and context" (Thompson 1994:66).

VULNERABILITY

Historical research assists greatly in determining the conditions within which a given hazard takes place and in establishing the degree of vulnerability of the affected society. Vulnerability is usually understood as the physical risk in the presence of given hazards, which has in part led to mistaken concepts, such as "a natural disaster." Vulnerability should be understood as the degree to which groups and social classes, communities and regions, even whole nations, are differently susceptible to risk in terms of their specific social, cultural, economic, and political conditioning factors (Westgate and O'Keefe 1976; Winchester 1992). Vulnerability is, in reality, a characteristic of certain social and structural processes resulting from a complex relationship between people, environment, and forms and means of production (Maskrey 1989, 1993a).

Including vulnerability as a key concept in disaster research over the past decade or so has "become a rallying point for alternative visions" of disaster:

> Society, rather than nature, decides who is more likely to be
> exposed to dangerous geophysical agents...[Thus] disaster
> depends upon social order, its everyday relations to the envi-
> ronment and the larger historical circumstances that shape or
> frustrate these matters. (Hewitt 1997:141, 143).

Vulnerability is and has always been the result of social and economic inequalities. It involves several levels that together characterize
what has been called global vulnerability, including natural, physical,
social, economic, political, cultural, ideological, and educational levels
(Wilches-Chaux 1993). An increase in disasters means, in reality, an
increase in the vulnerability of the societies that suffer calamities.
"Some populations prepare their future disasters systematically"
(Moseley 1997:72). It is not that the world has become more hazardous
or more risky; rather, it has become more vulnerable in the face of disasters, as "we are day by day creating communities of victims," as Chris
Dyer said at the SAR Advanced Seminar.

The concept of differential vulnerability is useful, since not all
groups are equally exposed to hazards and risks, nor do they have the
same resources for coping with emergency. Social, cultural, and economic factors are involved. Group or ethnicity, gender, age, and even
status (Blaikie et al. 1994; Torry 1979a) are often determining factors.

Mexican history offers many examples in this regard. One very
general case is the absence of information, particularly in official documents, on the damage suffered by the Indian population that lived in
Mexico City when earthquakes occurred. During the colonial period,
as in the nineteenth century, Indian populations lived on the outskirts
of the city; indeed, at times special laws prevented them from living in
the center. Mexico City occupied what is now the city's downtown, a
high-risk seismic area due to the particular characteristics of the sub-
soil. The city sits on the muddy bed of the ancient lake basin system,
and its underpinning is moist and fragile. In past calamities, consequently, damage must have been considerable in the residential areas
inhabited by the Indian population. However, native peoples were not
taken into account in either urgent or semi-urgent reconstruction projects and were not even mentioned in official records. When collec-
tions in money or in kind were made to help affected populations,

there was practically never any mention of the resident Indian population. The Indians had to face the consequences to their dwellings and habitat brought on by the earthquakes in isolation, surviving and reconstructing with their own scarce resources. Perhaps they were able to achieve this more efficiently than the rest of the population, but the available documentation does not allow us to make any estimates.

Another example concerns epidemics. We know that epidemics were responsible for the demographic decline after the Spanish invasion in the sixteenth century (Borah 1975), but in fact epidemics prevailed during the entire colonial period. The association of epidemics with agricultural crises was established recently. Particular attention has been paid to the epidemic of *matlazahuatl* (exanthematous typhus) that occurred between 1736 and 1739 and covered a large part of New Spain. Molina's analysis (1996, 1998, forthcoming), like many others associating typhus with food scarcity, malnutrition, and hunger in *ancien-régime* Europe, clearly shows that the most vulnerable people during agricultural crises were those whose daily lives included hunger and overcrowding. Even this causality is not generally accepted (Molina 1998:156ff); what Molina calls the "trinomial hunger-epidemic-hunger" was in fact associated with New Spain's agricultural crises of 1734–1735 and 1741–1742. Similarly, Oliver-Smith developed the idea of "five hundred years of disaster" or "the earthquake of the five hundred years" from his research on the terrible Peruvian earthquake of 1970, which could be understood as an event that began five hundred years ago with the Andean conquest and colonization; "this region's accentuated vulnerability is a phenomenon socially created, a historical product produced by well-defined forces" (Oliver-Smith 1994:21).

Capacity for Recovery and Adaptive Strategies

Closely linked to the concept of vulnerability is the capacity for recovery. This capacity is also differentially distributed and often determines the real scope of a disaster. Recoverability capacity should not be limited to economic factors, as is often done in disaster analyses, especially those that only study the exact moment the emergency takes place. As McCabe's case study shows, the capacity for recovery from drought among East African pastoralists depends not only on resources but also on social organization, social links, and the manipulation of kinship systems (see McCabe, this volume). So the capacity for recovery includes social, cultural, ideological, and sometimes even political, as well as economic, aspects. Recoverability capacities materialize to a great extent through the adaptive strategies that a community adopts. Discovering and determining those adaptive strategies, which in some cases act as "risk management,"[4] comes about in the same way discovering vulnerability does—from the socioeconomic context in its spatial and temporal dimension. Analysis of adaptive strategies, diachronically and comparatively, allows us to understand the specificity of the disaster and even to offer viable alternatives often ignored by scholars as well as those in charge of aid.

At any historical moment, every society has certain ways of facing the effects of given hazards of a natural origin. These adaptive strategies depend on knowledge about handling the natural surroundings as well as on the degree of dependence or independence people have in utilizing the resources their physical, social, economic, political, and cultural surroundings provide.[5] Often, disasters stemming from physical hazards are added to the daily "disasters" that certain communities, regions, or countries experience, showing that

> The natural extremes involved are, in a human ecological sense, more expected and knowable than many of the contemporary social developments that pervade everyday life...In most places and segments of society where calamities are occurring, the natural events are about as certain as anything within a person's lifetime. (Hewitt 1983:25, 26).

In this sense, criticism and contributions from anthropologists are quite revealing (Torry 1979a:46). The anthropological record, ethnographic in approach, and the historical one, based on documents, confirm that individuals are not unaware of the hazards that exist in their communities. They have lived long coping with them and have developed adaptive strategies, even in times when hazards were considered acts of God. Drought registers in Mexican history clearly show, for example, that peasants are, and have always been, aware of the potential of drought, and over centuries have developed strategies to avoid hunger, the worst effect of extensive droughts. Historical records show that during periods of prolonged drought, those who suffered the worst effects, like high prices and scarcity, were low-income urban dwellers. Those who lived in rural areas resorted to various tactics that allowed them to face disaster more efficiently.

At the end of the Mexican colonial period, for example, between 1785 and 1810, there occurred several agricultural crises when the crop most affected by droughts and frosts was corn, the mainstay of New Spain's people, especially its indigenous populations. Droughts resulted in higher corn prices, which in turn elevated the prices of other basic products such as wheat, beans, and meat. However, the effects of this critical situation were not the same for all. Large landowners were able to store food in the enormous silos they constructed on their properties. This allowed them not only to face the situation but actually to aggravate it, since they waited until scarcity was at its peak and then, together with shopkeepers, placed their stocks on the market at the highest price possible.

Those who resided in the most severely affected rural areas, specifically the Indian population, resorted to two types of strategies to avoid starvation: they intensified gathering, hunting, and fishing and used food substitutes such as wild fruits, cactus fruit, prickly pear leaves, and roots. The Spaniards and Creoles considered this fare "abominable" and harmful and even attributed some of the diseases the Indians had to it. Meanwhile, those who lived close to rivers or lagoons intensified fishing and aquatic collection, an activity that, from pre-Hispanic times, had added important animal protein to the Mesoamerican diet.

There are two other examples of dietary substitution, the second strategy historical documents allow us to identify.[6] Evidence shows that, during these crises, wheat was more expensive but not scarce, and was used as a substitute for maize in tortillas in Mexico City and Guadalajara. References have been found to other types of food substitutions such as mixing kernels of maize with corncobs, grilled wild roots of the maguey plant, or oatmeal in order to make tortillas (García-Acosta 1994).

Historical disaster records of hurricanes in Mexico and other parts of Latin America reveal many other adaptive strategies linked to worldview among pre-Hispanic and early colonial Mayas (Campos 1994). Examples include worldview and disasters in the colonial Andean world (Camino 1996); religion and earthquakes in late-colonial Mexico

City; epidemics, agricultural disasters, religion, and governmental responses in eighteenth-century Mexico City (Molina 1996, 1998); and the organization of work, rains, and droughts in northern colonial Peru (Aldana 1996). Records show that societies develop multiple adaptive strategies and that they fall into five major types: social, cultural, political, ideological, and economic. As all the adaptive strategies developed to cope with disasters are culturally constructed over time, they must be understood and studied historically.

LAST REFLECTIONS

Since disasters serve as social laboratories, revealers, and sometimes triggers of critical preexisting situations, emphasis should be placed on understanding the surrounding and prior sociocultural context and vulnerability to the effects of a certain hazard. Examining one of the key theoretical issues in any disaster research—the multidimensionality of disasters as expressed in the concept of socially constructed vulnerability—deepens our knowledge of hazards themselves. It is necessary to distinguish between sudden and slow-impact hazards; to determine the causes of calamitous incidence, recurrence, and probability; to differentiate scale, intensity, and duration; to understand how to face disasters or avoid them. Handling hazard and emergency are just as important as attacking the direct causes that increase social and economic vulnerability.

As social scientists, we are hindered from carrying out all these tasks. To have a more complete understanding of the natural and social contexts and their structural and historical dimensions, it is absolutely vital to carry out multidisciplinary disaster research, based on the study of the interrelationship between vulnerable context and hazard,[7] focusing on the "relation of mutuality of the natural and social worlds" (see Oliver-Smith, this volume).

As stated earlier in this chapter, disasters as processes, as diachronic phenomena, can serve as the thread on which we, through ethnography, can weave many cultural histories. Historical perspective makes possible a synthesis of all these. In the same way that anthropology deals with other, contemporary cultures, history deals with other cultures in time, enlightening a sequential perspective, trying to show not only what happened, but also how and why it happened.

Anthropological and historical disaster analysis clearly demonstrate that earthquakes, droughts, frosts, and other hazards are not, and have not always been, chronic or "normal" disasters. They may be the "norm," but they should not necessarily become "disasters." It is only by distinguishing hazards from disasters, by recognizing disasters as multidimensional processes and studying them in a historical perspective, framing them as diachronic, that we can advance in the theoretical and methodological development of this discipline. To a considerable degree we will also be able to decrease the growing effects of the encounter between hazardous agents and vulnerable populations.

Notes

1. CIESAS (Research and Higher Studies Center in Social Anthropology, Mexico) has made a systematic and continued effort to carry out studies on disasters from a social perspective in both historical and contemporaneous terms. CIESAS's research has operated along the lines of the so-called alternative approach and adjusting them to the Mexican reality.

2. Similar hypotheses appeared for the first time, worded in different ways, in several of Hewitt's publications in 1983, as well as in the results presented by the CLACSO group (Caputo, Hardoy, and Herzer 1985).

3. Description and analysis of the type of sources used in the formulation of the catalogues of historical earthquakes and agricultural disasters appear in introductory studies on this topic (García-Acosta and Suárez Reynoso 1996; García-Acosta, Pérez and Molina, forthcoming; Escobar, forthcoming).

4. See Paine's (this volume) ideas on the concepts of risk management and "no-risk" strategy in Israel.

5. An interesting and clarifying review of different perspectives on the relationship between human beings and nature, the need to distinguish between nature and environment, and the proposal of a mutuality of society and nature in disaster analysis is found in Oliver-Smith's chapter in this volume.

6. As McCabe shows in this volume, among the Turkana pastoralists, diet always changes during the dry seasons.

7. An example is a joint study of the 1568 earthquake in Mexico, carried out by anthropologists, historians, and seismologists (Suárez, García-Acosta, and Gaulon 1994). This study could not have been approached in an integral fashion if a multidisciplinary focus had not been available.

4

Danger and the No-Risk Thesis

Robert Paine

> There are times when it is foolish to ask what the cost is.
> —The heroine of Bo Widerberg's film *Elvira Madigan*

This chapter side-glances catastrophe. It is about the handling of risk, perhaps about living in risk of catastrophe, but not about catastrophe itself. Specifically, I focus on risk to explore the paradox that, in situations of extreme danger, risk may be discounted.

Roy Rappaport (1988), rather than Giddens (1991), Beck (1992), or Douglas (1992), underwrites this paradox, insisting that "intrinsic to all transmission concerning risk" is the "social and cultural processing of information" aside from the technical assessments of experts. The recurring emphasis is on "adaptiveness" to risk—"the adaptive value of amplification or exaggeration under some circumstances, the adaptive value of playing down danger in others" (Rappoport 1988:190); in short, on how people are active agents of their own condition. The emphasis on "active agency" contrasts with the position adopted by Douglas and Wildavsky (1982:80) that "[people] manage as well as they do, without knowing the risks they face, by following social rules on what to ignore: institutions are their problem-solving devices."

In accord with the notion of active agency, this chapter uses several case histories—one of which, concerning Israel and Zionism, I explore in some depth—to highlight how people distinguish between *risk* and *danger* and how risk may be discounted. First, however, I treat the analytic distinction itself.

DISTINGUISHING DANGER AND RISK, AND THE NO-RISK THESIS

To foreground the analytic imperative of recognizing the risk-danger distinction, I turn to the Batesonian aphorism "the map is not the territory" (Bateson 1972), in the sense that "what we map is [the] relationship in which we participate, and not a direct representation of the things 'out there'" (Harries-Jones 1995:59). Thus map is to territory as risk is to danger: Risk we construct between ourselves, danger is "out there." The very notion of risk introduces options (the options of mapping); indeed, it requires them. Risk, then, pertains to probability calculations about danger and, hence, to the "cost" of a projected undertaking. One has options: to proceed as originally intended, to proceed in a modified way, or to abort.

The first option—proceed as originally intended whatever the odds—was, in fact, my actual point of entry into the matter of risk and danger. I came to it through thinking about Zionism in its formative period, the travails of the state of Israel, and how Israel has presented itself to the world. Initially, I supposed that Jewish Israelis would be self-consciously living with risk, that risk would be a compelling issue to them. I still believe this is so, but not in the way I originally expected. I have instead been struck by the ways, in a world that is so risky, that risk consciousness in Israel has been repressed. This leads into the no-risk concept.

Given that how one views risk is culturally constructed, my premise is that we must allow for the existence of cultural contexts—and a cultural logic—in which effort is put into *not* constructing risk. The no-risk thesis is one of cognitive repression of risk. It returns us to the crucial distinction between danger and risk, for the crux of the thesis is the stopping of the translation, or flow, of danger into risk. As we will see, there are notable cognitive implications.

There is one qualification. It entails the place of risk avoidance alongside risk repression in the cultural scheme. The no-risk thesis is one of risk repression with regard to an ultimate goal. There may be risk avoidance at the practical level, but it enters only to better ensure the attainment of the ultimate goal.

What does this imply in practice? Above all, it implies the preclusion of doubt and the effective elimination of ambiguity. It means the shutting out of perceptions of the world, and of what is or is not possible, that others may hold. It also involves shutting out the perceptions other people have of those who embrace no-risk; the notion of insulation is thus crucial. A person or group, then, that proceeds and persists with its enterprise despite its associated danger and does so without risk calculations, ideally embraces the no-risk thesis.

The case histories that follow tell their own stories, but let me emphasize two general points. First, embracement does occur. Second, there may follow embracement of danger itself as generative of value (Paine 1989), as zealotry and martyrdom demonstrate. So we are dealing with a logic of extreme behavior in extreme circumstances.

There are two further points to note. First, the extreme behavior may itself promote, even intentionally, the extreme circumstances. Second, behavior that looks "extreme" to an outside observer is likely to be understood as "adaptive" in the minds of the committed. This last point raises its own question about adaptiveness. What is adaptive in one set of circumstances or at one point of time, for example at a project's inception, may become maladaptive over time. The necessary insulation may deteriorate into ostrich-pose isolation, with an accompanying loss of political realism. This means that a strategy of risk repression may itself engender further or new danger. Again, while such a consequence may be evident as a "fact" to those on the outside, it may be repressed by those on the inside.

CONTRASTING NO-RISK SCENARIOS

The tight logical premise of no-risk thinking is found in a diversity of cultural contexts. By way of preparing for the Israel and Zionism case history and alerting readers to the range of variables we may encounter, I summarize and compare, in this section, four different cultural settings of no-risk logic. The first two are drawn from the ethnographies of Joseba Zulaika (1988, 1981), himself a Spanish Basque; one is on the Basque ETA, the other on Spanish trawlermen. The other two draw upon Sharon Stephens's (this volume) research on radiation protection and Anthony Oliver-Smith's (1986a) work among avalanche survivors.

Basque ETA

The ETA *(Euskadi Ta Askatasuna)* is an armed Basque nationalist group at war with the Spanish state, which views its members as terrorists. They see themselves as engaged in a conflict of "ultimate ends" (Weber 1949) in which rational calculation of means would not only be politically ineffective but would fail to express the Truth that is at stake. Rather, the ETA "terrorists" are guided by the "morality of sacred ends" in which the "fallen" in the struggle are "invested with the sanctity of sacrificial death" (Zulaika 1988:333, 334).

This ETA logic of no-risk is at one with the Basque cultural ethos, in which "sudden, partial, arbitrary acts are more decisive than the progressive summation of a process" (Zulaika 1988:178). Thus "[t]he very act of joining ETA implies...a radical personal decision of a yes-or-no kind. The self is faced with an all-or-nothing alternative, which does not allow for middle ground" (Zulaika 1988:323, 32). Danger is invited, risk is not calculated. What I have referred to as insulation and removal of ambiguity are indispensable correlates. Danger is embraced for its cleansing and fortifying properties, and these underwrite "the morality of sacred ends" (Zulaika 1988:334).

Spanish Deep-Sea Fishermen

In *Terranova* (1981), Zulaika draws upon his experience as an enlisted hand on a Spanish trawler in the northwest Atlantic waters. The trawlermen insist that they cannot predict when or why their nets will be full or empty; in their view there is no objective cause-and-effect relationship that can be applied when dealing with "uncertain natural resources." "Luck" is the determinant: "[N]o working disposition, no concrete method, no known technique can provide success 'until the right time comes'" (Zulaika 1981:66). Accordingly, these deep-sea fishermen do not make calculations about risk, and a no-risk disposition is engendered, not simply with respect to economic uncertainty and loss but also, quite crucially, with respect to physical fatalities and even death. The fishermen, writes Zulaika (1981:82, 70), "are there to offer their work and their lives in order to receive the gift of fish," and this means "they are defined by what they cannot control." Ultimately, it is their sense of being that is entwined in this enterprise.

Luck differs from mere chance. It comes "at the right time," and a necessary precondition is the devotion of the crew both to proper conduct—life onboard is regulated by taboos—and to continual work— "the continuous dragging of the net day and night" (Zulaika 1981:66, 81–82). Luck has its own (secret) certainty. No effort is made, for example, to tap into fisheries science for information that might reduce or explain the prevailing uncertainty (Zulaika 1981:82). Similarly, risk avoidance is weak or even absent. Life at sea is sensed as a "constant danger." Sometimes men are lost overboard; often there are no fire extinguishers on board, despite cases of fire (Zulaika 1981:66, 89). Yet the trawlermen are resigned to such dangers.

Thus a situation that one might well suppose would be riddled with ambiguities and uncertainties, along with a numbing sense of risk, is largely saved from these by the insulation from human decisions and flows of information (be they helpful or misleading) afforded by this principle of luck. Luck becomes "a quasi-cosmological concept offering some cognitive order" through bridging the gap between effort and result, between the human and natural orders (Zulaika 1981:66–67; personal communication 1997). In warding off uncertainty, however, it "*prevents* the search for, and eradication of, possible causes of danger" (p. 89; emphasis added).

COMPARISONS: 1

In both these situations, ritualized behavior tends to take the place of rational calculation, and in neither case is risk calculated; but the similarity ends there. If among the trawlermen the governing ethos is "what *must* be, will be" (Zulaika 1981:72), then among ETA it is "what we *will*, must be." Where the one is passively compliant, eschewing purposive action, the other is aggressively purposive; where the one is resigned to danger, the other embraces it. Thus the two have different linked ontologies of certainty and the future. The deep-water trawlermen's is habitual and both immediate and repetitive, whereas the ETA's is action-motivated and, in the long term, predicated on change.

Radiation Protection Experts

Sharon Stephens (this volume) leads us to consider how "experts," as opposed to the lay public, may publicly handle uncertainty, both their own and the public's. I suggest that this may lead to their calling on an approximation of the no-risk thesis. The radiation protection experts flounder for a politically acceptable way of letting an anxious and suspicious public know that there are risks attached to nuclear energy and nuclear accidents, and that their knowledge is none too reliable. Yet the message the experts send to the public is essentially: Stop thinking about risks, everything is under control (see the reference to Douglas and Wildavsky, above).

The problem, as the experts see it, is exacerbated by a public that is "irrational, uneducated, emotional, and sometimes even 'hysterical'" (Stephens, this volume); so a crucial implication within the message is for individuals to stop thinking individually (see Wallman 1998). Much attention is paid to the (re)structuring of "normality." In one respect, at least, there is no such restructuring: "Normality" remains, in the experts' view, a matter of "averages" within an undifferentiated population (Stephens, this volume).

It is, of course, because there *is* risk, but no politically acceptable way of transmitting such a message, that the strategy of risk repression is adopted. The practicality of the strategy depends in large measure on insulation—in this case, the experts' insulation. Insulation reigns over the experts' knowledge and its uncertainty, but also over the experts themselves as "invisible" persons (see Paine 1992a).

Staying "Put"

Anthony Oliver-Smith (1986a) draws attention to postcatastrophe decisions, decisions that themselves could be touched with catastrophe. The town of Yungay in the Peruvian Andes was obliterated by an avalanche that slid off the nearby mountain, leaving but a few hundred survivors out of a population of several thousand. People were faced with the question of whether to stay or leave, that is, rebuild their lives *in situ* or start life again elsewhere. There were risks attached to both options. Some people left, others stayed. Far from institutions delivering the answer (Douglas and Wildavsky 1982), it was "the threat of relocation by the government" that "stimulated a remarkable sense of common purpose" (Oliver-Smith 1986:236). In this way, "survivors" of the disaster were able to regain "a sense of participation and control over their own lives and society" (1986:263). Relocation, on the other hand, was seen as bringing further disruption and new risks.

Oliver-Smith (1986:265–66) sees this resistance to resettlement as "an adherence to the known, the proven, the secure" and "an affirmation of their identity," even though "the known" includes the possibility of another avalanche from that same mountain. Thus, along with that "affirmation" came the repression of risk vis-à-vis the mountain and risk avoidance vis-à-vis the outside world. To this day the mountain itself remains "part of the people's self-definition" (Oliver-Smith, in seminar). As does another mountain for another people and another cause. An ETA member explains the emplacement of her commitment in these terms: "because we were born here, because that mountain was born in me and I from that mountain, simply because of that…" (Zulaika 1988:259). This speaks to the strength and the "intense particularity" of emplacement (Feld and Basso 1996:11). But what of the costs of this "mapping" of territory? In Yungay, people also refer to their mountain as "a vile traitor…a cowardly assassin" (Oliver-Smith, in seminar). However, once the decision to stay has been made, calculation of risk serves no point. Indeed, it would likely undermine their situation. The issue becomes one of protecting a worldview. The cultural ideal becomes reality. To leave betrays that ideal, and if danger is part of that reality, so be it.

COMPARISONS: 2

The construction of normality and the lengths to which people will go to preserve and continue with "the normal," left implicit in the accounts of the Spanish trawlermen and the Basque ETA, now emerges as a dominating issue. It has much to do with shapes of knowledge and who is in the position to shape knowledge; it is on this account that the politics over "the normal" differ decisively in these last two cases.

For some who decide to stay in Yungay, it may be a matter of a trade-off of risks. They leave and risk the loss of their personal sense of emplacement, or, believing there is nowhere else where they can see themselves being themselves (Tuan 1984), they stay and live with the possibility of another avalanche. All who stay must find ways of preserving, of continuing with the everyday "normal" that they knew before catastrophe fell. Their "will be" emerges, we may say, out of what "had been."

In the case of the radiation experts, the salient feature is the attempted control of others' shapes of knowledge, and hence control over their sense of normality. In practical terms, the option to stay or to move is appreciably less plausible in the case of a radiation scare, and the withholding of information from the public, as reported by Stephens, further diminishes the likelihood of any exercise of choice. The experts' message is, of course, that continued normality removes any need to choose.

And Zionism

Here I call attention to issues of place from four ethnographic scenarios in the Zionist/Israel case study that will follow. Both the shaping of knowledge and the construction of the normal will feature centrally, but in ways different from those described thus far. I give prominence to the notion of "beyond," for even as they were energized by a powerful ideology of emplacement, Zionists moved "beyond" what had been. And moving beyond implicates a reshaping of knowledge. Furthermore, the truth about this beyond was not, as happened in the radiation case history, "taken out of sight" (Bauman 1989:97);[1] rather, the truths of Zionist visions have been kept very much in open evidence and have energized individual and group commitment.

These are common issues in Zionism, but "Zionism," in practice, is not one unified ideology. Ideological differences exist between secular and religious Zionists, and also within each of these groups, stretching even to ideological incompatibility. Yet the no-risk thesis applies to all, although in significantly different ways. Thus the *meanings* given to knowledge and normality are not necessarily shared; they are given different shapes. It is in the task of elucidating these forces of ideological division that I return to the "what must be" versus "what we will" predications.

The Case of Zionism, and then Israel

The early Zionists coming to Palestine took the momentous step of not just leaving their ancestral culture but embarking on a journey into virtually unknown and very foreign territory where there was another people already living. There they would sustain themselves on a new ideology of collectivism. This was a "root-and-branch" step. They cut themselves off from others, especially from many of their own people.

The project was risk-full. Those taking up the endeavor dealt with the risk by turning their backs on it—by living "beyond" it. They did so as part of the process of remaking themselves through the remaking of their culture (Wallace 1956b) and, in doing so, unceremoniously upending the verities of some of the institutions that had been Jewish life. These Zionists were colonizing a novel future (Giddens 1991); what they were *not* doing was counting the risk.

It was not that there were no practical precautions (risk avoidance), or that the early Zionists did not know risk emotively, or that they were blind or indifferent to moral questions posed by the perception of risk. Rather, their precautions had a matter-of-factness about them, and risk as an emotion was significantly played down. People tangled with the moral issues on their own rather than in public fora, and the risk of their being unwanted implants in an Arab world was, more often than not, repressed.

Journeys Beyond

The secular Jewish immigrant came with a determination to live in a present of her or his making, beyond the past with its disasters and humiliations and also its obsolescence. He or she also came beyond the thought of failure in the future ("what we will"). "Those who...went to Palestine, did not just flee from pogroms nor were they bent on economic safety and success—Ottoman Palestine was hardly an economic paradise. They were seeking self-determination, identity, liberation within the terms of post-1789 European culture and their own newly awakened self-consciousness" (Avineri 1981:13). To the same end, Vital (1975:10) speaks of "the attraction of a radical solution" so that "the further removed one was from the direct influence of traditional Jewish society, the starker appeared the contrast between the ancient glories and the contemporary degradation and between the social and political conditions that obtained for other peoples on the one hand and the depoliticized, broken-backed framework of Jewish national life [in the Diaspora] on the other" (see also Almog 1987; Segre 1980).

The religious immigrant came with equal intensity of conviction, but in this case it was to live beyond the present for a future that was promised aeons ago in the covenant God made with His chosen ("what must be").

It follows that by their own understanding these Zionists, secular and religious, were visionaries, even as there is a crucial difference between them as indicated: religious Zionists recognize themselves as among God's chosen; secular Zionists choose. Whereas the former condition is that of an eschatological imperative whose outcome is prefigured (although not without trials along the way), the latter emerges out of a political imperative whose outcome is a matter of human achievement. Zionist commitment by either of these routes returns us to the quintessential prerequisites of no-risk politics and its culture: preclusion of doubt, shutting out others' perceptions of the world and of what is possible and what is not, and, not least, shutting out the perceptions others have of "us."

Thus, in the process of its making, Zionist Israel (religious and secular) becomes an exception to some general statements about the condition of contemporary Western society. Niklas Luhmann (1993:vii), for example, is not alone in seeing the world around him as offering "a future about which nothing certain can be discerned"; Hermann Lubbe (1993:31) even avers that "there has never been a civilized community that has understood the conditions of its own life less than we do." The prevailing cognition in Israel has been that the future must be and therefore is (as in a vision), that the great national project will continue (even as it changes), and that the people themselves believe they have understood the conditions and the meaning of their existence. For them, it has been a matter of making these lived-with issues into "self-evident truth," truth of the kind that "commits the knower to the social system in which his knowledge is guaranteed" (Douglas 1975:209).

What happens to risk in these circumstances, as I have painted them, of Zionist Israel in its formative phase? If there is only one thing to do, risk does not have a place even as danger does. "Yes, we live dangerously...There is no choice! But we are free!" editorialized Amos Elon (1981:224) on the Zionist condition. Others might see this as a contradiction, yet for the committed it is no such thing. This cognitive stance is buttressed by the circumstance that without engagement with an other, whether a partner or adversary, risk is altogether less measurable and more easily set aside. More important still is that with an already unshakeable commitment to a project, the mind is closed to the opportunities of other ventures and thoughts to which risk-taking lends itself. Instead, one is alert to the danger of the truth's being subverted by such opportunities.

Yet the preclusion of doubt has to be taught, and self-evidency has to be cultivated. Although true both of the chosen and those who themselves choose, these matters were a particular burden to the early secular Zionist communities. While the learning process was diffuse, the key was to forge a moral group identity through the fusion of personal identity with social identity (Evens 1980; Talmon 1972).[2] "We behave as though only a plural exists" (Hareven 1988:10); "We don't like to be alone; we literally breathe each other. What does 'I' mean?" (Rubinstein 1984:133). At the end of a day's labor in the fields people might dance the hora, "linked arm in arm, and shoulder to shoulder, moving in a steady circle, with accelerated tempo, driven by the pressure of each against the other, a pressure that demanded uniformity of step and rhythm" (Diamond 1957:95). In school, "[t]he Zionist leaders and educators [of my youth], focused so intently on the monumental implications of our ancient tribe's return to its land, were not concerned with cultivating the solitary self, the lyrical personal voice of the individual" (Ezrahi 1997:22). A linguistic "antistyle" evolved, concerned that words could be "at the expense of a commitment to deeds" (Katriel 1986:24, 29). In this there was a deliberate distancing from the Talmudic tradition of involved discourse that recognized the "many-sidedness of issues and the inherent ambiguity of human affairs" (Katriel 1986:18).

But what if the Jew from Eastern Europe, now a Zionist in Palestine, felt lost? David Ben-Gurion issued frequent epistles of this kind: "[W]e who have come to settle in the Jewish state have taken a leap [back] in time which makes us feel closer to David, Uzziah, and Joshua bin Nun than to the *shtetl* in Cracow or the nineteenth-century ideologists of Warsaw" (in Weiner 1970: 241). Pedagogically, every effort was made to replace Yiddish with a "native" Hebrew (Even-Zohar 1990).

Notwithstanding the essential emphasis on a collectivized identity, the sacredness of individual life was (and is) revered, especially when in service, as soldiers, to the common good and against the common danger. As a feature writer in the *Jerusalem Post* (May 25, 1985) put it: "The Israeli soldier is not to become a mere nameless number: he must always remain an individual with an individual name." In the newspaper of the same date there was this endorsement by Yitzhak Rabin, then minister of defense: "There is a 'supreme value' and that is that every soldier sent on an operation should know the State, the Cabinet, the Army are behind them." Hence the lengths to which the State of Israel has gone to secure the return of prisoners of war (or their bodies) in enemy hands (Paine 1996).

Not all who joined the Zionist project stayed with it, however. Many left, in some years exceeding the numbers that came (Paine 1993:237 n. 9). In a backhanded way, this attests to the rigor of the ideal of the project.

NORMALCY

Ultimately the State of Israel was achieved in 1949 by Jewish force of arms in the post-Holocaust world, and its fifty years have been scarred by wars and threat of war. These circumstances influence what is accepted as "normal." Consider, for example, the political rhetoric through the years. Elon sees "the towering urge for self-reliance" (1981:199); the Israeli chief of staff declares, "We have decided not to live by the sufferance of others" (Rubinstein 1984:90); and Prime Minister David Ben-Gurion would say, "It's not what the *goyim* [non-Jews] think that matters but what *we do*" (field notes). Thus the "shutting out" process is forwarded. Crucial is the attitude regarding "blame"; to blame others is to posit a relationship with them. Blame may also disperse responsibility. What was being said here is that, henceforth, we are responsible to and for ourselves, as are other nations.

One qualifier of this thesis of shutting out others and of going it alone is Ben-Gurion's wartime use (1941) of what Amitzur Ilan sees as the Zionists' "theory of catastrophe": "Our misfortune in the world is increasing. But [says Ben-Gurion] Zionism's power stems from the increase in the Jews' misfortune" (in Ilan 1984:127). Against that is Ben-Gurion's statement in 1957 that "German anti-Semitism, the

Dreyfus trial…persecution of Jews in Rumania…they represent events from the past in foreign lands, sad memories of Jews in exile, but not emotional experiences and facts of life which educate and direct us" (Liebman and Don-Yehiya 1984:55).

In 1960 the Israeli historian J. L. Talmon saw, even among the secular settlers of that period, "a kind of divine and creative madness which not only stills all fear and hesitation but also makes for clarity of vision in a landscape bathed in a lurid, distorting light" (cited in Elon 1981:198). Elon's (1997:269) comment on this passage is that it "accounted for much of the daring and energy of the young state…But after 1967," Elon continues, "it was also one of the causes for much of the narrow-mindedness and sanctified nationalistic egoism that came in the wake of the Six-Day and the Yom Kippur wars—the paranoia, of 'the entire world is against us' and the disregard of Palestinian rights and of international opinion" (Elon 1997:269).

Such infusion of values around the Zionist project and the making of its state reminds us again how notions of "the normal" are selective constructions. For example, in the Zionist case the construction tends to render invisible things that exist in the eyes of an outside observer and, reciprocally, to reveal things that are not there to the outside observer (Tuan 1984). I found religious Zionists "reading" or "seeing" the landscape in this way:

> We stand on a Samarian hillside. Our guide is a Jewish religious settler. In the landscape before me I see, to my left and along a stony elevation, an Israeli settlement, and in a fold in the valley in front of me, a Palestine village. I turn to listen to our guide. The landscape he "sees" apparently contains neither the settlement nor the village: what he is telling us to "see" is the site where Jeremiah was born and where the Maccabees—just across the valley—fought and defeated a Roman legion…neither the village nor the settlement are used as orientation points. (adapted from 1983 field notes; see Paine 1995b:161)

There is good reason to suppose that the selective process will be especially evident and pressed into service in situations of strain over a principled commitment. People cling to their "normal" despite what is happening around them (Paine 1992a; Zulaika 1981; also see Douglas and Wildavsky 1982). During the *intifada* of the 1980s on the West Bank, Stanley Cohen, a criminologist at the Hebrew University of Jerusalem, noted to his distress how among people—secular for the most part—who associate themselves with a "sane, decent Zionism with a conscience," there was, nonetheless, "a refusal to believe what is happening. Life goes on" (Cohen 1988:62; Ben-Ari 1989 is an auto-ethnography of this situation). This is normalcy as insurance (Douglas 1990); the insurance is against thinking about a risk, the risk of ethical ambiguity compromising the Zionist project.

RELIGIOUS WORLDS

For religious Israel,[3] the messianic fulfillment has yet to be and, therefore, the no-risk thesis remains unimpaired to this day. This follows from the unchanging principles of eschatology that govern and inform religious Zionism. Prefigured knowledge, as already mentioned, is the key: All is in the Torah; God is omnipotent and omniscient. Thus, "It has to be understood that nothing accidental happens to Jewish people. This is a fundamental tenet of Judaism" (Rabbi Yitzak Peretz in Paine 1992b). In the religious context, the no-risk thesis is far from being a contemporary Zionist invention; rather, it has helped Jews to sustain their faith through the centuries, whatever might befall them. Thus Jacob Katz (1961: 214), historian of the European Jewish Diaspora, writes: "Even the gravest events [e.g., the massacres in Russia in the seventeenth century] were not likely to evoke reactions transcending the framework of traditional [Orthodox] modes of thought and actions." We are left understanding that all was overshadowed by divine providence—the pogroms and Cossacks did not come of themselves but by the direction of God. People re-intensified, if anything, their life of devotion.

However, this does not mean that unanimity has to prevail among those whose lives are fortified by a no-risk ideology. For example, troubling contradictory eschatological conclusions regarding the Holocaust are mooted (Fackenheim 1987; Mintz 1987). Was the Holocaust a divine signal of imminent redemption? Or was it a signal of divine displeasure (and the delay of redemption)? Separate messianic circles have their own answers (Mintz 1987; Ravitzky 1997), each of

which is held by those who espouse it to be unequivocally eschatologi-
cally informed: "Only an explanation that purports to be absolute,
total, and final can balance the demonic loss and justify it" (Ravitzky
1997:127). Each is anchored in the imperative of the removal of impu-
rities among the Jewish people; they differ, however, over the identifi-
cation of the impurity.

In one view, the impurity is the State of Israel; in another, it is the
Jewry of the European Diaspora. The first is the view held by those
Ultra-Orthodox *(haredim)* who oppose all efforts to activate "Zionism"
as a political project. For them, the redemptive promise of Zionism will
be fulfilled in God's own time, and Jewish "passivity" in this matter
(e.g., no attempt to resettle the holy places in Judea and Samaria [the
West Bank]) is "a heroic decision that must be daily reaffirmed." For
them, the Zionist state is "an insolent human attempt to usurp the pre-
rogative of the Creator Himself" (Ravitzky 1997:63).

The other view is found in those religious circles that would purge
the Jewish being of all such passivity, which is seen as the mark of
Judaism in the Diaspora. This view holds that the "footsteps of the
Messiah" are already heard; witness the "miraculous" outcome of the
1967 war. This means that Redemption is nigh and Jews—in service to
God—must do what they can to bring it about. Hence the imperative of
Jewish return, *now,* to Judea and Samaria. (As the state itself is often
found wanting in its political Zionism in terms of this agenda, political
partnerships are entered into with the irredentist Greater Israel wing of
secular Zionism; see Aran 1989.)

Thus within the world of Jewish Orthodoxy a telos of "what must
be" faces a telos of "what we will." Duty in the one is to wait on God's
will, in the other it is to activate His already-declared intention. The
Gentile world is irrelevant in both cases. It is simply "shut out."
Responsibility for the ultimate fulfillment lies exclusively with the
Chosen. Delays in redemption are not blamed on the Gentiles. Where
there is blame it is between the Chosen along the lines indicated, and
between them and the Jewish public that has lapsed into secularism:

> Of particular significance to our present inquiry has been the
> politically active alternative centered around the Gush Emunim
> ("Bloc of the Faithful"), for whom politics is a mode of religious

> expression: My husband and I are convinced that we are living in a most fateful period. If we prove to be the exclusive propri- etors of Eretz Israel [i.e. West Bank]...it will hasten redemp- tion. (Gush Emunim spokesperson, in Weissbrod 1982:269)

> We are commanded by the Bible, not by the government ...Settlement is above the law of the Knesset. *(ibid.)*

> We did not initiate the freeing of *Eretz Israel* [in this context, the West Bank], it was brought upon us and we afterwards saw it as an act of God: He wishes us to build. (A leader of the Gush Emunim, 1983, field notes)

> The purpose...is not the normalization of the people of Israel—to be a nation like all other nations—but to be a holy people, a people of the living God. (Rabbi Yehuda Amital, in Rubinstein 1984:105)

Here, we find the eschatological consequences of no-risk stated unmistakably and dramatically. They are consequences that may work for war, that is, for a cataclysmic fulfillment of redemption:

> [W]e may see in the state of war between us and the Arabs the hand of providence. (Rabbi Chaim Peles, in Rubinstein 1984:114)

> When will peace come? I don't know. But what if it takes gener- ations. We are here until the end of time. (Field notes, Hebron, 1983)

Meanwhile, there has been the attempt to blow up the Mosque of Omar in Jerusalem in the 1980s (for what peace is it, went the reason- ing, that leaves the Temple Mount in the hands of Islam?)[4] and the mas- sacre in the Tomb of the Patriarchs in Hebron in the 1990s.[5] This is "the blazing landscape of redemption" after centuries of "a life lived in deferment" that Gershom Scholem warned about (1971:35). And, as though commenting on the "what we will" telos within no-risk ideology, he asked "[w]hether or not Jewish history [and what else with it?] will be able to endure this entry into the concrete realm without perishing in the crisis of the Messianic claim" (Scholem 1971:36).

A final point. What should not be lost from view is that the messianic claim of either telos, and the no-risk ideology with it, is a claim of perfection, and perfection does not suffer compromise. Especially illuminating in this connection is the depth of meaning given to the Hebrew word for peace, *shalom:* "derived from a root denoting wholeness or completeness,...[it] is bound up with the notion of *shelemut, perfection*" (Ravitzky 1987:685).

Particularly worthy of note is the contemporary adoption of the historical (from the Middle Ages) "elevation" of the idea of peace "to the level of the cosmic, the metaphysical, the divine" (Ravitzky 1987:688). So for there to be peace—a condition of perfection—the imperfect, seen as the unpeaceful, has to be destroyed. The question on which religious Zionists are divided is that of the means by which the destruction should be accomplished.

SECULAR WORLDS

Among secular Zionists, in contrast to the religious Zionists, several criteria of project fulfillment exist, and, more than ever before, they are the subject of open debate. This situation prompts the question of whether the no-risk thesis is still tenable in today's secular Israel. Would J. L. Talmon, for example, still see Israel as a place of "creative madness which stills all fear and hesitation"? Today there exists an "Israeli" society, diverse and fractured though it is. With it, in the view of many Israelis, Zionism has achieved its aim. It is yesterday's slogan; project days are over. "Most Israelis wish to be a people like all peoples: they seek the same recognition from their neighbours, the same certainty in their permanence, that the French, English, Russians, and Chinese enjoy" (Kramer 1997:95).

Note, however, several cautionary points. First, much the same had been said before (Rubinstein 1984:70). Second, the trend may very well suffer backlash leading to a volte-face—indeed, some would say this is already the case (after his electoral defeat to Netanyahu, Peres was reported as saying: "Well, the Jews defeated the Israelis!"). And third, there is the paradox: The "certainty" vouchsafed here, being in the political domain with its bargains, carries risk with it.

That much said, a war-weary people may well wish now to be "a people like all peoples," yet this means a change in Israel's understanding of itself. In his forceful and important book about risk and political realism, Yehoshafat Harkabi (1983:xv) is quite clear as to what this has to mean: Nothing less than "the *secularization* of Jewish history and destiny." Harkabi ventures a historical explanation of the origin of this particular no-risk mind-set: "As objects of history, the Jews were also its victims" and "Jewish misfortunes were transformed into a cosmic predicament" (1983:134, 133). He continues: "This perception of non-responsibility, of innocence in history, is liable to become a matter of habit, continuing unnoticeably into the present when, with the establishment of the State of Israel, we Jews returned to being *subjects* in history" (1983:134). The irony is that the pioneer and militantly secular Zionists brought this no-risk philosophy with them from the Diaspora that they scorn!

Harkabi warns that the loss of "realism," meaning, among other things, the loss of probability calculations characteristic of a no-risk political philosophy, could court catastrophe. To avoid such an outcome, a sense of risk is needed. Certainly, Israel deploys the risk factor forensically (Douglas 1990) as a means of bolstering financial and military aid, from the United States in particular. But the government has seldom done so in the public arena—hence the storm following Prime Minister Golda Meir's coupling of Israel with a "Masada complex" (*Newsweek*, March 19, 1973). Subsequent decades brought Camp David and the Oslo Accords, which were not convened on a no-risk basis. On each occasion there was inclusion of an adversary, and bargaining ensued.

Aside from what is or is not happening within and between governments, there is emerging among broad sectors of Israeli society a willingness to recognize risk of both loss and failure. This willingness comes with a new sense of individual opportunity and awareness of the chance of lost opportunities. Entwined in this is the move of mainstream Israel, as part of its wish to be a people like other peoples, from its earlier collectivist ethos to one of individualism (see especially Ezrahi 1997).

This does not imply a loss of social conscience. On the contrary, one hears more than ever voices of reasoned conscientious dissent and protest. The invasion of Lebanon (1982) was not accepted as a "war of necessity"; with the *intifada* came more soldiers' refusal to serve in the West Bank. Of particular note is the public discussion of the distribution of risk as illustrated by the dilemma of Israel's northern frontier abutting Lebanon. Military deployment in southern Lebanon keeps the Hezbollah at a distance from the Israel border, but not without a cost in soldiers' lives. Mothers of these young soldiers want the government to make the oft-debated decision to withdraw to the Israeli border, but to forsake this "Israeli security zone" would bring more Israeli communities within range of katyusha rockets (see Postscript, below).

Much of Ezrahi's emphasis is on Israelis' struggle to redefine perceptions of power and violence and their application for political ends. "[I]n their first general war, Israeli Jews still seemed to perceive force from the point of view of victims...All that began to change in the aftermath of the war of 1967...the narrative of victimhood...ceased to make sense" (Ezrahi 1997:188). Now there begins to emerge "[a] readiness to actually reframe the conflict, to see it not as a war of survival but [with the *intifada* in mind] as a struggle between a civilian population and an occupying force" (1997:215). For the first time in the history of the Zionist project and of the State of Israel, perhaps the public has to face a confrontation of values, "the sin of occupation" versus territorial withdrawal as "an act of betrayal" (Ezrahi 1997:10). As though echoing Harkabi, Ezrahi reminds us that this amounts to a direct challenge to the "Jewish visionary epic" of "elevating politics from earth to heaven" (1997:198) and takes away from "certainty" its earlier self-predicting ontology. The majority of Israelis are no longer living "beyond" and no longer "shutting out" the rest of the world. Even so, there is the ideology of "Greater Israel" in the West Bank with its persisting no-risk mindset in which some secular Zionists, along with the Gush Emunim, are mired. Their numbers may be small, but the ideology "justifies the use of any and all available power" (Ezrahi 1997:198).

For what is now surely mainstream Israeli society, however, the changes beckon a profound change in psyche, and perhaps the key is the new and growing ability among Israelis to adopt an outsider stance (Cohen 1988:96)—seeing their society as if from the outside without abandoning their insider's sense of belonging. The most poignant register of this happening is when one can say, in good faith, "My culture lets me down," instead of "I let my culture down" (Paine 1992b:197). Only in the former case are persons free to set about changing their culture. Of particular concern here, such thinking sabotages the no-risk mind-set with its closure against the rest of the world that, I have suggested, empowered the will of Zionists.

A consideration of a different order plays in here as well. In today's Israel, the no-risk thesis is seen by many as a frighteningly insufficient adaptation in a Middle East of nuclear and chemical weapons. In yesterday's world, the collective drew a defiant brand of comfort from noting how Zionism "survives in spite of all odds, therefore there are no odds for survival"—so one didn't think about risk (Don Handelman, correspondence, January 18, 1998). Today the individual is aware that "the nuclear cloud now looms seriously on our horizons for the first time" (ibid.). Aware of the possibility of catastrophe (which had no place in the Zionist lexicon), Israelis now do begin to wonder about the "odds for survival." The Gulf War was a telling example. People in Tel-Aviv slept in their cellars, gas masks at hand, and Iraqi missiles came through.

SOME CONCLUDING OBSERVATIONS AND QUESTIONS

The association of no-risk with crisis warrants discussion, as does the question of the likely life-span of any no-risk project. I begin by attending to the issue of contextuality in relation to no-risk.

A premise throughout this essay has been that risk is socially constructed (Ruck 1993) and thus contextually sensitive, but how far does the characteristic no-risk closure to the world allow for that? For instance, can a no-risk strategy be applied sector-wise to particular groups within a given society? I suppose this to be most unlikely. It might seem that the radiation case (Stephens, this volume) is a sector-wise application of no-risk; however, the subject population did not know (though some may have guessed) the full implication of the experts' message to them. Certainly the no-risk disposition in the making of Zionist Israel was not sectoral but inclusive. Yet there is a sense in which the question—no-risk as a sectoral phenomenon within a society?—is a false one, for the closure that no-risk entails generates its own social and cultural boundaries, its own society. An example is the profound value separation between Zionist groups in Israel, each with their own no-risk reasoning. Of course, it is with the weakening of the no-risk disposition among a population that sectoral patterns are likely to emerge. Such patterns are in evidence in today's Israel, along with concerns over the distribution of risk in which risk avoidance—"Why should I take the risk?"—wins out over risk repression (Hirschberg 1998) and people begin to ask whose fault is it that they face risks (Halevi 1997).

Then there is the question (requiring more research) of how contextually inclusive a set of no-risk precepts might be. Within the routine of a day or a year there will be different domestic contexts of risk, say, which seemingly have no bearing on the particular no-risk situation. Still, might there not be a psychological "contagion" factor, as with the Spanish trawlermen or ETA members, for example, who cannot put aside their fatalism and driven behavior even while they are at home? Out of the realm of the hypothetical, the question is discursively addressed (with no easy answers) by Ben-Ari (1998:xi) respecting "the transition [in Israeli society today] between civilian and army lives."

No-risk is associated with crisis, but, as our cases showed, this relationship is itself variable. A crisis may descend upon a group of people; alternatively, it may be intentionally provoked by them. It may cause bewilderment and despondency, or it may generate clarity in a situation and dispel ambiguity.

The ETA resorts to the making of crisis to reduce indeterminacy. A crisis is manipulated, used to punctuate and highlight the otherwise long-drawn-out "battle" with the Spanish state. Then there is the crisis that the radiation experts fear and wish to avoid. It is one of uncertainty, and inasmuch as it reveals a life-threatening lack of knowledge, it generates not clarity but ambiguity and moral panic; no-risk is introduced as the antidote. For the Spanish trawlermen, crisis has yet another "grammar"; theirs is a world from which both ambiguity and crisis are effectively banished. Should crisis befall them, one can expect resignation. In Israel, crises can spell clarity, but of different kinds. For the apocalyptic messianist, it is the clarity of heightened expectation ("what must be"), while among the early secular Zionists and today's Greater Israel advocates a principal function of "clarity" has been to keep the sense of "project" alive at any odds ("what we will"). (Note that the Six-Day War, with its overwhelming and, for some, "miraculous" victory, served both these ends.)

Finally, there is the question of life span. On account of its imperatives of closure, one would suppose no-risk adaptations would have limited life spans. Yet, as with crisis, there are singular differences. With the ETA ideologues, the issue is their will to pursue into the future their "what we will" no-risk commitment; the probable answer is that it persists for as long as danger is cultivated as a value. In the case of the Spanish trawlermen, with their ethos of "what must be," an indefinite continuance of their no-risk adaptation is all that one sees at present. As for the survivors of Yungay who elected to stay put, they took a decision that launched them into a certainty clouded by an uncertainty: They chose to remain and rebuild their town ("what we will") in the shadow of the mountain ("what must be"). Quite a different situation, however, is unfolding around the radiation experts. They introduced a no-risk mode as a holding operation against uncertainties, but, as Stephens makes clear, the clock is ticking on that strategy.

What of Israel? Perhaps a majority of the secular-motivated Zionists have outgrown the need to pursue the "certainty" of the Zionist vision and hence the no-risk mode; that, however, is far from being the case with the core of the messianically motivated, whose "what must be" is embedded in eschatology.

POSTSCRIPT

This essay was completed in 1998. Of course, in the case of Israel, "politics" have continued at a pace (withdrawal from southern Lebanon, a second *intifada,* and the like). I have chosen not to update the political narrative, for I do not see that doing so would appreciably enhance or alter the argument put forward.

Notes

I thank my fellow seminarists at the School of American Research for their insightful comments on the original presentation of this paper; I also benefited from comments proffered at subsequent presentations in the departments of anthropology at Memorial University and the University of Tromsö and at the 1997 meetings of the American Anthropological Association. Jean Briggs, Gerald Cromer, Itamar Even Zohar, Don Handelman, Iris Jean-Klein, Stuart

Pierson, Peter Sinclair, Jonathan Skinner, Sandra Wallman, Shalva Weil, and Joseba Zulaika were kind enough to read drafts of what became this chapter; my thanks to them, one and all. And a special thank you to Susanna Hoffman for her skillful editorial surgery.

1. The phrase "taken out of sight" is from Zigmunt Bauman's 1989 study of the Holocaust. Judged as a no-risk campaign, the Holocaust combined risk repression with meticulous risk avoidance.

2. There is a degree of cultural selection in what follows. Their secular perspective aside, these accounts focus on immigrants from Eastern and Northern Europe—the Ashkenazim. For a fuller account and bibliography, see Paine 1993.

3. My treatment is of necessity selective and abbreviated. See also Friedman 1990; Landau 1983; Paine 1992c; Schweid 1985; and Willis 1992, among others.

4. Segal (1988) is a firsthand account of the so-called "Jewish Underground"/"Jewish Terrorists" by an erstwhile member; for an account of Jewish terrorism by a Judaic scholar, see Greenstein 1985; on violence in Judaic tradition, see Shapiro 1985.

5. See Paine 1995a for the ideopolitical background, including the coming of Rabbi Kahane to Israel, on which see especially Cromer 1988 and Ravitzky 1985.

5

Bounding Uncertainty

The Post-Chernobyl Culture of Radiation Protection Experts

Sharon Stephens

"Science establishes the physical and biological facts of radiation. Culture and politics come in with the setting of socially acceptable or tolerable limits of exposure" (Alan Martin, Cambridge lectures, July 10, 1995; unpublished). These are foundational claims in the field of radiological protection as they have been institutionalized within the International Commission for Radiological Protection (ICRP) and diverse national radiation protection agencies (see Taylor 1979; Caufield 1989). In contrast, many recent works in the anthropology of science (for example, Traweek 1988; Martin 1994; Nader 1996; Gusterson 1996) have made compelling arguments for the ways in which culture and politics enter integrally into the very formation of what counts as a "fact" in science and how the seemingly given boundaries that underlie the framework of the ICRP, such as between nature and society, scientific facts and value judgments, or experts and the general public, are constituted.

The Chernobyl nuclear accident was a disaster of global proportions. In the aftermath of Chernobyl, some authors (Gould and Goldman 1991; Beck 1987; Haynes and Bojcun 1988) have claimed that it challenges the international scientific community to reevaluate dominant paradigms of radiation science and risk assessment and that it calls into question basically nondemocratic, "top down" practices of radiation policy formation (Gould 1990). But while Chernobyl might have led experts in the field of radiological protection to question certain basic assumptions and practices, I argue here that the accident has resulted instead in increasingly vigorous expert assertions concerning the solid scientific grounds for current policies and the expert control over areas of uncertainty. Such assertions of normalcy and control are as much within the province of an "anthropology of disaster" as are processes of disaster-related cultural change, reinterpretation, and restructuring (Oliver-Smith 1996).

This chapter explores the topic of the "post-Chernobyl culture of radiological protection experts" through a case study of the ways that recognized leaders in the field communicated their understandings, primarily to middle level professionals in government and the European nuclear industry, during the Sixth Residential Summer School on Radiological Protection offered at Magdalene College, Cambridge, United Kingdom, July 10 to 14, 1995. Anthropological inquiry into discourses among national and international radiation experts and various communities "on the ground" about the nature and significance of Chernobyl fallout can provide insights into the cultural grounding of issues of expert knowledge and risk assessment and perception.

DESCRIPTION OF THE COURSE

The Radiological Protection Summer School was organized by IBC Technical Services, Limited, a private, London-based firm that specializes in developing courses and providing scientific/technical information for government and business communities in the UK and, increasingly, the European Union (EU). According to the preliminary brochure, the course was intended for "professionals who had responsibilities in radiological protection, nuclear safety, public health or related subjects in industry, government departments and local authorities…to serve as a refresher course for those well established in the field or as a thorough introduction to newcomers." There were thirty-five "delegates" (the organizers' term for participants): twenty-four from the UK, two each from Sweden and Norway, and one each from Canada, Spain,

Switzerland, the Netherlands, France, Belgium, and Germany. Most held middle-level positions in government (for example, in the United Kingdom Ministry of Agriculture and Department of Environment and the Swedish Radiation Protection Institute) or in the nuclear industry (for example, Scottish Nuclear, Limited, Nuclenor Spain, and British Nuclear Fuels). The term "delegates" referred, I think, to the notion that course participants were representing their institutions rather than acting on their own behalf. The four-day intensive course cost 1,225 British pounds, a sum that would tend to discourage individuals paying for it themselves. It would also, I suspect, deter most "delegates" from environmental organizations with antinuclear views.

Topics covered included radiation dosimetry, biological effects, radiation risks and their acceptability, the setting of standards for protection of workers and the general public, radioactivity in the environment, detection and measurement, emergency planning and response, and the safety features of various nuclear power plants in the EU. The course brochure stated, "The course will be addressed by an authoritative panel of speakers who will provide a review and update of the concepts and practice of radiological protection. Recent developments in the understanding and assessment of radiation effects will be discussed and their implications for protection standards will be considered." Here I note a selection of the "authoritative experts" whom I will quote below: Chris Huyskens (Director, Radiation Protection, Eindhoven University of Technology, The Netherlands), Keith Baverstock (World Health Organization European Centre for Health and Environment, Italy), Sam Harbison (Director of Nuclear Safety, Health and Safety Executive, UK), Michael Thorne (Scientific Advisor, Nuclear Technology Division, Electrowatt Engineering Services, UK, and former secretary of the ICRP), Alain Brissaud (Head of Radiation Protection Group, Electricite de France), Robin Ward (Station Health Physicist, Trawsfynydd Power Station, Nuclear Electric, UK), Marion Hill (Partner, Kane and Hill Consulting Scientists), Michael Segal (Head, Food Safety Radiation Unit, UK Ministry of Agriculture), and Mark Dutton (Group Head, Containment and Radiological Group, NNC, Limited, UK).

The Chernobyl accident was never explicitly featured as a topic for discussion, but it figured significantly in the ways that the experts framed their presentations and especially in discussions of the "management" of post-Chernobyl public fears about nuclear safety. The course occurred at a particularly sensitive moment in the history of nuclear power in the UK, as the previously state-controlled industry was on the verge of privatization and debates were taking place in the media about what the "rationalization" of nuclear plants might mean for trade-offs between cost-effectiveness and public safety. This was also a period of intense discussions about what the "harmonization" of different national radiation policies within the EU might mean for nuclear industry accountability to diverse national publics. Within such a context, Chernobyl-inspired public fears about nuclear safety came to be seen as potential obstacles to "rationalized privatization" and international "harmonization."

My own "delegate" status in the course was somewhat anomalous. At the time, I was the coordinator of an international and interdisciplinary research program on "Children and Environment" at the Norwegian Centre for Child Research, where we were developing a research unit and international network on children and radiation issues. Our concern was how a focus on children, in many ways the population most vulnerable to radiation risks, calls for new sorts of interdisciplinary scientific understandings of radiation effects and raises fundamental political questions about how policy makers can legitimately define what constitutes "socially acceptable risks" without developing new ways of taking into account public concerns about children's safety and well-being (Stephens 1993, 1994; Christensen and Stephens 2000). At the time, I was also engaged in my own anthropological research on the social consequences of Chernobyl fallout in Norwegian Sami areas (Stephens 1995). The Sami are Scandinavia's indigenous minority population, with their own set of culturally framed vulnerabilities to Soviet nuclear testing and Chernobyl fallout. These research interests, both of which involved the ways that particular populations are differentially vulnerable to radiation risks, had led me to explore debates between "alternative" and "establishment" radiation scientists and to question the sorts of economic and political interest implicated in the institutionalization of international radiological protection within the ICRP.

My aim here is not to argue for certain scientific and policy models over others. Rather it is to explore the ways that cultural and political judgments enter into radiation science and standard setting at every step of the way. These occur, I would argue, within both "alternative" and "establishment" camps. The Chernobyl disaster led the former group to radical statements about large numbers of "excess deaths" and wide-ranging health problems resulting from the accident, not just within the former USSR, but around the globe (Graeub 1994; Gould and Goldman 1991). However, it is the reassertion of normalcy and control in the "establishment" groups that is my concern here.

My analysis of the Cambridge course is based primarily on my own notes. (I was not able to tape class presentations and discussions.) The organizers and teachers of the course also provided extensive accompanying written materials, and I draw upon these in my discussion as well. An important part of the culture of scientific experts is that they do not read from prepared texts, but rather use transparencies outlining the main topics they intend to cover and speak more or less extemporaneously from these. I was especially interested in gaps between written texts and oral presentations, precisely because it is in the latter that speakers are more likely to acknowledge areas of uncertainty, to speculate about the role of politics in the framing of scientific concepts and models, and to mention explicitly the link between the Chernobyl accident and escalating expert concerns about the management of "irrational" public fears.

RADIOLOGICAL PROTECTION PRINCIPLES AND THE ICRP

The course began with a brief discussion of basic principles of radiological protection (RP). It was taken for granted that course participants were already familiar with the ICRP, whose status as the primary source for authoritative scientific information about radiation effects and standard setting was simply assumed. In fact, it was not until the last discussion of the last day that one of the course participants asked, "Who exactly are those people, and how did they come to have so much power?"

As background to a discussion of basic RP principles, it is useful to give a brief history here of nuclear regulatory institutions (see Caufield 1989). Every country with a nuclear industry has at least one nuclear regulatory agency. The United States has at least sixteen federal agencies and twenty congressional committees, and each of the fifty states has its own regulators. The United Nations has four main agencies concerned with radiation exposure: the Scientific Committee on the Effects of Atomic Radiation, the World Health Organization, the International Atomic Energy Agency, and the United Nations Environment Programme. In addition, radiation protection issues are addressed by a host of scientific and medical societies, university laboratories, government-funded research institutes, and industrial associations. "Together, these groups make up what its supporters call the radiation protection community and its critics refer to as the nuclear establishment" (Caufield 1989:167). The EU is a new player in this field, with its own European Commission of Radiological Protection and a developing set of EU directives.

At the center of the radiation protection community is the ICRP, a group with no legal power but tremendous international authority. The commission is a private scientific body established in 1928 to provide doctors and scientists with guidelines on radiation safety. The ICRP's apparent independence from governments and the prestige of its expert members have made it attractive to nations in need of credible radiation protection standards. Its recommendations have been adopted with only minor modifications by virtually every country in the world. The ICRP regularly publishes documents about state-of-the-art radiation science and makes explicitly political judgments, not only defining the risks of different radiation exposures but also stating how much risk is acceptable. As Caufield (1989:167) notes, "Before the Second World War, commission members were accepting risks on behalf of themselves and their professional colleagues. But now, in recommending standards for blue-collar workers and the general public, the commission accepts risks on behalf of millions of people who don't even know it exists."

The commission does not aim for absolute safety. This would obviously require banning all radiation exposures, which would conflict with the basic institutional philosophy that the benefits of nuclear technologies are too important to lose. As Michael Thorne noted in his lecture on basic ICRP recommendations (July 11, 1995), the aim of radiological protection is to provide an appropriate standard of protection for humans, without unduly limiting the beneficial practices giving rise to radiation exposure. These "beneficial practices" refer primarily to nuclear power.

The basic aim of ICRP is to make recommendations that would prevent "deterministic radiation effects" (the result of exposures large enough to lead "deterministically" to organ malfunctioning and eventual death) and to take all reasonable procedures to prevent "stochastic effects" (biological events that result from lower level exposures that may lead, with varying probabilities, to hereditary defects or cancer). The guiding principle here is "ALARA"—the reduction of exposures to levels "as low as reasonably achievable." According to Thorne, ICRP's stance is that no practice involving exposures should be adopted unless it produces sufficient benefit to exposed individuals or society to offset the detriments.

The ICRP does not conduct research but bases its recommendations on the evaluation of existing data and the expertise of its members. Four fifteen-person standing committees, each headed by a member of the main commission, prepare the detailed technical reports and policy recommendations, which, after approval by the commission, are issued as *Annals of the ICRP*. Keith Baverstock asserted in his lecture (July 11, 1995) that ICRP recommendations are not primarily about preventing exposure but about planning for it (and controlling the damage in case of accidents). This, he noted, is what RP tools and models are designed to do, and if we do not recognize this, we will not be able to understand or use these tool and models knowledgeably in the practice of radiological protection. For example, when the ICRP introduced the concept of a "tissue weighting factor" (discussed below), it did so for a reason: to plan for the level of exposure that a worker in the nuclear industry can safely experience.

This would seem to me to be a recognition of the ways that political ends enter into the formation of scientific models and facts themselves. Nevertheless, the main message of Baverstock's lecture, and the dominant message of the course as a whole, was that it is crucial to distinguish clearly between solid scientific knowledge about radiation doses and biological mechanisms, on the one hand, and the politically inflected risk limits that are developed on the basis of this knowledge, on the other. As Michael Thorne stated (July 11, 1995), there is a gulf between the measurable quantities of things like radiation dosage and the "substantial imponderables" that characterize the setting of "safe" or "socially acceptable" risk limits. While the ICRP engages in both science and policy recommendations, it resolutely affirms the boundary between the two domains. It also affirms differences among discipline-based knowledges that organize studies within the larger areas of science and policy formation.

DOSIMETRY: THE REALM OF RADIATION PHYSICISTS

According to Chris Huyskens in his lecture (July 10, 1995), the description and quantification of the amounts of radiation is the province of physicists, who study the radiation-related mechanisms of electronic excitation and ionization and the specific physical characteristics of different sorts of radiation (e.g., gamma rays, X rays, and ionized particles from various substances). "The results of dosimetry," he noted, "are the starting points for decision making." Much of the scientific literature on radiation effects focuses on Japanese atomic bomb survivors, but these studies have had to be rethought in recent years in light of new models of the amounts and kinds of radiation doses survivors received.

Although there is a general division in RP between science and policy formation, there are also occasional admissions that there are more or less "scientific" (i.e., solidly factual, clearly measurable and calculable) domains within the "science side" itself. Radiation physicists deal with the complexities of radiometric and dosimetric quantities and with the mechanisms of energy deposition, but it is radiation biologists who must deal with the less clearly measurable aspects of what happens to radiation energy once it is deposited in human tissue. There are numerous less clearly measurable aspects and value judgments involved in this most "scientific" of all RP domains.

RADIATION EFFECTS: THE DOMAIN OF BIOLOGISTS

According to Keith Baverstock, again in his lecture of July 10, 1995, the transition from physics to biology in RP is far from smooth. A major problem is that once the discussion of radiation effects inside the body is moved, it must deal not only with the facts of ionization collisions but also with the intricacies of biological processes. It is crucial, he argued, to distinguish between deterministic effects, which are clearly dose related (i.e., a certain amount of radiation will predictably result in cell or organ death), and stochastic effects, which are not linearly dependent on the size of dose. There are no absolute threshold levels for stochastic effects, such as radiation-induced change in one cell that may result in a series of malfunctions in other cells and organs. Here the issue becomes *probabilistic* effects, which tend to increase with increasing dose. That certain levels of exposure are likely to be safe in a statistical sense can be said, but it is scientifically impossible to say that they will be safe for any specific individual. Baverstock noted that this is one of the most difficult points to get across to laymen, who tend to associate radiation exposure with cancer, irrespective of dose levels and probability curves.

The fundamental concept for RP, according to both Baverstock's and Thorne's lectures, is the "effective absorbed dose," that quantity of radiation absorbed by a particular organ or tissue. Here, said Thorne, the ICRP takes a "nonpurist view." Because of the tremendous difficulties and uncertainties involved in trying to specify a point source exposure and its subsequent biological pathway, the ICRP has developed the notion of an "average organ/tissue dose." The average dose determination is achieved through the use of various "weighting factors," what Thorne calls "regulatory conveniences that subsume a lot of radiobiology." The notion of "absorbed dose" multiplies the external dose at incidence by a weighting factor "to take account of the relative effectiveness of the different types of ionizing radiations at the low exposure levels encountered in radiation protection practice." There are also various "tissue weighting factors" that take into account the different sensitivities of specific tissues and organs, for example, bone marrow, the thyroid gland, the liver, and the kidney.

The complexities of these calculations go far beyond the scope of this chapter. The important point here is that they are based on models of biological effects developed by "averaging out" specific effects on specific individuals within various populations under study. Thus, for example, the tissue weighting factor for the human breast ignores differences between males and females, and tissue weighting factors as a whole ignore differences among the organs of people of different ages. My notes indicate that the values of tissue weighting factors are rounded and simplified values developed for a reference population of equal numbers of both sexes and a wide range of ages (Thorne lecture, July 11, 1995). According to Huyskens, in his lecture of July 10, 1995, these models are not "science in its most pure form," and they are certainly not effective for predicting specific health effects for individuals. By extension, in my opinion, neither are they effective for predicting specific health effects for different *groups* of individuals.

Nevertheless, argues Baverstock, "for radiological protection purposes, it is seldom necessary to go into microscopic detail about what is happening to particular individuals or organs. Rather what is needed are quantifiable terms that are good enough for the purpose at hand: the formulation of radiation protection standards for nuclear workers." (May I note here that the majority of such workers are adult males). "Beyond this," he declared, "our confidence in weighting factors has to be low. These are just tools for planning the exposure of individuals in the workplace. But it makes no sense to say that any one individual has had an 'effective absorbed dose' of a certain quantity. This would tell us very little about the sort of biological effects we might expect to see."

The problems are compounded when the matter of "collective effective absorbed dose" arises. What do we really know, asks Baverstock, when we add together individual effective doses? Any population will include some individuals who are especially resistant and others who are especially sensitive to radiation. It should be observed here that when differences among individuals were mentioned, these were presented as natural and individual differences in sensitivity. Differences among groups with different histories and social locations never entered into the discussion; for example, poor children with diets lacking in calcium, a deficiency that leads to greater bone absorption of radioactive strontium, since it "acts like" calcium in the body. Discussion of radiation effects in relation to RP shows dramatically, I would argue, the ways that large assumptions may be packed into the seemingly most precise and scientific facts. This is not to say that these facts are *only* cultural and political constructions. Rather it emphasizes that it is not just "working models" but the "facts" themselves that are tools created for particular purposes. Huyskens, in his lecture of July 10, 1995, acknowledged as much, when he stated that "the danger in numerical calculations is that we forget the real meaning of the numbers, where they came from and what they were designed to do."

In discussing complex terms such as "tissue weighting factors," it is crucial to remember that these are terms developed by the ICRP on the basis of its current understandings of biological mechanisms of radiation at relatively low exposures and its review of epidemiological studies. The fact that there are major disagreements about these studies and their conclusions went almost unmentioned at the Cambridge course. As noted above, the dominant model for radiation health effects has come from studies of A-bomb survivors, who experienced relatively high-dose radiation at one point in time. Scientists then extrapolate linearly downward to develop models of health effects at lower doses (see Baverstock and Stather 1989; Jones and Southwood 1987).

But what if the biological mechanisms are qualitatively different at lower doses? This is the argument of some scientists in the "alternative camp" (Graeub 1994; Gould and Goldman 1991), who argue that nuclear testing, nuclear accidents, and routine leaks at normally operating nuclear plants are resulting in widespread immune system damage and mutated strains of viruses. These are a result of the "Petkau effect," the formation of cell membrane–damaging free radicals at relatively low-dose exposures. Discussion of the Petkau effect never entered into any of the formal lectures. When asked about it, Baverstock simply dismissed the topic without further discussion as "more politics than science."

PSYCHOSOCIAL ASPECTS OF EXPOSURE: THE DOMAIN OF PSYCHOLOGISTS AND SOCIAL SCIENTISTS

Media-supported and -driven "political science" did come to the fore, however, in discussions of the psychosocial aspects of radiation exposure. This is a problem, according to a number of lecturers, that has become much greater since Chernobyl, emanating, in particular, with claims that the fallout has been associated not only with increased risks of cancer and hereditary problems (according to the ICRP, the primary risks involved in radiation exposure), but also with increasing immune system problems, hormonal disturbances, increased vulnerability to other diseases (such as tuberculosis), and accelerated aging.

Baverstock, in his lecture of July 11, 1995, reported that when the International Atomic Energy Agency sent representatives to the Chernobyl region to investigate claims of a wide range of health problems following the accident, they found no effects other than cancer (in particular, an increased rate of thyroid cancers in children) that could be directly attributed to radiation. The investigatory group did, however, identify a wide range of reported health problems that could be associated with the psychosocial stress of the accident. Baverstock specifically called attention to the stresses associated with massive relocations of populations in the region (on the problematic basis of avoiding what was, in effect, a doubling of one lifetime's exposure to natural background radiation) and stresses linked to fears of possible long-term health consequences for current and future generations. Such fears, he suggested, are often associated with changes in lifestyle, for example, more smoking and drinking, that have detrimental health consequences and with a tendency to attribute any health problems that occur to radiation.

Baverstock asserted that the greatest problems resulting from Chernobyl in the immediate region of the accident and especially in Europe are psychosocial rather than medical. Psychosocial effects are enormously increased, he claimed, by scientifically unsubstantiated media claims and sensationalism. In order to combat such media-related problems and the significant health problems that might result from them, the radiological protection community needed to direct increasing attention to "managing" the media and shaping public understandings about radiation risks.

Part of the problem, he admitted, could be attributed to certain gaps in knowledge about the biology of low-dose exposures. More significant, however, were national differences in the definition of "safe" or "acceptable" exposures. When the public learns about these differences, they assume that there are even greater gaps in knowledge that actually exist, because people do not understand the important division between science and politically inflected standard-setting. These misunderstandings feed into people's fears and psychological problems. "A primary task, then, is to unlock this spiral," stated Braverstock in his lecture of July 12, 1995, "to move forward with harmonizing our standards across the European Union." The alternative may be not only escalating public fears and psychological problems, but also threats to public order as manifested, for instance, in reports from Poland of people stealing iodine after the Chernobyl accident in order to counteract the effects of the fallout.

The crucial message from this course was that people must not confuse the health effects arising from two separate routes—the mental perception of radiation risks and the actual doses to target organs. The former are likely to loom increasingly large in the foreseeable future, putting additional burdens on both national radiation protection agencies and the ICRP. Perhaps, suggested Baverstock, the radiological protection community needs another international agency to deal with radiation-related psychosocial effects. Such an agency could deal with the tangled issue of public risk perceptions and leave the problems of radiation science and scientific risk assessment to the ICRP.

RISK ASSESSMENT: THE DOMAIN OF THE ICRP AND NATIONAL REGULATORY AGENCIES

"The first thing we have to recognize is that public logic is not the same as scientific rationality," observed Sam Harbison in his talk of July 11, 1995. There is a high "dread factor" connected to public conceptions of radiation, which means that in the UK, and Europe more generally, inordinate amounts of money and time have been put into nuclear plant safety features, although the actual risks from chemical production are much greater. Michael Segal, in his presentation of July 13, 1995, introduced a pie chart, indicating that in the UK in 1995, 47 percent of the radiation exposure of the "average person" came from the "natural background radiation" of radon. After this come cosmic rays and medical exposures, and finally exposures from fallout, occupational doses, and routine discharges from nuclear plants. The last three sources account for less than .1 percent of the total exposure. However, according to my understanding, although radon is "naturally" emitted from the earth, amounts of radon exposure are affected by what people do to the earth with activities such as mining and by building codes and structures. By emphasizing the "naturalness" of radon and cosmic ray exposure, experts are suggesting that these are radiation risks people take on every day without being unduly concerned about them. Thus, fears about the much smaller risks from nuclear energy can be considered as the "irrational," or, as one of the other presenters declared in his lecture of July 14, 1995, even "hysterical" concerns of an uneducated public. In discussing the topic of radioactivity in food, Segal noted various measures that have been taken to protect the general public after major nuclear accidents: the 1957 Windscale factory fire in the UK, the explosion of a high-level nuclear waste tank at Kyshtym in the USSR in 1959, the core meltdown of a nuclear plant at Three Mile Island in the US in 1979, and the Chernobyl reactor fire in 1986. Although such events are statistically extremely rare, he noted, it is the fear of such major disasters that fuels public concerns about the everyday operations of nuclear plants.

The problems of educating the public in scientific risk assessment are enormous, considering the complexities involved in risk quantification and comparison, asserted Harbison in his talk of July 11, 1995. First, the radiation hazard must be identified and quantified. Then calculations must be made of the probability of such an accident occurring, models must be constructed of the possible exposure pathways for humans, and the various probabilities calculated of exposure by these different routes. Then the experts must specify and quantify detriments to the "targets" (affected organs/tissues), followed by calculations of quantified risks to individuals and to society.

Harbison stated that while probabilistic risk assessments may appear highly quantified, people should not forget how much they are based on estimates and assumptions along each step of the hypothetical exposure route. Take, for example, the quantification of "social risk," broadly defined as the total detriment to the present and future health and well-being of a specified population. Obviously, it is not possible to quantify and weight all contributing factors, so the experts fall back on using estimated numbers of fatal cancers that might result from a particular radiation exposure. "This is a necessary and adequate move from the regulatory perspective, though it is difficult to communicate to the general public why other factors are not being taken into account," Harbison observed.

A major problem at this juncture is the relationship between experts and the public, which is mediated largely by journalists, themselves inadequately informed about the complexities of radiation health effects, risk assessments, and the principles of radiological protection. The issue for the experts, therefore, becomes public education. In his address on July 12, 1995, Robin Ward discussed exposure of the public by nuclear power stations in the UK. He asserted that even though routine plant discharges are trivial in terms of their health effects, they can loom large in the public eye. The average member of the public, he remarked, tends to see radiation limits as specifying what is "safe" or "not safe." Thus, if a plant is reported to be discharging 95 percent of its allowable limit, the public tends to think that this means that the plant is on the edge of safety, while the experts recognize these discharge levels as far below anything that might cause significant health or environmental problems.

As the course reached its third day, discussions of the safety of nuclear power stations in the EU and of the need for more sophisticated public information and education advanced to the fore, and I began to wonder if the middle-level professionals who were the primary "delegates" in this course were being recruited as an important part of this stepped-up educational effort. Mark Dutton, in his lecture of July 13, 1995, discussed the ALARA ("as low as reasonably achievable") principle underlying ICRP recommendations. In practice, he said, the operative principle most often becomes ALARP—"as low as reasonably practical." There are always going to be further safety precautions that are technically achievable, but he reminded the audience that the ICRP aimed at providing "an appropriate standard of protection for man without unduly limiting the beneficial practices giving rise to radiation exposure." The job of RP experts, therefore, is to develop safety precautions that are not only "reasonable," but also "practical" in terms of their costs—"a very important consideration in these days of privatization and industry rationalization."

By the end of the course, "the public," sometimes presented as a potential opponent and obstacle to nuclear development, but more often as an undifferentiated group to be cajoled and convinced by "public relations experts in the RP field," as Dutton declared, loomed large in discussions. It is worth noting here that "the public" was never broken down in these discussions in terms of gender, class, age, ethnicity, or nationality. Nor were such distinctions deemed relevant in assessing possible risks. As previously noted, the science of RP is aimed mainly at developing probability assessments of what might happen to "average" tissues, organs, individuals, and populations. In contrast, the main concerns of many members of the public center precisely on risks to individuals, men and women, people of different ages, particular social groups and environments (Bryant 1995; Chugoku Newspaper 1992). While RP experts are concerned with the public's incapacity to understand probabilistic risk assessments, cost/benefit analyses, and expert safety recommendations for "tolerable" or "socially acceptable exposures," at least some members of the public are explicitly concerned with differences that are largely "averaged out" by expert calculations. What will happen to my children? How are certain groups, engaged in particular activities, eating certain diets, having access to different sorts of medical care, differentially vulnerable to various sorts or radiation risks? Who is entitled to decide what is a "tolerable" or "socially acceptable" risk, if it is acknowledged that risks are not evenly distributed across society? And, given a history of changing expert statements about what is "safe" or "acceptable," why should the public simply trust expert judgments and assurances that an accident like Chernobyl "could never happen here?"

Significantly, these are all questions that were never addressed in course lectures and were only touched upon in course discussions. The question posed by one of the course delegates about the ICRP, "Who exactly are these people, and how did they come to have so much power?" was answered by Alan Martin, course organizer, in a lecture on July 10, 1995. Martin said that ICRP is composed of independent experts who can provide the scientific base required for credible policy recommendations. "Someone has to make sense of the chaos of radiobiology. The ICRP does a good job. There is no really convincing epidemiological material that shows the nuclear industry has ever harmed the public."

Thus, the self-evident problem for RP experts becomes that of bridging the "credibility gap" between experts and the public, or raising "public risk perceptions" toward the level of scientifically grounded "expert risk assessments." Insofar as this is a primary aim, the "real disaster," according to Mark Dutton in his lecture of July 13, 1995, is disparate national safety limits, which erode public trust in the authorities. Such differences are unavoidable, he observed, when dealing with countries at very different levels of development. "Ultimately, each country has to decide its own level of risk. A country like Bulgaria may well be willing to accept a higher level of nuclear risks in order to reduce energy production costs...How much a society is prepared to pay to save one life varies enormously from case to case." Here, he stated, is where social scientists can be useful in clarifying the economic, political, and cultural constraints on radiation policy decisions. The development of the EU, with a common European culture and integrated economy, holds out the possibility of harmonizing national radiation standards and presenting the experts as "one-voiced," at least within one region.

CONCLUSION

At least half of the Radiological Protection Summer School course dealt with safety features in European nuclear plants. Lectures included a case study of pressurized water reactors in France (Alain Brissaud), radiation monitoring and practical application of the ALARA principle in nuclear power stations in the United Kingdom (Robin Ward), protection measures related to solid and effluent nuclear wastes (Ward), and safety features of nuclear fuel cycle facilities (Partington). The overriding message throughout these lectures was that the probability of "Chernobyl happening here" was virtually negligible. Left out of course discussions was any mention of RP challenges in relation to nuclear weapons testing, an omission all the more striking because at that time France was resuming its nuclear testing program in the Pacific Islands.

I have argued here that major challenges for the "establishment" radiological protection community in the present era include, first, the reassertion of scientific control over an apparent chaos of reported health and environmental consequences of the Chernobyl accident, and second, the management of Chernobyl-related public fears and concerns. The omission of nuclear weapons issues makes sense in this context, because the consequences of nuclear weapons testing are even more disputed and politically charged than the health and environmental consequences of nuclear energy production. They are also outside the realm of international monitoring and scientific control.

In the wake of Chernobyl and other widely publicized nuclear accidents and near-accidents, the international community of RP experts seeks to return to normal operations, but within a changed social and political context that results in the reinvention and restructuring of what "normality" involves. RP experts vigorously affirm the naturalness of boundaries, for example, between science and policy formation and among the discipline-based knowledges appropriate to different RP domains, that they could once take for granted. Similarly, the unquestioned authority of the ICRP is now seen as in need of buttressing through the explicit "harmonization" of national radiation protection standards throughout the European region.

In the post-Chernobyl era, the range of concerns that need to be routinely included within the realm of radiological protection has swelled to include psychosomatic effects, public education, the analysis of culturally inflected risk perceptions, and management of the popular media. Some experts argue that the domain of RP has expanded so quickly and drastically that the ICRP can no longer be expected to maintain its authoritative leadership role in all areas and that it may well be time to establish another international body dealing with psychological and social issues related to radiation risks. However, in doing so, the basic divisions between science and society, facts and values that structure the current ICRP worldview would be reproduced and confirmed.

Carol Cohn (1987) has suggested that the worldviews of "nuclear defense intellectuals," that is, experts in US nuclear weapons policies and strategies, are organized by a logic of containment, manifest in written materials and formal policy declarations about "clean, surgical strike scenarios" and elaborate calculations of the amount of "collateral damage" (i.e., human deaths) that might be expected in different circumstances of nuclear weapons use. Cohn gives striking examples about how the language of bodies, everyday life, and religion enters into informal discussions, for example, in the sexualized imagery of certain bombs giving "more bang for the buck," the domestic imagery of nuclear weapons sites colloquially referred to as "Christmas tree lots," and the religious imagery of the nuclear defense community as the "nuclear priesthood." In psychological terms, this might be described as a kind of "return of the repressed," whereby the experts refer, often jokingly or ironically, to those aspects of reality that are systematically excluded from their formalized worldviews.

I would argue that something similar goes on among RP experts. It was only after the course was over that I began to reflect upon the disparities between the ways people talked within the classroom and outside of it. During coffee breaks, shared meals, and social events, such as punting down the river, experts and "delegates" relaxed with stories about their families, anecdotes about their own personal histories, and discussions of the architecture and intellectual traditions of Cambridge—precisely the sorts of individual-, place-, and history-specific concerns that were excluded from formal discussions. Moreover, there were significant gaps between the formal, scientific aspects of the RP worldview emphasized in written course materials and the informal comments of lecturers, often delivered as joking "asides." After a discussion of the difficulties involved in quantifying and balancing costs and safety benefits according to the ALARA/ALARP principles, Dutton laughed and said, "I guess in the end, it is value judgments that go in and value judgments that must come out."

During discussions of the safety feature of various nuclear plant designs, I was struck by the reliance on "compartmentalization" planning as the key to ensuring worker and public safety. The aim is to contain and control routine leakages that occur in everyday operations and to be able to close off whole areas in the event of accidents. RP philosophy itself seems oriented to containing and controlling conceptual "leakages" as well, for instance, between disciplines and domains, and to "closing off" and neutralizing the effects of larger-scale accidents such as Three Mile Island and Chernobyl.

Cohn's ethnographic analysis of "nuclear defense intellectuals" emphasized gendered dimensions of their practice and language, and gender considerations seem equally important to me in the analysis of the culture of RP experts. Of the thirty-five "delegates" present, only six were women, though this imbalance was not immediately evident from the delegate list, which includes only last names and first initials. Only one of the expert lecturers was female. The course organizers were male and were referred to by title and last name, in contrast to their female secretaries, who were referred to only by first name. At the end of the course, the secretaries received bouquets of flowers from the course organizers, in gratitude "for attending to all the small practical details that made our larger discussions possible."

I realize that these gendered dimensions of the course are so expectable as to seem petty in their recounting, but gender also figures significantly in the international structuring of the RP community of experts and the division between experts and the general public. Consider the makeup of the ICRP itself. Since its founding, the ICRP has been closely tied to users of medical radiation. About half the commission's members have been medical doctors, with physicists the second-largest group. Only a handful of biologists, geneticists, or specialists in environmental or occupational health have ever served on the commission (Caufield 1989:175). "A large fraction of members of ICRP have been and are radiologists, employees of the nuclear establishment or have large contracts with the nuclear establishment" (quote from Karl Morgan, who worked for thirty years with the ICRP and the Atomic Energy Commission, in Caufield 1989:176). There has never been a woman on the commission, nor a representative from one of the "softer" social sciences, such as psychology, sociology, or anthropology. In contrast to the masculinized experts, the public is often portrayed in terms of stereotyped feminine characteristics, as irrational, uneducated, emotional, and sometimes even hysterical.

Evelyn Fox Keller (1990), one of the most eloquent and thoughtful commentators on gender and science issues, argues that cultural constructions of gender enter into the very formation of scientific models and facts and into the ways that uncertainties are bounded, "leakages" controlled, chaos normalized, certain voices silenced, and questions dismissed. The international community of RP experts, and the RP worldview that informs their practices, have certainly been deeply gendered from the beginning. They have also been significantly structured by race, class, culture, and world region differences. One of the reasons that RP experts are so sure that "Chernobyl could never happen here" is that technologies, managerial techniques, and systems of education, referred to as "theirs" and meaning less developed or non-Western countries, are so vastly inferior to "ours," meaning Western Europe and America.

An interesting question is whether these divisions have become more pronounced in the aftermath of the Chernobyl disaster, which raised the specter of an irrational, feminized public as a potential obstacle to the continuing authority of the RP community and to the nuclear industry it regulates, supports, and depends upon. It appears to be no coincidence that at a historical moment when public opposition to nuclear power comes from activists differentiated by culture, gender, race, class, and nationality in the form of indigenous people's organizations, women-based groups, and organizations fighting against "environmental racism," the RP community is reasserting the scientific grounds for "averaging out" these differences in the analysis of biological effects, developing "risk management" approaches in relation to generalized "mass publics," and calling for the concentration and centralization of expert control at regional levels that are increasingly distant from people "on the ground." Analysis of the post-Chernobyl culture of radiological protection experts suggests that disasters can have profound and far-reaching effects, especially when they remain unacknowledged as disasters.

6

The Monster and the Mother

The Symbolism of Disaster

Susanna M. Hoffman

> The study of signs [is] at the heart of social life.
> —Ferdinand de Saussure, *A Course in General Linguistics*

Whether a society encompasses few people or multitudes, whether its landhold is remote and its records without letters or its reach global and its renown etched in ink, disaster contradicts its members' definitive knowledge. No matter if the disaster stems from nature or errant technology, is experienced or merely expected, no one, neither sage nor scientist, preacher nor president, can wholly tell the why or the where of a calamitous event. And so, no matter what place in the world it occurs, what form it might take, whether singular or chronic, peoples' explanations of disaster tend to rely on creative, often mythological, imagination. The belief systems of people experiencing or expecting calamity are rife with symbols dealing with their situation, and their cosmologies are vibrant with metaphor.

Like all symbols and metaphors, those dealing with catastrophe reflect the mental processes of a collective people and the fruits of both creative impulse and sense-making reasoning. They give an ethnological picture of how disaster is seen, interpreted, and utilized prior to, after, and in preparation for an event. Some scholars have proposed that symbolic values have a cathartic effect for cultural modification

(Turner 1974; Lakoff and Johnson 1980; Laughlin 1995; Prattis 1984; Campbell 1949), but the cathartic value of disaster symbolism is even more primary. The imagery surrounding disaster implements cultural and personal survival. It provides a compass of orientation on how to think about calamity and gives an orbit of persuasion on how to cope with and survive it. Behind the symbols lies a logic that classifies the event and gives it cause. Once ordered and given reason, a calamity can be given context, content, emotion, and meaning, all of which figure significantly in understanding the cultural response to disaster. There is, after all, a point to communication even when it is denotive. In the case of disaster, that point is double-tined: Disaster symbolism enables the conservation of a sociocultural world, and also its transformation.

I have titled this chapter "The Monster and the Mother" because the same sort of dualism many people characteristically evidence in their symbolic schemes often surfaces in disaster symbolism. As one would expect, the dualistic schemes frequently overlap with those already present for environment and mirror those bespeaking the opposition, where it occurs, between nature and culture. Because of the circumstance, however, the dualistic schemes surrounding disaster commonly appear in new guises and bring up subtle features not otherwise manifest. Frequently, they take on special embodiment. Cyclical schemes including both grand and implied allegories of beginnings and ends, apocalypses and revivals also arise in disaster symbolism, and I will touch here on both the formal and informal sort. I then turn to technological disasters because they bring forth particular, convoluted, and chilling symbolic issues.

Generally one premise begins and underlies this study. If we are to follow certain scholars (Turner, Douglas, Levi-Strauss, Derrida, Geertz, Cohen, and I think their point is well taken, especially in much disaster symbolism), then *because* the paradigmatic systems by which many people organize their reality involve *false* divisions, the systems incorporate perpetual disequilibrium. Culture, for example, is not in fact truly separate from nature, only categorized so by certain people. All human endeavor takes place on a physical plane, and in all too numerous ways that physical plane converges into what people have distinguished as the cultural, continuously confusing their tidy arrangement. In the face of catastrophe, the disequilibrium becomes acute. Indeed, it erupts.

Whether the scheme appears as a static social and cosmological arrangement or is expressed within a process of a cycle from start to scheduled end, the environment roars up implacably to demonstrate that the divisions by which the people regimented reality are illusion. In order to reestablish cultural sense in such situations, victims must strive to reformulate distinctions and reconstruct order to their world.

One might ask how the examination of disaster symbolism relates to other aspects of disaster study, such as issues of vulnerability, political ecology, disaster response, and mitigation. Symbols are, in the first place, highly pertinent to a people's reaction to disaster. Symbols influence shared behavior. Equally important, symbols can be utilized and manipulated by different factions involved in a disaster and thus become political. Disaster spoils pattern, and matters in the state of disruption become less restricted. The potential for change becomes greater, to the point that disorder itself can become part of pattern (Douglas 1966). Cultural symbols can be also seen as exclusive systems of coercion and control, and as inclusive systems of melioration and order (Prattis 1997:xi, 1-20).

People experiencing disaster stand on a pivot differentiating a model "of" and a model "for." A model "of" is the symbolic presentation of the existing relationship between elements in a social system. A model "for" creates the image of a postulated reality that would be realized in social practice (Geertz 1973:93). Different groups in a society can embody the "of" and the "for." The dominant can produce models "of" and impose models "for" for the less powerful. Moreover, because of the ambiguity of symbols, the same images and forms can be used by any and all sides in a conflict.

As for individuals facing or experiencing catastrophe, they engage the symbols evoking their predicament in an almost visceral manner. Lakoff and Johnson (1980:145) point out that the symbolic process provides a continual feedback system in which symbol must be integrated with experience if a deeper understanding is to be the end result. Human experience can and should be considered under the scheme of a constructed metaphor, since people start to comprehend experience in terms of metaphor, which, when they begin to act in terms of it, becomes a deeper reality. Understanding the occurrence is exactly the task disaster victims, as well as students of disaster, undertake.

To illustrate this chapter, I rely primarily on my experience and research with the Oakland-Berkeley firestorm of October 1991. I incorporate material from other disasters as well. The data on disaster symbolism are sparse. In the midst of rubble, few, victim or researcher, think to write down the content of ceremony or form of imagery. Nonetheless, picking through the embers, mud, and detritus of a calamity for what signs and allegories can be found is, I believe, a relevant and necessary step to further the study of catastrophe and culture.

THE OAKLAND FIRESTORM

> *By midnight, gas-jet flames dotted the blackened hills where the houses had been. Over 1,600 acres had burned. Hundreds of pets were lost. Property damage was estimated at $1.5 billion.*—Patricia Adler, 1992

> *May We All Be Restored And Renewed*—Message tied around a tree, Oakland, 1991–92

As the sun moved toward mid-morning on October 20, 1991, in Oakland, California, the day was already dry and blistering hot. Unusually turbulent winds were blowing in from the east. In the midst of this torrid condition, about 11 o'clock, a spark from a blaze that had ignited atop the town's graceful hills the previous afternoon—a fire that firemen thought they had extinguished—rekindled. From that spark developed a ferocious firestorm that swept down the heights, leaped two multilane freeways, and, although it burned for two more days, in four hours destroyed some three thousand dwellings. Though the fire skipped homes and blocks here and there, across much of the extensive burn zone only chimneys stood. Flats, bungalows, condominiums, and three-story houses were reduced to eighteen inches of ash. Melted automobiles listed into metallic puddles. Twenty-five people died, and more than six thousand were left homeless. Since the temperature of the fire reached over 2,000 degrees Fahrenheit, most survivors lost almost every possession they owned.

In contrast to most disaster victims, the inhabitants of the destroyed area could largely be described as well educated and relatively affluent, middle to upper middle class. The majority were of European background, but the community was mixed, with many Asians, a considerable number of African Americans, and a wide range of ethnicities living throughout. With its unique homes, the area had attracted doctors, lawyers, teachers, social workers, business owners, and artists, as well as people with other callings. Among the victims were a number of notables: a member of Congress, a state senator, a former mayor, a famous sports star. Some of the victims probably possessed substantial wealth, but most depended on salaried jobs, albeit good jobs, and some struggled to make ends meet. Sprinkled throughout were students attending several colleges.

The community was highly familial. The modest to large, mostly older homes had been constructed to accommodate children, and about one-fourth of those burned out were minors. A number of single individuals, single parents with offspring, returned older children, other extended family members, and childless couples, both hetero- and homosexual, also lived in the zone. Residing so near a renowned university (the University of California–Berkeley) and an elegant city (San Francisco), most of the victims could be said to follow socially pro- gressive tenets and practices. Most men and women gave at least public voice to racial, gender, and age equality. Many were highly committed to political causes. Ecology, human rights, and concern with education were popular issues. Families were small. Most women not only worked, but worked as professionals. Most residents had eschewed intense kin- ship bonds and socialized far more with a network of friends. People were familiar with contemporary trends.

Most of the victims, though not the students and some elderly, had home insurance. Almost all, however, quickly discovered that they were seriously underinsured. The animosity that erupted following the cata- strophe did not focus, as is usually the case, on aid givers and govern- ment agencies, but rather on the insurance industry. In due time most victims won settlements from insurance companies, though not with- out considerable struggle, and the victims' efforts to effect sweeping changes in insurance industry practices shortly died out. Faced with what they considered unfair regulations, victims did have the forti- tude—and political wherewithal—to change a number of federal laws governing disaster victims.

As is almost universally the case after a calamity, most of the sur- vivors returned to dwell again in the disaster zone. Most rebuilt homes on the same sites as before. Some re-erected near-replicas of their former residences; others let their imaginations and architects loose. A number purchased and built on different lots or bought undamaged houses within the fire zone, while some of the survivors moved to other communities near and distant. At this point, nearly a decade later, about three-quarters of the community is reconstructed and reoccupied, with over half the residents probably fire survivors and the others newcomers.

Affluent or not, sophisticated or not, the inhabitants of the Oakland and Berkeley hills nonetheless suffered a devastating disaster. In the following months and years, like disaster victims everywhere, they faced the enormous task of reconstituting their lives from residence to reasoning, macadam to meaning. These people resided in an urban, industrialized, far from parochial situation. By anyone's standards they led very worldly lives. Yet ritual arose among them immediately. They built shrines, invented ceremonies, and told sagas. A newspaper with fire-related news, survival information, calendar of events, personal accounts, columns, and fire-inspired poetry and fiction sprang to life. A book of disaster writings and photographs appeared. Shows of firestorm art and videos surfaced in galleries. The city erected a permanent memorial to the event constructed from tiles designed by survivors. Some tiles display artwork, others names or words, but every one illustrates a firestorm thought or tale. Interaction among the survivors and between them and others—the surrounding community, insurance agents, aid workers, builders—went through an intricate, albeit predictable, social pavane of unification and segmentation that revealed much about their perception of the human community. Survivor talk consciously and unconsciously advanced their concepts of time, space, place, the cosmos, and the calamity.

I began my research into this particular catastrophe as a decidedly involuntary participant observer. The research "trip," however, has proved one of the most enlightening I have ever tackled, as well as the most intense and lengthy. It will endure, I warrant, the rest of my life. I am an anthropologist, but I am also one of the survivors of the Oakland firestorm. In the fire I lost my home, all my possessions, and two pets. Since my office was in my home, I also lost twenty-five years of anthropological research, seven manuscripts not yet submitted to publishers, slides and photos, lectures, course notes, and my entire library. I have witnessed and taken part in disaster recovery as both a victim and scientist, undergone and overviewed the reconstruction of community, the enactment of celebration, the exploration of explanation, and the reconstitution of a once again sensible world.

The disaster aftermath continues to this day. Ceremonies still emerge, as do fables, now ever more metaphoric as history passes into myth. Magazine and newspaper articles describing and analyzing the event continue to pour forth, often taking an increasingly revisionist and allegorical point of view. Victims and officials mark the anniversary of the disaster with convocations and tributes that glow every year more emblematic. Politics and other factors color the replay. I have seen how the Oakland firestorm community dealt with the disaster, its eventualities and effects. I have taken note of how victims, and others, "enciphered" the catastrophe verbally, behaviorally, artistically, and architecturally and continue to do so.

What the Oakland firestorm survivors underwent and how they behaved does not differ greatly from survivors of other disasters. All display much the same sort of symbolic expression and metaphoric solutions, as do people who live in zones of chronic calamity. The residents of Oakland themselves dwell in a region of chronic disaster. They were expecting a calamity, only the calamity they anticipated was what they had experienced two years earlier—an earthquake. The area had as well undergone prior firestorms. In 1923, 584 homes in a 72-block area of Berkeley succumbed to a fierce blaze (Cerny and Bruce 1992), and in 1970 a less drastic conflagration destroyed 37 Oakland homes within the zone that reburned in 1991. Citizens had also intermittently undergone California's other two recurring mishaps, flood and mudslide. California is, indeed, so disaster prone, some call its four rotating afflictions—fire, earthquake, flood, and avalanche—the state's version of annual seasons. Still, echoing Paine's description of risk denial and mediation (this volume), only the specter of a monster earthquake loomed in Oaklanders' cultural itinerary. Fire, though prevalent, did not enter their consciousness.

With the aid of symbolic thought, the Oakland firestorm survivors had formed a fiction to deal with and "defang" their environment. Utilizing oppositions, embodiment, and metaphoric description, they swept aside the hazards about them and, in the days and years following the firestorm, spun the chimera again. I deal largely with their postdisaster symbolism, as the prior was inert. The actions, utterances, palaver, rituals, writing, and art that fiery Sunday initiated "outed" it.

In surviving the disaster and researching it, I interacted with the firestorm survivors on many levels. I attended almost all community gatherings. I participated in the postfire neighborhood association for my residential block and the larger ones encompassing adjacent neighborhoods. I served on a panel exploring why my district lacked water adequate to fight the blaze. I organized and led a group of those with my same insurance company through their settlements. These associations, which included people of both genders, every age, and many ethnicities, continued for several years. I also belonged to a large group of women survivors organized by the women architects of the area and to a small, phenomenal, self-organized support group of twelve women that met every week and still occasionally gathers.

Because of the circumstance of my research, I cannot avoid that I represent here a number of "voices." To separate them I have chosen to use the pronoun "they" to mean the victims of the firestorm, despite the fact that I am one of them. I use "I" in reference to my own experiences, reserving "we" to refer to students of disaster. I give ethnographic data, but my approach is strongly analytical, and much of my discussion is correspondingly filtered through that screen. I apologize from the onset for any disequilibrium in my own dualities. It is difficult, often perplexing, to be both actor and ethnographer; along with ethnographer, by strong bent ethnologist; researcher and unwitting survivor.

THE REEMERGENCE OF DUALISTIC SCHEMES

One eventually begins to wonder whether Nature herself does not abhor disjunctive groupings.—J. S. Bruner, J. J. Goodnow, and G. A. Austin, 1956

The cultural distinction drawn between humanity and its obverse, animality, or between the safe and orderly and their antithesis, the wild, gives rise to a fundamental opposition between nature and culture, an operation that Levi-Strauss argues is latent in all peoples' attitudes and behavior (1963a, 1966, 1969, 1973). Others disagree, positing that this schematic division is not universal (Strathern 1980). Still, many people do employ it, especially those involved in any version of Western society, which so pervades globally today.

Even among those who do construct this opposition, who abstract matters cultural from matters natural, however, the physicality of life behind the cultural remains at some level undeniable (Levi-Strauss 1963a, 1966, 1969, 1973). To overcome the logical paradoxes that exist when nature is divided from culture and to reduce dialectic tension, people use symbolic codes. Generally the symbols they create assuage the inherent problem by rooting perceptions about cultural formations within nature. In other words, people pluck features from the physical world and employ them as a model for cultural arrangements. This, at any rate, is what has been posited as the workings of nonindustrial societies. In industrial societies such codes have been assumed to become obsolete. People in technologically developed situations, so the thought goes, are sufficiently removed from their immediate natural environment to lift themselves away from borrowing elements from the physical world as a way to regiment the social one. They use other matter for their models, barbers over bears, class over clans (Levi-Strauss 1963b, 1966:109-34).

But when a disaster occurs or threatens, not even people in industrial communities can ignore that their living circumstances are founded in the physical realm. Nor can they ignore how far they have fashioned, in fact have struggled to fashion, themselves separate from that reality. Very quickly in the face of a physical upheaval, the fallacy of their segregation from nature comes to the fore. Both nonindustrial and industrial people must once again deal with their fundamental grounding and with the urge to vault themselves apart from that material purchase. They must again impose separation between nature and themselves, and in so doing generate again the disequilibrium that teeters within that division.

At the time a calamity occurs or threatens, be the people industrial or not, they inevitably already have in place a plan that arranges and explains the world to them. It is by and large this blueprint, or elements of it, that emerges in the presence of calamity. The emblems representing catastrophe overlap with cosmological and environmental symbols. This was certainly the case in Oakland. In all manner of terminology and representations, in ceremony and behavior, the survivors of the Oakland firestorm resurrected deep environmental precepts to paint a symbolic portrait of their misfortune. Without a grid of totems, the images expressed were nonetheless reducible to nature and culture and to the fundamental division between the two.

To begin with, the survivors of the firestorm immediately cast the fire as a phenomenon from nature's sphere. The fire was characterized as wild and uncontrollable. It was further instantly posed as oppositional to culture. One of the first and most pervasive statements to arise was that the fire should never have encroached upon an area variously described as "cultivated," "landscaped," or "residential." Though the area destroyed by the conflagration was as earthbound as any, it was styled "city," a refined area of homes constructed for human occupation, a "civilized" region lifted from nature and humanly formed.

Survivors blamed the inferno on a combination of several factors, all of them deemed conditions of nature. Strangely enough, they resounded of the four primary components of nature Aristotle set forth long ago. Besides the fire itself, they faulted the air; it was blowing. The earth, too, conspired; it was arid. Water played a role. There had been a drought, and although Oakland's reservoirs were full, its ancient fire hydrants were unable to pump—a cultural failure.

Some cultural causes were cited, but they were contextualized on a nature-culture slide rule. Houses had been erected too near untamed parkland, that is, culture had been "too close" to nature. Shades of Mary Douglas (1966), it was matter on the margins, not quite within nature and not quite cultural, that was often cited as the "dangerous" factor. "Nobody should be allowed to have a house that close to the unkempt park," said one survivor to me. "There should be a border area." Many said natural elements, such as weeds, within the cultural, such as yards, should have been prohibited. The spark that flared into the conflagration apparently arose from a culturally set fire—workers burning off weeds, but therein lay another error. A natural thing, like a fire, should have never been employed to solve a cultural problem, like an overgrown yard. "Why didn't those workers just use a machete?" was the rhetorical question I heard over and over. Only a cultural means, a tool or human labor, should have been used to remedy a cultural predicament.[1]

Once the Oakland fire was "put out," rituals arose stunningly quickly to "culturize" the advance of the physical. Survivors gathered upon or as close to the burn zone as possible. There they spoke and heard uplifting and allegorical words about how they would rebuild the domain of culture again. "We will return the area to the garden it was," said one speech maker. The gatherings and ceremonies employed customary cultural formulas—prayers, convocations, and appearances by public officials—and displayed accouterments of culture's persistence—a stage, music, cooked food. Within households, people constructed shrines of cultural items that passed through the inferno and emerged recognizable again. They included keys, vases, dishes, and bits of photos. Pictures of "before" were set up evoking the reconstruction of the same, as if the fire between were a mere interagent.

At the same time, what was left of nature within the burned-out area was mollified with cultural gifts. Surviving people turned surviving trees into cultural altars. They bedecked the few that still thrived with vases of cultivated flowers, ribbons, trinkets, and messages. People paid homage to burned-out lots with similar paraphernalia, transforming their charred property into semi-chapels and meditation sites. "I take flowers and a cushion. It's the only place I'm comfortable," a woman in the architect's group told me. I admit, I visited my lot in a similar manner. This same spectacle was noted by Oliver-Smith (1986:192–95)after the avalanche in Yungay, Peru. People brought flowers to the muddy scar and adorned it with crosses of wood and stone. Four surviving palm trees were turned into a chapel. In time the town moved its official ceremonies to take place there, so that the physical remains of the event evolved into a culturized, wholly sacred monument. In Oakland as well, the victims of the disaster became seeming crusaders in reclaiming nature's detritus back into culture. One postfire landscaping company entitled itself "Cul'ture, n." (*Phoenix Journal* 1993–94).

Of highly charged concern to the victims of the Oakland firestorm was "disorder." The fire left a chaotic scene, messy and undifferentiated, whereas cultural things are generally, or at least to people's minds, more tidily arranged. Nature may be awesomely beautiful, but part of its magnificence and danger is its seeming disarray. The mess left after the fire was simply too tousled for the comfort of many survivors. At all early gatherings, the rubble and its cleanup claimed absolute topical immediacy. Who would remove the mess, and when would the removal take place? Many victims, unable to wait for the city's cleanup program, rushed to "clean up" their lots themselves, until tidy rectangles of delineated lots once again spanned the space nature had torn through.

If disordered space was disturbing, so was disordered time. As one fire poem stated, "We return and sift through/the ashes of our homes/archaeologists/how many centuries have passed/since yesterday" (Cooney 1992:90). "In those first hushed days after the containment of the October fire, the most ordinary routines seemed remarkable," wrote another survivor. "The simplest chore felt like a rare privilege" (Adler 1992:i). Day and night, a moon's month, a year are natural temporal spans. The rest, hours, minutes, weeks, are culturally imposed. For the survivors, the drift away from cultural to natural time unnerved. Torn from schedule, their lives had become discultural and dysfunctional. The opening of an aid station with its clear and circumscribed hours became a focus of community. Meetings scheduled at specific times hypnotically lured.

But nothing seemed to grip the firestorm victims so powerfully and so symbolically as the matter of domestic animals gone feral. Survivors were obsessed with the possibility that because of the fire, once acculturated animals had returned to a wild state. The effort to bring animals now gone wild back to tame was so intense it spurred a three-year rescue mission and the publication of a 171-page expositive book (Zompolis 1994). Pictures of found animals were displayed at the survivor-aid station. A telephone pet "hot line" was activated. Foster homes were provided while owners were located and adoptions set up for the unclaimed. One of the final editions of the *Phoenix Journal* announced that all retrieved but ownerless "fire" pets had been taken into good homes (Zompolis 1994; *Phoenix Journal* 1993–94).

Other dualisms emerged in survivor imagery and action as well. The struggle to recover was portrayed as a trip "upward," while the disaster was painted as a "down" fall.[2] A schism between male and female with older, traditional gender behaviors resurfacing (Hoffman 1998). Death versus life also came into play. Victims sketched the disaster in chiaroscuro, as "a dark episode" and "going through hell." The climb to renewal was portrayed as the "light at the end of the tunnel." Oliver-

Smith (1986:195) reports that death loomed in cultural importance after the Yungay disaster also.

EMBODYING THE SYMBOLS—THE MONSTER AND THE MOTHER

To embody something is to give it understanding.—Franz Boaz, 1940

"Them hills almost killed you."
"They saved me, too. Those hills were a real mama to me."
—Quote from Kai Erikson, 1976

I don't think I want to keep living here when these big monsters keep coming along.—G. B., interview, California, 1997

Oakland firestorm survivors evoked yet another symbolic operation. As with all people in a new situation, they had only so many symbolic tools at hand, and in their extremity, they utilized the symbols already in the schematic corpus and applied them to epitomize alternate applications. Levi-Strauss (1966:15–16, 21, 1995) submits that people use symbols like classic handymen, *bricoleurs,* who have only so many devices in pocket to handle whatever repair comes up. Likewise, people in every society use signs they possess from within their limited assemblage to represent changing contexts and content as the need arises.

People in a dire situation are particularly pressed to slide the signs about. Faced with critical and novel issues on both physical and conceptual planes, they grab images from within the stock of their tradition and employ them for erratic and urgent demands. The firestorm survivors were no exception. Most notably, they shifted the constitution of content and meaning behind the basic nature-culture dualism. They performed this tidy slippage by employing embodiment.

The symbolic repertoires of all peoples incorporate some, if not considerable, embodiment. The corporealness of a jackal to represent a band of hunters, an elephant for a political party, a snake for the enemy, makes both social groups and abstract concepts more describable and embraceable. When embodying a symbol, a people can bedeck ideas with distinction and persona. In Oakland the firestorm victims came into the fire's aftermath with an image of nature already in place, that of a gentle and nourishing mother. The image was not new. Harvey (1996:121) points out that members of Western society inherit the humanization of nature from the tap roots of Christian culture, which favors domination. From that deep source comes Mother Nature. Even before Christianity, Western tradition linked nature to mother figures, and of late, it seems in culturally progressive sites such as Oakland, even prior to the fire, nature has reascended as a mother figure. Nature, also called "earth," has again come to represent wholesome and proper living along with "real" nourishment that is not the product of technology. Many in the US have come to revere and worship nature, to the point that rarely has nature been a more potent image, politically or otherwise.

Most of those in Oakland conceived it their duty to nurture nature. Nature loomed so large that "she" was viewed not just as a mother, but as a battered one. Many in Oakland lay the blame for the fire not on nature's whim alone but on the abuse of the environment, and after the fire they initiated and lobbied for more correct and respectful treatment of Mother Nature. They replanted property with foliage proper for the environment and removed more flammable trees wrongly borrowed from other ecological zones.

Unable to disabuse themselves of nature as a possession under their control or rid themselves of a current cultural divinity, Oakland firestorm survivors could scarcely class nature entirely under the category of "nature," despite its fiery eruption. In their new iconography, they also perceived that they both needed to heal nature and needed nature's nurturing to recover. Hence, they were faced with a paradox, which they solved rather double-handedly. On the one hand, they cast the storm as an aspect of nature and depicted nature as wild and uncontrollable; on the other, they took the mother image and shifted nature almost entirely into it. Nature was quickly again referred to as fostering. People removed nature from blame and forgave it. Amending nature back into something cultured, survivors then had little choice but to transform that which was wild and uncontrollable about the physical world into something other. They appropriated something figurative and illusive. They seized upon a monster. In short, the Oakland firestorm survivors bifurcated nature and fleshed out the firestorm with body and unbody. As David Schneider (1976) reminds us, nature is entirely a cultural concept, and the firestorm survivors manipulated it.

With the natural realm under the category of culture, there was scant option but to see the storm as something *un*natural. Given nature as embodied and humanly ministerial, no path was open but to dehumanize the violent, anticultural side of the physical. Again, survivors had in traditional ideology a particular figure that was natural, yet unnatural, formed yet unformed, that had shape but was malshaped: the monster. Just as the embodiment of nature as a mother was not new, neither was the specter of the monster. Monsters and the monstrous have haunted Western mythology and literature for millennia. Legends of monsters dispatching legions of men arise in epics as far back as Gilgamish. From Beowulf to Melville to Anne Rice and Stephen King, in lore the monster devours the quick. Nor is the typification of disasters as monsters new in other societies. Those with gods of calamity, such as the Hawaiian Pele and Indic Kali, tend to clothe them as terrifying ogres. Bode (1989:111, 143) quotes the Andean villagers as calling the mountain that brought the avalanche "a savage." In our tradition, "Vesuvius is a monster not to be restrained by any man's cunning or ingenuity," wrote volcanologist Alessandro Malladra in 1913 (Time Life 1982:120). Descriptions of Stromboli vivify the mountain: "Up there lives a dragon, a sleeping monster" (Time Life 1982:125). Earthquakes are frequently described as roaring dragons, tornados as devils, floods as ghouls; and what English speaker has not heard the phrase "freak of nature?"

Oaklanders had no divinity to characterize the power and fear of a catastrophe. Still, survivors rushed to anoint the firestorm a freak. In oral and written words, they used terminology synonymous with monster—"a horror," "a terror," "ghastly," "eerie," and "uncanny." Just as there is sometimes no form to the monster, there is sometimes no proper noun. "The unnamed and unnamable," Clark (1996:40–41) calls it. "What is familiar, may not be properly known." Nonverbally, survivors further illustrated the firestorm as a devouring fiend. My particular favorite is a tile in the commemorative mural that portrays the fire as a half horse-dragon at the front, its hind quarters a blood red, all-consuming, spiraled swirl, not unlike a local artist's portrayal of the Yungay avalanche as a dragon on the cover of Oliver-Smith's 1986 book.

In daily vernacular, the next step, the linkage of the uncivil or monstrous with calamity, was already in place. With an overactive child called a tornado, an angry person a volcano, and a shocking disclosure an earthquake, little was needed to moderate the idea to suit the firestorm.

The amorphous monster constitutes a perfect symbol of cataclysm for industrialized societies, which typically have a less direct sort of symbolic scheme. In metaphoric nuance, even the formless can take on semiotic value, and in urbanized society, where a plethora of the formed, the bodied, and the categorized abounds, the formless is always more frightening. The illusion of the monster carries two other long-standing symbolic and highly applicable renowns. Quite infamously it conveys danger. Quite famously it stands as a category breaker. Cohen (ed., 1996:x) states that in myth and literature the monster is best understood as an embodiment of difference. Derrida (1974) describes the figure of the monster as one that breaks bifurcation and disassembles such constructed dualities as between nature and culture. The monster is a form suspended between forms, threatening to smash distinction, and as such is dangerous (Cohen 1996:6). The monster, such as Caliban, Frankenstein, and Grendel, refuses to participate in the classified "order of things." The monster muddles the clash of extremes as "that which questions binary thinking and introduces a crisis" (Garber 1991:11). Rather than appearing at troubled times, the monster, like an unexpected quake or hurricane, creates the exigency. Thus, when the firestorm shattered the disjuncture Oakland's residents had contrived between nature and culture and confronted them with that aspect of nature they could not command, the monster readily slipped into representational role. "Everything was fine until that monster firestorm came," a man in my insurance group complained.

In transforming the disaster into an unnatural phenomenon, the monster as an image again possessed ideal traits. The monster in mythology is always an unnatural creature. It exists at the boundary of humanization. It is not quite a person, yet does not exist without humanity. Disasters similarly hover at the edge of human community, yet do not measure as calamities without that community. Monsters and disasters both prey on humanity and destroy. Without a group of experts, the monster is a metaphoric way of "bounding uncertainty" (see Stephens, this volume).

The monster is a resistant Other known only through process and movement, never through dissectible analysis. Only when a monster looms and strikes does it give opportunity for intelligibility (Cohen 1996:4–5); the same holds true for disaster. The monster has ontological liminality (Cohen 1996:6). What fashions a monster or brings it out always remains unknown; what generates a catastrophe and ushers it forth remains as obscure. The monster also has antidiachronicity. All that is known about monsters is seen through hindsight and records; it can only be read backward from the present (Waterhouse 1996, and see García-Acosta, this volume). Equally, the majority of what is known about disasters derives from their incidence. Moreover, the monster makes a problem of temporality. No one can calculate the calendar of the ogre's appearance, and in a time-linear society such as ours, the certainty of a calamity's reappearance coupled with the uncertainty of when have made prediction an obsession of disaster researchers.

Both monster in myth and disaster in science resist capture. They stand at the limits of knowing. The true threat of the monster is its propensity to shift and to be unpredictable. Similarly, despite modern advances, both natural and technological catastrophes defy foretelling and pinpointing. Disasters spring up insidiously and ever more frequently. Moreover, the monster always escapes (Cohen 1996:4–5). After each appearance it turns immaterial and vanishes. So, ostensibly, does disaster, although the effects of both linger. A catastrophe lasts a few moments, days, or years and is gone. Both monster and disaster, however, always come back. Each time the grave or earth opens and the beast or quake strides forth, a message is proclaimed. Neither can be stopped. In the face of both ogre and cataclysm, scientific inquiry and ordered rationality crumble.

The anamorphic monster validates the "paradoxical virtues of defect" (Cohen, ed., 1996:xi; Prescott 1996). It brings to light unsuspected things about its victims, their nature, society, sins. In effect, so do disasters. In the environment the defect may be a slip fault, an errant ember, or a company dumping pollutants (Button, this volume). There are political consequences lying in the belly of the monster representation as well. In literature the monster presents an excuse for persons or factions to impose rules and controls upon others. In environmental matters, the representation of a monstrous disaster justifies the same enterprise. The monster brandishes an invitation to action, particularly of the military and governmental sort. Harping on the threat of calamity or its reappearance, persons and governments do the same. Use of the monster image allowed the massive water projects and concomitant despotic governing of China (Wittfogel 1953). The behemoth Mississippi River, embodied as an uncontrollable old man, validated massive funding for manipulation of its course by the Army Corps of Engineers. Monsters and disasters alike as well are characterized as "gobbling up" and used to evoke fear and suppress dissent (O'Neil 1996).

The monster delimits the social spaces through which people may move and prevents intellectual and geographic mobility. The fiend at the door makes people stay in their place and keep to the conservative. Dwelling in the shadow of a calamity likewise keeps people circumspect. The monster is a vehicle of prohibition (Cohen 1996:12–16). In belief systems, the causes that entice both monster and calamity to appear, sometimes immorality and corruption, sometimes innocence and virtue, echo remarkably. One never knows, so it's best to toe the mark. On the other hand, the specter of the monster as an "outside" enemy gives people the cause and symbol to unify, as disaster victims characteristically do (Erikson 1994, Hoffman 1999).

Of course, along with all else, the monster, like the mystique of a disaster, also represents a kind of desire. At the same time as destroying, the monster offers escape, the enticement to explore new paths and new and interconnected methods of perceiving the world (Cohen 1996:16–20). As noted earlier, Douglas (1966:9) mentions the identical feature for disorder. Beauty is enchanted by the possibilities of the beast; people are attracted to disasters and want to encounter them. Thousands of people poured into Oakland to see the damage the fire had wrought. Many uttered the wish that they had undergone the catastrophe.

ETERNAL CYCLE COSMOLOGIES—WHEN THE MONSTER COMES 'ROUND AND 'ROUND

Pachamcutin, which is to say the world turns around. For the most part [Andeans] say it when things are turned from good to ill, and sometimes they say it when things change from ill to good.—Garcilaso de la Vega, quoted in S. MacCormack, 1988

Social time places physical time into a socio-cultural context.
—T. Forrest, 1993

Along with dualistic systems, disaster symbolism arises within ideologies in which time forever rotates in cyclical fashion. When and where such temporal schemes prevail, disaster is almost universally depicted as culprit and creator. A cataclysm of one sort or another ends one cycle, yet begins another. Disasters also frequently appear repetitively to mark minor stages within major ones. Among some people such cyclical ideologies are highly formalized with mythologies that herald the length of periods and the horrors of terminating catastrophes. Among others, the notion that time and catastrophes repeat emerges in a more informal manner, almost an unmindful one.

All the religious cosmologies indigenous to India—Buddhism, Jainism, and Hinduism—characterize the universe as transiting cyclical time in an exact and formal manner. Over virtually incalculable periods of time the cosmos travels through a process of evolution and decline ending with calamity, only to evolve once more (Basham 1959:272). These beliefs continue in areas that Basham called "monsoon Asia," as Zaman's (1994) disaster research in Bangladesh documents.

The Inca of South America supposed time to elapse in great periods as well. At the close of every era, irrespective of human merit, a physical and social cataclysm took place, and the world turned upside down. Volcanoes, storms, and floods announced the apocalypse, after which new people with strange customs and replacement gods took over. The cycles were articulated within the concept called *pachacuti*, first referred to by de la Vega as *pachamucutin* (McCormack 1988:961, 988; also see Moseley, this volume). *Pachacuti* appeared in Incan imagery in monster form and also as a rainbow whose arc implied the beginning or reversal of a given order. The doctrine of *pachacuti* proclaimed that all humans would mutate into monsters at the end of time. Bode (1989:258) found many ideas reminiscent of Incan cataclysmic cosmology still expounded in the Peruvian highlands city of Huaraz after the 1970 earthquake.

In the Western conception, time is like a line stretching into infinity, and every event along that line is new, but for the Maya time was like a wheel. Everything that transpired at one point in time occurred at a parallel point in the next and replayed endlessly in cycles to come. Each cycle, short and long, ended with catastrophe (Freidel, Schele, and Parker 1993:60; Peterson 1990:11; Waters 1975:256–57). The Aztec continued these beliefs and developed the cosmology yet more (Coe 1994:149). At the culmination of every fifty-two-year loop, women were locked up to prevent their transformation into monstrosities. Within the core of the beliefs lay the conviction that if the Pleiades did not appear, earthquakes would ravage and terrible miscreations would be loosed to roam the land (Peterson 1990:37; Nicholson 1967:44). The Hopi and Ute tribes of North America, both Uto-Aztecan speakers, hold analogous cosmologies (Waters 1977).

Oakland firestorm victims also conveyed a belief in cyclical time, but the precept arose in their reflections in an informal rather than formal manner. Survivors disclosed, in fact, two strains of rotational theory. The first reiterated the belief, long extant in Western and Judeo-Christian thought, that disasters have occurred on a regular basis throughout time and take place because of moral malfeasance. To numerous firestorm survivors, or perhaps more so to the surrounding community, Noah's flood and Sodom and Gomorrah echoed close. Current sins, however, were judged not so much sexual as ethical. The affluent inhabitants of the fair hills had enjoined gluttony and pride and merited the disaster. "Those people in the hills deserved to be wiped out. It was God acting," said an Oakland flatlander to me, and he was not alone.

More commonly, survivors gave heed to a second form of cyclical belief, one that more subtly encapsulated time and disasters into repetitive pattern. They declared that the firestorm had been "due." It was, many proclaimed, the "seventy-year" fire. "It was bound to happen" was another iteration I encountered. The disaster survivors thereby shifted the blaze into a recurrent, rather than unique, form and gave it a calendar. The 1991 victims had merely tumbled into an unlucky year and, by that happenstance, were the unfortunate recipients of a persistent and rhythmic, if not exactly punctual, turn. Within a short time, fellow Americans underwent other such fitful yet periodic recurrences. They endured the "hundred-year flood" (the Mississippi) and the "five hundred–year flood" (Grand Forks), while every year experiencing the annual "season" of tornadoes occurring where they always occur, in "tornado alley." Americans should expect hurricanes to destroy much of the Carolinas, Long Island, and Florida in the next decade or so, according to predictors of hurricane sequences. Earthquakes and avalanches are not only due, but should they miss their deadline, "overdue." The informal cyclical thinking is perpetuated by scientists and their ominous yet vague forecasts. Through this informal system, Americans, like other peoples, culturally manipulate catastrophes so that they appear, both in prediction and certainly in aftermath, to be anticipated and normal. They become like drought to the Turkana (see McCabe, this volume).

Oakland firestorm survivors, like disaster survivors elsewhere, also whitewashed the time before their particular calamities and indulged in good time–bad time nostalgia. In doing so, they reinforced that informal as well as formal cyclical time ideologies begin and end with disasters as dividing lines. After the firestorm, Oakland survivors as well began to live their lives again—linguistically. Practically every verb spoken was launched with the prefix "re." Survivors recovered, rebuilt, replaced, and were renewed. In linguistic metaphor, they took a second spin on the wheel of existence, and everything they performed was a duplication of what had gone before. On top of that, survivors were avidly caught in anniversaries. One week, one month, one year, they celebrated and suffered every one. "I've gone to every anniversary," one woman told me. "They tell me what I was and who I am now." "As a unique time designation anniversaries are a special situation," Forrest (1993:455) writes of disasters. "Implied in the concept is the convergence of the past, present, and future."

Cyclical concepts of disaster mirror dualistic schemes in much of their symbolism. What differs is the operation more than the essential meaning. Almost more than dualistic schemes, cyclical ones disclose a fundamental opposition between nature and culture in their framework. However, rather than contrive a stark separation of the categories, cyclical metaphors spell out an arbitration between them. Each rotation processes one aspect of the dialectic into the other, mediating them into a continuum. Nature destroys culture, but simultaneously begins culture again. The same disequilibrium between false categories that dualistic schemes generate exists, but it is written into the tale rather than left in disjuncture. Nature and culture oscillate. With disequilibrium intellectually solved, the fallaciousness of the dichotomy does not entail disintegration when calamitous events ensue. Cyclical schemes formulaically allow nature to go back to nature. Survivors in Oakland tacitly acknowledged this feature of rotational schemes. They reaffirmed that "it was good for nature to be cleaned out," and that the fire allowed nature "to start again."[3] All told, cyclical metaphors offer more malleability for people in disaster situations, which perhaps explains why they are more prevalent where catastrophe is chronic.

Cyclical ideologies join the present to the past, so that current happenings are already preordained history. What appears unexpected is, in fact, expected. Events do not have to do with date but rather time. Extraordinary occurrences need not slip into myth, for they are already mythical when they take place (Levi-Strauss 1978a, 1989). In addition, calamity does not imply loss, for all returns. The unknown becomes known, for the plot is teleological. Acts of recovery, and the speed with which recovery takes place, are not of issue. Time, repairs, and mitigation merely fold into the crescendo toward the next calamity. The process of restoration from any calamity is like cooking. From the rawness of the natural, culture must once again cook, and cook till done (Levi-Strauss 1969).

Cyclical schemes, both formal and informal, place God in nature, which means that nature is in essence never really without mastery. Natural acts become purposeful ones arranged by deities, and all eventualities take on sacred, and thereby cultural, implication. Within recycling schemes, the dichotomy between gods and humans is also mediated, and life entire waxes spiritual. Psychologically, cyclical symbolism offers particular comfort to victims, for what occurs is preordained, not retributory. Politically, on the other hand, cyclical symbolism leaves people particularly vulnerable. Where people dwell and how, along with hazards of the physical environment, are not of consequence, since fate determines all that transpires and who holds power. Mobility, too, is rendered useless. Victims may be obligated to deal with the particulars of any calamity, but they remain powerless to alter overall or underlying circumstance. Preventive acts allay nothing.

Since cyclical ideologies conjoin nature and culture, their symbolism often presents both figures in one representation. The destroyer is also the regenerator, as in images like Kali or concepts like *pachacuti,* where the monster and the mother are united. If anything, in cyclical schemes it is people, both singularly and as a collective category, who stand on the margins.

THE PROBLEMATIC NATURE OF TECHNOLOGICAL DISASTER—WHEN CULTURE ATTACKS CULTURE

In the first place, disasters that are thought to have been brought about by other human beings…not only hurt in special ways but bring in their wake feelings of injury and vulnerability from which it is difficult to recover.—K. Erikson, 1994

Though the Oakland firestorm was not per se a technological disaster, some would say its overwhelming and unexpected devastation most assuredly stemmed from technological fiasco. The fire was not entirely a bolt from the blue nor a matter of living in a friable zone. It occurred to a certain degree as a result of direct human mismanagement of the environment, and the victims were aware of it. Besides inappropriate landscaping, building materials and frivolous placement of houses invited conflagration. Roads in the dry, hilly area were narrow and circuitous. Some terminated without egress. The water system was antiquated and inadequate. Typically, the folly of Oaklanders' ways and the nonchalant path to a "normal" accident manifested only in retrospect.

This is not to say that wholly technological disasters did and do not threaten Oakland. Technological disasters, those linked arm in arm with natural factors, such as the Buffalo Creek flood, and those materializing totally independent of environmental features, such as the Bhopal toxic spill and the Chernobyl nuclear incident, have descended on the modern world with chilling ominousness. Their growing incidence, coupled with their invisible menace, have seized people's imaginations to the point where they inspire universal fear. Apprehension of them, however, emanates not only from their insidious nature and destructive potential but also from their horrific symbolic implications.

As outlined in previous sections, much disaster symbolism expresses a separation between nature and culture. In many peoples' worldviews, historical chronicles, and symbolism, disasters have been reckoned as deriving from the category of nature. Flood, fire, wind, earthquake, or slide, all fit in peoples' minds within the category onto-logically considered their domain. Nature is the "proper" origin and phylum of disaster.

Technological disasters emanate from the wrong category. They emerge from the arena that is cultural, not its antithesis. They come from within the sanctuary and sanctity of the humanly managed, the category conceptually labeled "safe." They are not supposed to erupt from the constructed and contrived realm, the estate of humans. When they do, it is very hard, indeed nigh impossible, for people to give them differentiation and disjuncture. "Displacement is the genesis of sym-bolic behavior," says Cassier (1966), and technological disasters cannot be displaced. They dwell in the same category we do.

Symbolically, technological disasters portend still more. With tech-nological disasters, symbolically, the "culturechthonous" becomes an auto-da-fé. That is, something born from culture turns into a public execution. I borrow the Spanish Inquisition's euphemistic referral to a public execution as an "act of faith," for it applies in both its references to technological disasters. Above all, humans have faith in culture. Culture is the seat of human trust, the provider of protection. In conse-quence, when a calamity that culture creates falls upon people, in imagery and in reality it seems that culture turns upon its members and kills them. The fundament of faith executes those who have faith in it.

As stated earlier, disaster dismantles the false dichotomies that some people construct and eradicates the denial of the savage. When so-called natural disasters occur, ones from the correct and opposi-tional category, that denial can be reestablished; but disasters that spring from culture itself seemingly debar culture's hale return. If cul-ture brought the tragedy, how can culture become whole again? Denial of menace cannot be wholly reconstructed. Technological disasters pre-sent exactly what humans cannot tolerate and continuously endeavor to put at distance: They signify an incubus on culture's own back, a malignancy in the wholesomeness of the constructed world, danger within the secure. They represent a cultural betrayal. Matters that spoil pattern are the cause of fear, points out Douglas (1970), and techno-logical disasters mar the very heart of humanly ordained pattern.

It follows that in concept, technological disasters often take on the quality of the most dangerous and the most polluting, albeit they may be so in reality as well. Their silent undermining and invisible damage do not fade. Enemies from within always provoke continuous tension and require constant vigil, and that is the aura that technological disaster creates. Rajan discusses the continuing disquiet within victims of the Union Carbide accident in Bhopal (1999 and this volume). Stephens (1995) paints the same picture for the Sami of Norway. Paine (1992b) describes the increasing sense of risk globally, and Erikson (1976:255, 1994:11–21) the individual and collective trauma left by technological disasters. Included are both technological disasters that are abrupt and those that Erikson describes as gathering force slowly and silently.

Few sense-making images or explanatory metaphors satisfy when culture attacks culture. Hence, in their aftermath technological disasters also leave nearly unsolvable issues of how to reconstitute logic. In the first place they tend to be immeasurably disruptive physically. "From an ecological perspective, natural disasters rarely result in long-term disruptions of the relationship between humans and their biophysical environments, while a community's built and modified environments frequently sustain loss. On the other hand, technological disasters routinely disrupt the exchange between human settlements and their natural or biophysical environments, while in many cases resulting in comparatively little or no damage to built and modified environments," state Kroll-Smith and Couch (1991:355–66). In addition, they fundamentally disrupt conceptual order. Kroll-Smith and Couch (1991:361–362) go on to say, "Our conception of living and dwelling are psychically rooted in our relationship to the earth," but our methods of living are cultural, and a technological catastrophe alters them in a way not altered in natural disaster. "Humans experience their environment mediated by conceptual categories fabricated in social interactions," states Mary Douglas (1985:34). With technological disaster these interactions are permanently shaken. Levi-Strauss (1985) adds that should local ecology lead to change in one part of the story, the rest must follow, and that involves the symbolic system.

In consequence, as Malcolm Gladwell (1996:32) points out, technological disasters prompt particular rituals: "In the technological age, there is a ritual to disaster. When planes crash or chemical plants explode, each piece of physical evidence...becomes a kind of fetish object, painstakingly located, mapped, tagged and analyzed with the finding submitted to boards of inquiry that then probe and interview and soberly draw conclusions. It is a ritual of reassurance." What is, of course, occurring in the ritual is culture taking care of a cultural problem so that people can rest secure. The rituals imply that culture has understood and corrected its error and will prevent the event recurring.

Communities also resurrect a long known, though discarded, restorative, in a rather new form. They pry out the wrongdoers, but of a new sort. In the wake of a technological disaster, people search for the humans they can designate "inhuman." They seek those they can name responsible, not necessarily for moral reasons as has transpired before, but largely for errors in craft. It is not sins in the eyes of God that are denounced but miscalculations in the arts of culture. People take the callous chairman of the board or the iniquitous manufacturer out of the human category and categorize the malefactor as inhuman. The wrongdoer is a "monster." Those who should have mothered, blundered. The process is not unlike a witch hunt of old.

Technological disasters stand "ex" cycle. Though they fit within predictions of general disintegration in certain formal versions of cyclical time, they contradict specific formulas and, thus, defy God and time. They completely repudiate informal cycles. Events such as the Three Mile Island nuclear plant meltdown never reemerge as seventy-year floods. In keeping, technological disasters never pass from history to myth, but always stay history. Technological disasters also never receive beautification. Only catastrophes from the category of nature gain redemption from their stunning, if ferocious, bedazzlement. Technological disasters in symbolism and symbolic power leave lasting scorched earth.

THE BEAUTIFICATION OF DISASTER—CONCLUSION

> *People seek to clothe the nakedness of death with a cloak of opu-*
> *lence...The beautified corpse is a formality for the hardened*
> *survivors.*—M. Horkheimer and T. Adorno, 1972

In the long afterglow of the fire's embers, Oakland firestorm survivors launched two finalizing symbolic ships. They reinvented the disaster as "creative destruction." They claimed the storm cleared away the mess and was good for the environment. The fire allowed a new start, many said. Most declared the calamity was "good" for their lives. They now had "clean slates," as if their slates, whatever they were, had been sullied before.

They also redescribed the firestorm as awesome in its beauty. When people reinvent calamity as "creative destruction" or describe a violent act of nature as "terrifying beauty," they are doing what Horkheimer and Adorno describe for death rituals—seeking to clothe the nakedness of the unacceptable with a cloak of opulence. As people do for a funeral, they embroider a body and primp facts so the antithesis between life and death or nature and culture becomes less daunting. In gracing the fire with finery, Oakland's survivors performed a triple sweep. They blew away the ashes, scrubbed the ruins, and prettified even the concept of calamity. They turned the disaster into a comely corpse, and with that went on with their lives.

They further glamorized the calamity as a preservative boon, a preemptive strike that prevented a worse disaster from occurring. It was a warning, and with it nature had done good. Nature was not untrustworthy. Nature was just handing out a little well-deserved caution. Technological disasters are often depicted in the same manner. The anxious declare them omens that make the population conscious and caution people to change their cultural ways.

Already the Oakland firestorm has begun its fusion into fable. Though the victims remember its exact date, others have asked me, "Wasn't that fire about twenty years ago?" or "Wasn't that last year?" while across the country the blaze is almost forgotten. Disasters drift from the real to the unreal, and sometimes from the unreal to the real. The Greek villagers among whom I often work soberly told me how the red volcano behind them once erupted and threatened to pour death on everyone, but the Virgin Mary came and blew it out. In fact, the igneous remnant they nod to bubbled up over more than 20,000 years ago, long before the island was inhabited and a Christian virgin could have protected it.

Disaster is, of course, a symbol of itself along with all else, so while cataclysms indeed occur, in symbol they do not actually have to (Wagner 1986). The mere term "disaster" epitomizes disorder. The matter of disaster is also itself symbolic. Fire burning, air swirling, earth shaking, water spewing, even atoms in their fission, dirty streams, and foul air, all make for the making of imagery.

In examining the symbolism of disaster, I feel I have embarked on a Herculean task. This study seems only the first of a probable twelve labors. Not all cultures symbolize disasters in the ways I have described, but all use symbolism somehow as part of their operation to depict and explain them. I believe that in understanding the symbolism of disaster perhaps lies the key to comprehending certain inexplicable riddles disaster researchers encounter. Why, for example, do the victims of disaster return to the area wasted? Why do those living in regions of chronic disaster stay? Some have no choice; they are economically closed out of safer places to live. But students of religious symbolism have long since clarified that metaphor also leads to the process of ownership (Deshen 1970). If metaphors of the environment enable such a process, then place attachment becomes more sensible. How Laughlin (1995) speaks of religious metaphor further elucidates why inhabitants of disaster zones feel no call to act upon ecological or technological problems. Symbols and metaphors mitigate the need for change. Why not stay? Why not return?

Disaster researchers also operate symbolically. In most descriptions and analysis, culture and society are expressed in habitual past tense. Yet the strongest barrier to the recognition of human cultural activity is the immediate and regular conversion of experience into finished products the past tense conveys (Williams 1977:128–29). We in disaster studies speak in the past, although disasters are ongoing and are coming. We should not embrace the illusion of the bygone. We cannot afford to do so.

Notes

1. Similar characterizations arose around the great Chicago fire. Though never verified, in legend the fire was said to have been started by Mrs. O'Leary's cow, which kicked over a lit lantern. Nature, in the form of the cow, should not have been in an urban area, barn or no barn. Nor should Mrs. O'Leary have brought a natural element, fire, into that misplaced barn with that malapropos cow. In the Chicago situation, racism, classism, sexism, and religious prejudice all entered in the schema, in all of which respects Mrs. O'Leary herself figured

as lower and closer to animalism along with her cow (Bales 1997; Smith 1995; Sawislak 1995). The Chicago fire legend stands as a classic example of how disaster symbolism can assume political implications. In Oakland, political implications of the Chicago sort were thankfully absent, though the fire starters were reputed to be "Mexican."

2. Lovejoy (1964) points out that down is more animal and up more godly, at least in Western thought.

3. Levi-Strauss (1978b:198) notes that the transformation back to culture at the end of the cycles requires enactment, spatially, temporally, and acoustically. As a rule, this takes place through the destruction of cultural items—the smashing of calendars, icons, furnishings—followed by the reformulation of cultural matters—rekindling fire, replacing divinities, and refurbishing the home, such as was done by the Aztecs.

7

Popular Media Reframing of Man-Made Disasters
A Cautionary Tale

Gregory V. Button

Well, I think the oil companies were certainly getting their way with the media. They know how to use the media very well, and how to feed the proper sound bites and things at the proper time. As well as how to stage a good production. For example, the outer coast was pretty heavily oiled. Exxon...hired sixty to eighty local people to go there and clean a beach. They brought in all these helicopters and put everybody in their orange waist coats and flew them over there and put them on the skirmish line with their shovels. Dan Rather's crew came in from, I believe CBS, and flew over there. They got good footage over there for about a half an hour and they interviewed some very conscientious and concerned looking oil people and filmed them. Then they packed up their equipment and flew out. And that's what you saw on the evening news that night, Exxon's wonderfully orchestrated cleanup project. The next day all those people were laid off and they [Exxon] never, ever, went back to that beach. It was that kind of stuff that is maddening to local people.

  —Tom Bodett, writer-humorist and Homer, Alaska
  resident, commenting on the *Exxon-Valdez* oil spill.

  Like the residents of Homer, Alaska, victims of man-made disasters and their families struggle not only to regain control over their lives but to refute the "objective" frames of the disaster offered by the media and other social institutions. This struggle to assert counter-definitions is a perduring theme of man-made disasters in recent times. Just as victims of the *Exxon-Valdez* oil spill constantly struggled to reframe the media's and Exxon's framing of the event, victims struggled to do likewise in the tragedies surrounding Bhopal (Rajan, this volume); Love Canal (Levine 1982); PPB poisoning in Michigan (Eggington 1980); ground water contamination in Legler, New Jersey (Edelstein 1988); and the Santa Barbara (Molotch 1972), *Braer* (Button 1995; 1999), and *Sea Empress* (Button 1999) oil spills.

Community victims must contend not only with reframing journalistic and corporate accounts of their story but also, in some cases, with popular media accounts, such as Jonathan Harr's best-selling book *A Civil Action* (Random House 1996). Harr, a sophisticated, highly accomplished writer, wrote a riveting tale of a class-action case that pitted the victims against two of America's largest corporations. The book was based on a 1986 legal battle over whether toxic groundwater contamination was to blame for the deaths of several children in the Boston suburb of Woburn. It won the National Book Critics Circle award for nonfiction and was made into a successful movie by Disney's Touchstone Pictures. Both the book and the movie, described by critics as compelling legal thrillers, are particularly potent examples of the reframing of a catastrophe because of their enormous influence on the culture at large. In fact, the general public only came to know of the Woburn tragedy as a result of these media productions.

Many of the Woburn victims have been deeply disturbed by Harr's book. Some argue that both the book and the movie exclude their story and thereby distort the meaning of the events. Anne Anderson, one of the central players, believes the story, which involves the death of her son, is rightfully hers. She is upset because of her lack of inclusion: "It's frightening. I don't own the story; I don't even own anything they are going to do with it" (Goldberg 1998). Several other members of the Woburn families were upset that, at first, Disney did not involve them in the production or compensate them for their stories. After these families reframed the issue in the Boston-area press as partly an issue of ownership, the studio agreed to pay some of the families and consult with them during the production.

It is not, however, the notion of the ownership of a story per se that is of central concern here, but the adequacy of a frame's explanatory power to explicate a disaster. The exclusion of the voices of disaster victims is constraining in this and other ways. As I have argued elsewhere

(Button 1995), it makes a crucial difference whose interpretation is heard in the aftermath of a man-made disaster and whose interpretations are excluded. The outcomes of important questions—who is to blame, who is to be compensated, who suffers disproportionate risk exposure, and who should be involved in essential decisions such as remedial treatment and preventative policies—pivot on whose voices are heard.

In this chapter I examine the alternative perspectives or arguments that are undermined by the frames employed by the media to explain disasters. Beyond the specifics of the Woburn disaster, it seeks to explore how the reframing of a man-made disaster alters the public perception and discourse of disasters in general. The way people employ frames to construct knowledge is central to this undertaking. In strictly Foucaultian terms, we need to be mindful of the role reframing plays in reproducing ideologies. It is important to pay attention to the role of framing in reproducing ideologies and reinforcing the privileged positions of authority. This chapter seeks to remind us of how writing participates in the practices that maintain systems of power.

Narratives of conflict, such as the struggle of the residents of Woburn to seek compensation for the harm inflicted on them, are particularly potent domains in which to explore the legitimation and reproduction of ideologies. Examining such events provides us with insight into social power structures within our own culture. Contemporary anthropologists (Briggs 1996) have argued that narratives of conflict provide us with privileged sites from which to examine the social order. While these anthropologists examine stories of more traditional anthropological forms, such as gossip and trickster tales, I argue that major media events package accounts of a man-made disaster into culturally preconceived frames.

Historian Robert Darnton (1975) states, "Newspaper stories must fit the cultural preconceptions of news." Like other mediated accounts in our popular culture, Harr's courtroom/suspense drama of Woburn fits the cultural preconceptions of society. The book's failure is that it does not challenge these preconceptions and attempt a more critical and creative narrative. Instead, the standardized "plot" imposes a meaning on events that elide the meanings victims attach to the disaster, which, coupled with a political-economic analysis, would provide us with insight into the social order.

How the media packages information and participates in the construction of reality informs us of some of the ideological elements that seek to maintain the status quo in the wake of a disaster. Such packaging also reminds us of the often overlooked fact that disasters are not merely phenomena of the material world but are grounded in the politically powerful world of social relations. This analysis also underscores the fact that disasters are not only socially and physically disruptive; they are also political events. Thus, disaster analysis must involve the analysis of political power relations among those affected as well as among the various agencies and institutions that stand in relation to the event and the victims.

Whether labeled "man-made" or "natural," disaster events highlight ongoing power struggles in society. The control of information in the media or in public discourse, as well as the attempt to control the social production of meaning, is an attempt to define reality in accordance with a favored political agenda and therefore must be seen as a distinctly ideological process. This struggle becomes more pronounced in the wake of a technological disaster. The framing process both constructs and reconstructs meaning in a selective manner that legitimizes some accounts while obscuring others, privileging some political agendas and negating others. Hegemonic ideologies are, however, as Gitlin (1980:256) observes, "extremely complex and absorbing" and can thus incorporate a patina of liberalism like the one Harr employs in his narrative account of a crusader challenging the system.

The way the media frame an event strongly mediates how the public thinks about that event. Frames are the packages in which the central focus of a news story is developed and understood. Although "largely unspoken and unacknowledged" (Gitlin 1980:7), they help journalists organize the world; they also strongly shape how we, as readers, perceive the world. Frequently frames are unchallenged assumptions about the world. Rather than the cultural constructions that they are, frames usually appear to both reporters and news consumers as natural constructions. They present seamless, seemingly objective accounts of the given world, neither revealing their underlying subjectivity nor showing how complex disaster events really are. The contestation over the meaning of a disaster and the struggle to interpret it commonly result in a struggle to frame the event, the outcome of which is often dependent on who has access to the media.

One way to unpack frames, particularly of news-related stories, is to think of them as products of culture, which has built-in assumptions about what categories are considered relevant. For instance, the "who," "what," "when," "where," and "why" that a news story is supposed to address should be investigated—that is, the people defined as "who," "what" things are accepted as facts, the geopolitical boundaries constituting "where," the time-line constituting "when," and "why," which constitutes an explanation. The news media and many of our cultural frames highly restrict this latter category as well as most others (Schudson 1995:14). For most new stories, the "why" is predicated almost solely on motives, thus precluding looking for the causes of disasters in the broader social patterns. For example, Harr's framing limits his explanatory mode to "motives," thereby restricting the explanation of causes to an individual plane. Moreover, as I shall also discuss, Harr's "who" almost excludes the voices of disaster victims and their families, thereby collapsing our full understanding of the disaster.

Technological disaster frames also tend to focus on individuals, just as Harr, in his book, focuses almost exclusively on attorney Jan Schlichtmann. Individualism, the "mainstay of capitalist ideology" (Cormack 1992:53), obscures the categories of class, race, gender, and age, which are essential to understanding and explicating the politics of disaster. Needless to say, such an approach also excludes the agency of social movements such as the one born in response to the contamination in Woburn.

This emphasis on the individual accomplishes at least two things. First, it displaces any systemic account of the disaster and its causes because it relies on anecdotal, individualistic accounts that decontextualize the larger sociopolitical conditions in which the tragedy occurred. Second, narrative discourse makes individuals appear to be passive victims rather than active agents struggling politically to redefine events and reframe official accounts of the disaster. This approach is galvanized by the media's tendency to rely disproportionately on official accounts of the disaster while dislocating the voices of the victims and their families.

In order to analyze the controversy surrounding the framing and reframing of the Woburn story, it is first necessary to recount the basic events surrounding the disaster. The community of Woburn is located approximately twelve miles north of Boston and has approximately 37,000 residents, most of them working class and lower middle class. During the mid-1970s, some residents began to notice what they thought was an unusually high rate of childhood leukemia in the community. Jimmy Anderson was one of twenty-six children diagnosed with this disease between 1979 and 1985. Like Jimmy, most of them lived in East Woburn, eight of them within a half-mile radius, six within one block. [According to the National Cancer Institute, the average incidence of childhood leukemia is 3.74 cases per 100,000 children (DiPerna 1985).] Adult leukemia and renal cancer rates in Woburn were also high. Soon Woburn, like Love Canal in New York and Times Beach in Missouri, became a bellwether hazardous waste case.

The residents of Woburn had to struggle with corporations as well as with local, state, and federal agencies in order to gain recognition of the seriousness of their situation. In many ways, the story of Woburn is even more remarkable than Love Canal. Although we still do not know for certain whether anyone died because of the contamination at Love Canal, we do know that many people, young and old, died in Woburn. Woburn stands as a benchmark toxic waste disaster not simply because of the death rate (which is only one indication of severity), but also because it was the first time lay and professional researchers worked together on an epidemiological research project. Woburn also allowed for substantial information to be gathered on the probable causation between specific kinds of carcinogens and leukemia.

The unfolding events in Woburn were in many ways contiguous with the sequence of events in Love Canal. When the problems in Woburn were first being noticed, the story of Love Canal had not yet come to either local or national attention. By 1979, however, Love Canal emerged as the toxic waste story of the decade, and it was not until several years later that Woburn also made headlines. The policy implications of Love Canal had tremendous impact on Woburn as well as other communities whose disasters subsequently came to public attention.

As was true of Love Canal, the Woburn story began largely because of the efforts of one mother, Anne Anderson. She began to notice an unusual number of childhood leukemia deaths in her neighborhood after her son Jimmy was diagnosed in 1972. Anderson had difficulty in getting anyone, including her husband, to take note of the emerging cancer cluster, so she took her concern to her minister, Bruce Young. He soon became convinced that her assessment was accurate. They began gathering information from other families and asked state officials to test the water.

In May 1979, workers found 184 fifty-five-gallon drums of waste in an empty lot near the Aberjona River in Woburn. The Massachusetts State Department of Environmental Quality Engineering (DEQE) investigated and found that wells contiguous to the river contained carcinogenic organ compounds (Brown and Mikkelsen 1990). The wells, known as G and H, were the main water source for Anne Anderson and her neighbors in East Woburn.

The state ordered the wells to be shut down. Only a month after the wells were closed, a DEQE employee driving by an industrial site not far from the wells noticed activity he believed to be a violation of the Wetlands Act. The Army Corps of Engineers and the United States Environmental Protection Agency investigated and found violations and contamination on the site, including dangerous levels of heavy metals. However, the EPA did not notify the town or its residents of this danger. Not until four months later, when a local reporter broke the story, did the town learn of the contamination.

These events reinforced Anne Anderson's and Bruce Young's hunches about the possible cause of illness in the community. Young, in consultation with Jimmy Anderson's physician, composed a questionnaire and drew a map of the immediate community of East Woburn. When they plotted the leukemia cases, Anderson and Young realized that of the twelve cases they uncovered, half were within just a few blocks of the Anderson home. This discovery launched a grassroots community group, For A Cleaner Environment (FACE).

The Woburn city council asked the United States Centers for Disease Control (CDC) to investigate. Shortly thereafter, the Massachusetts Department of Public Health (DPH) issued its own report rejecting the cancer cluster model of FACE. Although the DPH study found that there had been 18 cases of leukemia (among all age groups) in the preceding decade, compared to an expected total of only 10.9, it concluded that there were no abnormal rates of leukemia in the community (Brown and Mikkelsen 1990). The CDC's study commenced in May 1980, and the report was issued in January 1981, just a few days after Jimmy Anderson died. In fact, by that time, nine of the twelve children in the original cluster had died (DiPerna 1985). The CDC cited 12 cases of childhood leukemia in East Woburn, where the expected rate was 5.3. The DPH rejected the CDC study as inconclusive and argued that the instances of leukemia did not correlate with groundwater contamination.

The controversy and indeterminacy of the studies, which are common in a man-made disaster, led to uncertainty and concern within the community. They also increased FACE's resolve to press for further studies. After Anderson and Young presented their data to a seminar at the Harvard School of Public Health, FACE members and researchers at the school launched a lay epidemiology project. The Harvard/FACE study focused on twenty cases of childhood leukemia diagnosed in Woburn between 1963 and 1984. Project members also incorporated DEQE's models of Wells G and H. In the most innovative and controversial aspect of the study, three hundred community volunteers were trained to conduct telephone interviews with 57 percent of the community's households.

It wasn't until early 1984 that the results of the study were announced. A consistent pattern of positive association was found between the availability of water from Wells G and H and the incidence of childhood leukemia, stillbirths, sudden infant deaths, and some birth defects. Furthermore, children diagnosed with leukemia had an average of 21.2 percent of their yearly water supply coming from Wells G and H compared with 9.5 percent of children without leukemia (DiPerna 1985).

While this study was going on, the EPA conducted a hydrogeological study of the community's groundwater. The EPA study lent considerable plausibility to FACE's case when the agency found that the bedrock under East Woburn was bowl-shaped and sloped to the southwest, exactly where Wells G and H were located. Two toxic plumes of contaminants were also identified in this region.

Based on this evidence alone, eight families of children diagnosed with leukemia filed a lawsuit against W. R. Grace Company and Beatrice Foods Company, both of which owned facilities the plaintiffs claimed were the source of the plumes detected in the EPA study. The suit argued that subsidiaries of the two corporations dumped toxic waste into the water supply, thereby causing death and harm to the community.

The case was tried before a jury in U.S. District Court in 1986. The most persistent problem the plaintiffs faced stemmed from the decisions of Judge Walter Skinner, who, according to many observers, consistently gave the corporations every advantage and ruled favorably on most of their motions (Brown and Mikkelsen 1990). His rulings became controversial in September of 1985 when he imposed a gag order on the suit's participants. The Massachusetts Civil Liberties Union argued successfully against the extent of the gag order, and the judge modified it a month later. By February 1986, after substantial media coverage, the order was lifted (Brown and Mikkelsen 1991).

The plaintiffs' case was also adversely affected by the judge's ruling that the trial was to be divided into three parts, beginning with consideration of whether the defendants were responsible for dumping the waste. Only if the jury found that responsibility existed could the trial proceed to the second part, in which the jury's task would be to decide if the dumped chemicals caused leukemia. The third segment of the trial was to be the jury's consideration of the award of damages.

The plaintiffs' expert witnesses testified that the source of the plumes was indeed the subsidiaries in question. Hydrogeological evidence was also introduced that demonstrated the flow of underground water from the plants to the wells. Attorneys for the defense argued that the plant operators were not responsible for the dumping, which must have been caused by trespassers. Their case seemed to deteriorate when the plaintiffs proved that at the Woburn Tannery plant, owned by Beatrice Foods, contrary to the testimony of former owner John Riley, he had foreknowledge of the presence of toxic waste. Workers and managers at the Cryovac plant, owned by W. R. Grace, also testified to witnessing the frequent dumping of trichloroethylene at the plant.

Toward the end of the first stage of the trial, Judge Skinner made another controversial ruling. He declared that Beatrice could be found guilty of dumping only after 1968, while Grace could be found guilty of dumping as early as 1964. This was the first time a Massachusetts court held a corporation (W. R. Grace) accountable to strict liability. Beatrice

Food's liability was restricted merely to negligence, since the court ruled that there was no evidence of the subsidiary plant dumping waste. The jury found W. R. Grace guilty but Beatrice Foods not guilty. It was anticipated that the trial would then proceed to the second stage. Instead, Judge Skinner ordered the case to be retried because he decided that the jury had not understood the hydrogeological data (Brown and Mikkelsen 1990). This decision placed the plaintiffs at a severe disadvantage, considering the expense of another trial and the deep pockets of the corporations. In September 1986, the families settled out of court with W. R. Grace for $8 million. After legal expenses and fees were deducted, each family received approximately $450,000. After the settlement, the plaintiffs learned that the EPA had withheld a 1983 report lending substantial support to the families' claims (Brown and Mikkelson 1990; DiPerna 1985). Furthermore, another court found that Beatrice Foods had suppressed evidence during the trial. A newly released EPA report also demonstrated that the Beatrice facility was the most polluted site in the well area. Appeals were filed amid charges that the EPA obstructed the appeals process by refusing to allow an EPA employee who had witnessed dumping at Beatrice to be subpoenaed. After many other legal maneuvers, all appeals were denied, and in 1990 the United States Supreme Court refused to hear the plaintiffs' case.

Meanwhile, between 1982 and 1986, seven more children in Woburn were diagnosed with leukemia. The settlement with W. R. Grace was only a partial victory for FACE and the original eight families. But the Woburn families succeeded in setting a precedent in community activism: They conducted two lay epidemiology studies that established the existence of a leukemia cluster, brought national media attention to their case, and brought a case to trial.

Harr's book presents a reasonable account of the litigation of this case but provides very little information on the community and its struggle outside of the trial. His focus is almost exclusively on the trial and backroom intrigue, with the plaintiff's attorney, Jan Schlichtmann, as the principal character. The afflicted families and the members of FACE play a minor role in Harr's narration; in more than five hundred pages, Harr devotes only a single, thirty-eight-page chapter to the story of the community and the individual families. The voices of community members appear in Harr's text only on fifteen separate pages. In his afterword, Harr notes what happened to only one Woburn resident, even though he mentions several of the courtroom participants. His failure to mention the fate of many of the other Woburn residents underscores how little attention is given in his text to the victims of the disaster. He briefly, and almost in passing, records the disbelief and disgust of the Woburn families when they learn that Judge Skinner has barred their testimony from the courtroom. Inexplicably, Harr does little to probe the meaning of this decision for the case or the underlying legal grounds on which the decision was handed down.

Thus, in *A Civil Action,* the Woburn disaster victims end up in the same place as almost all disaster victims in media accounts of man-made calamities (Button 1999) such as Bhopal (Rajan, this volume) and the *Exxon-Valdez* oil spill (Button 1993), with reporters relying largely on government and corporate sources. The failure to record the voices of disaster victims is a common oversight of the press in its coverage of such events. Seldom do we hear directly from the victims themselves, as we do in Lois Gibbs's (1982) account of Love Canal or Susanna Hoffman's (this volume) account of the Oakland fire. Relying on government, corporate, and professional sources often prevents disaster victims from providing competing accounts. The consequence is that some people's accounts are valorized, while other accounts are marginalized. Sharon Stephens's (this volume) account of the failure of victims of nuclear radiation exposure to find a voice in the international scientific community illustrates this point nicely.

In his book, Harr makes little of the disenfranchisement of the Woburn residents and, in fact, reproduces it by devoting so much attention to the testimony of experts and so little to the accounts of the Woburn victims. By downplaying the central significance of social action in the story of Woburn, he reinforces the cultural ideology of maintaining the status quo and promoting civil order.

The larger point to be made here is not to find fault with Harr's success or critique his book. Harr's depiction is merely a reflection of our popular culture at large and its presentation of man-made disasters, its proclivity to place man-made disasters within prepackaged scenarios that reproduce our cultural ideologies and prevent us from having a finer analysis of disasters. Such scenarios keep us from asking questions about the risks that disaster victims face, including the question of why disaster victims are vulnerable to such risks in the first place. Moreover, constraining frames prevent us from comprehending how disasters are produced by our social and political processes and are not merely to be considered "accidents." As noted earlier, limiting the investigation of "why" to the human motivational causes of disasters prevents further inquiry into the social patterns of our society that are responsible for the production of disasters.

Disaster narratives that media people employ in their descriptive accounts often reiterate a standardized story that can fit a wide array of calamities. If we situate the construction of news in a broader arena than the organizational setting of a newsroom and employ Gramsci's notion of hegemony, then we take into account the decisive political/economic influence of certain interest groups (Ryan 1991). The underlying cultural logic of disaster narratives tends to reinforce the hegemonic forces of society (Iyengar 1991). It is unavoidable, then, that our discourse about disasters becomes a discourse about the politics of disasters. Such an analysis underscores the political nature of disasters and highlights the extremely political processes of controlling access to information and the construction of meaning.

While technological disaster narratives vary from incident to incident, certain recurring themes emerge—themes that reinforce the dominant hegemonic forces of society. In so-called environmental disasters such as the *Exxon-Valdez* oil spill, the focus is generally on the effects on the ecology, ignoring the effects on human communities. This attempt to naturalize the disaster is often taken a step further by having the disaster narrative place the spill outside human control. In effect, this turns discussions of responsibility and blame away from government agencies as well as corporate entities. The response to disaster is depicted as a valiant and often vain struggle with Mother Nature, a scenario that places much responsibility outside of human control. The resulting reification makes the event appear all the more like an accident rather than the result of human negligence (Tuchman 1978).

Finally, standard disaster narratives ignore the long-term continuum of a technological disaster and tend to report on the event in an episodic fashion. They ignore the longitudinal evolution of the disaster and serve to reinforce the neglect of systemic forces and the long-term effects of disaster on human communities. This results in little nonlocal follow-up as the disaster story continues to unfold over the coming months or even years. Seldom do nonlocal newspapers publish ongoing stories in the ensuing months; most stories that appear after the initial event are "anniversary" stories rather than in-depth follow-up features.

The media treat technological disasters as they do most news stories. Stories quickly become dated and are abandoned for other, "breaking" stories. Obviously this precludes any systemic analysis of a social problem. In the case of technological disasters, this treatment is most unfortunate. The continuum of these particular phenomena, unlike many disasters, often unfolds slowly, and it can take years for the effects to become manifest, as the story of Woburn attests.

Harr framed the story of Woburn in a standardized cultural trope, thereby establishing cultural legitimacy and lending coherence for the average reader. After all, as Darnton (1976) points out, a prepackaged courtroom drama frame meets our cultural preconceptions and, equally importantly, guarantees, as it did in Harr's case, a profitable best-selling book and movie. However, in the process of choosing this selective frame, he tailored the story to rely for its dramatic action on lawyers, judges, and corporate figures, just as journalists are overly reliant on government officials and experts. Harr's frame also emphasizes the heroic action of one man, Schlichtmann, over and above the heroic actions of the residents of Woburn. Individualism, a mainstay of our culture, is given prominence over the collective actions of a social movement. The text glosses over the political actions surrounding the disaster as well as the importance of local knowledge in bringing attention to an often neglected, unrecognized environmental calamity.

The book also elides the political action of Judge Skinner by skimming over his highly controversial decision to keep the plaintiffs out of court and thereby skew the case in favor of the corporations. Ironically, Harr buries the trenchant observation of Skinner's behavior by Charles Nesson, a Harvard Law School professor who served as a member of Schlichtmann's legal team, in the afterword to the paperback edition: "I used to believe in the idea that justice would prevail if you worked hard enough at it...I thought if judges saw cheating in front of them, they'd do something about it. The Woburn case gave me a depressing case of reality."

Obviously, Harr chose not to give us a "depressing case of reality" by framing the Woburn story like a Frank Capra movie, thereby avoiding calling into question the political-economic system that produces man-made disasters. Instead, he provides us with another example of the media discouraging "discursive alternatives" to our discourse about society (Fiske 1989:178). What is lost in this approach is what is so extraordinary about the Woburn saga: the unprecedented lay epidemiology project that compiled sufficiently compelling evidence to bring the case to trial. An examination of this brings us to a deeper level of analysis of the exclusion of not only the voices of Woburn residents, but also the voices of many man-made disaster victims.

The reasons for these exclusions are historically and culturally derived. In the 1920s, for instance, the rise of science made reporters distrustful of the "reasonableness" of public opinion because such opinion was no longer viewed as the "articulation of reason" (Tuchman 1978:210). In anthropological terms, this represents the displacement of local knowledge. As Brown and Mikkelsen (1990:149) have so aptly observed, professionalism has come to embody "a high degree of informational control." Basically, this control involves the exclusion of laypeople. A similar point is made by Kroll-Smith and Floyd (1997:197): "A principal axiom of modernity was the separation of lay and expert knowledge." Local knowledge is contextual and not merely "lived"; that is, the knowledge base is derived directly from the environment in which it is situated. This powerful dichotomy of lay versus professional knowledge not only excludes the voice of individuals, but also ignores communities and their historical, cultural, and environmental experience.

In our highly professionalized culture, the public debate over controversial topics is overwhelmed by privileged arguments. Civil disputes, whether they are about the siting of toxic wastes, nuclear power facilities, or disaster charged issues, are seen as being only for experts to debate. The lives and voices of everyday people are excluded from legal decisions and policy debates that affect the nonexpert. Stephens (this volume) testifies to the same problem in the international scientific community.

Harr's exclusion is very much like the exclusion of local knowledge that was common in the wake of the *Exxon-Valdez* oil spill, when Exxon officials and government agencies discounted the predictive local knowledge native and fishing communities possessed on the tides, marine life, and remedial measures (Button 1993). The exclusion is also similar to the dismissal of crucial local knowledge about the environment and public health concerns that were reported by the public but ignored by United Kingdom officials after the *Braer* oil spill in the Shetland Islands (Button 1995). Certainly the health reports and lay illness stories that were ignored in the aftermath of the Bhopal explosion illustrate this same point (Rajan, this volume). Another example of the intrinsic importance of local knowledge in studying disasters is offered by McCabe (this volume). A thorough, comprehensive knowledge of the delicate complexities that exist between people, culture, and the environment during and between cycles of drought and famine can be derived only from the kind of anthropological investigation that relies on, rather than rejects, the local knowledge of a pastoral society.

Seen from this anthropological perspective, it is somewhat more understandable how Harr's framing of the Woburn story both draws upon and reproduces ideological ideas within our culture. This division between "rational" knowledge and local knowledge is perhaps threatened most in the case of Woburn, where local lay participation undermines this division in direct collusion with professional knowledge. The fusion of local knowledge with the knowledge of professional biostatisticians comes tenuously close to collapsing this separation altogether.

Popular accounts like Harr's may be highly entertaining, but at the same time they are severely obscuring. The imposition of standardized frames over disaster events by the media and our popular culture undermines alternative discursive frames of explanation and precludes us from analyzing disasters in a way that would allow us to fully unpack the politically powerful world of social relations in which all disasters are grounded. The media's tendency to rely on official accounts and experts reinforces the cultural division between professional and lay knowledge. The stock frames serve to reproduce our cultural ideologies and keep us from inquiring why victims are vulnerable in the first place. When the "why," or causes, of disaster events are limited to the notion of "motives" (while culturally reproducing the notion of individualism), notions of class, race, gender, and age are obscured, as is the possibility of examining the political-economic system in which the events are embedded. As Oliver-Smith (this volume) has written: "Disasters, in many senses, have become a kind of metaphor for processes and events currently unfolding." While disasters serve this metaphorical role for our era, we also need to remember that our accounts of disasters are, in turn, reflective of our culture.

8

Punctuated Entropy as Culture-Induced Change
The Case of the Exxon Valdez *Oil Spill*

Christopher L. Dyer

> *There was not food, the corn was trampled down*
> *The flocks and herds had perished; on the shore*
> *The dead and putrid fish were ever thrown;*
> *The deeps were foodless, and the winds no more*
> *Creaked with the weight of birds, but, as before*
> *Those winged things sprang forth, were void of shade*
> *The vines and orchards, Autumn's golden store,*
> *Were burned;—so that the meanest food was weighed*
> *With gold, and Avarice died before the god it made.*
> —Shelley, *The Revolt of Islam*

Disasters are playing a growing role in shaping the social and cultural fabric of the human condition. Disasters include global changes that are brought on by human abuse of the biosphere and compounded by demographic realities of an expanding world population. As human populations expand, stressing available resources, they enter into new and often precarious states with their environments that increase risk and leave many vulnerable to disaster. Meanwhile, developed economies put marginal human populations and environments at risk as they strive to increase productivity and create new markets for the juggernaut of world capitalism. With the UN Division of Humanitarian Assistance declaring the 1990s the "decade of disasters," providing solutions to the dislocation of human communities in the global village has become a vital task. This task requires a holistic approach that takes account of cultural differences while recognizing common causes of disaster.

Anthropology—the most holistic of the social sciences—provides a framework for understanding worldwide cultural dislocations brought on by disasters. Anthropologists are latecomers to the disaster scene, however, and their voices have yet to receive significant attention from disaster managers and policy makers. Moreover, in their struggle to cope with the increasing severity and frequency of contemporary disaster events, disaster managers and organizations require rapid, practical advice that recognizes the complexity of the problems they face and offers timely and appropriate solutions. Anthropologists have yet to provide such advice. In particular, anthropologists and other students of disaster have failed to consider the "interaction of the social, technological, and natural processes that produce hazards and disasters in our accounts of human environmental adaptations" (Oliver-Smith 1996:304). Anthropology *has* begun an in-depth ethnography of disaster that spans the cross-cultural range of disaster adaptation and response (Oliver-Smith 1996). The present challenge is to apply such ethnographic knowledge to the conceptualization, testing, and application of general theories and models of disaster response and mitigation.

This chapter grew out of the observation (echoed in Shelley's poem, above) that as disaster events increase in frequency and severity, recovery from certain kinds, or combinations of, disasters becomes increasingly difficult, if not impossible. This phenomenon is not new; throughout history, civilizations have faced ecological and cultural collapse resulting from drought, disease, or earthquake (see Moseley, this volume). It is made more cogent, however, by the rapidity of modern culture change and the increased risk associated with human-induced catastrophes, also known as technological disasters. Debacles such as Love Canal, the *Exxon Valdez* oil spill, Three Mile Island, and Chernobyl threaten the very sustainability of industrial society and call into question the adaptive value of modern technology.

Developing societies, meanwhile, are in a precarious state as they face natural and technological events that put them at risk. The increasing severity of contemporary disaster events can exceed the local adaptive resources of societies and communities, requiring some external response to achieve recovery. Developing populations experiencing a disaster are frequently at the mercy of externalities that interfere with crucial aid, and over which they have little or no control.

Populations experiencing disaster are often (1) dependent on media constructs (Benthal 1993) ("it's not a disaster until we say so"), (2) jeopardized by practices that threaten environmental sustainability (e.g., the recent peat fires of Indonesia), (3) blackmailed by a Western political ecology that links aid to "democratic correctness" (e.g., the famine in "Marxist" Ethiopia), or (4) ignored (or receive inadequate assistance) due to oversaturation of aid agencies working in a climate of increasing stress to the human-environment relationship (Benthal 1993). Outcomes include rising mortality from disaster events in the developing world, ecological collapse of life-sustaining systems, and overwhelming recovery costs from both natural and technological-induced events worldwide.

Disasters may exceed the capacity of developing societies to recover without enormous outside assistance (Torry 1978b). Average income losses from recent disasters in some developing countries (e.g., Sri Lanka, Bangladesh, and Nicaragua) are ten to twenty times greater than in disasters in the United States (Haas et al. 1973). In some cases, such as the 1972 earthquake in Managua, Nicaragua, postdisaster recovery was hampered by a predisaster imbalance in the relationship between the built infrastructure and the resources necessary to recover those infrastructures.

The most severe cases of nonrecovery come not from loss of built infrastructure but from degradation of the natural environment, which poses an unmitigated hazard to human survival. Hazard is defined as anything that threatens the health and survival of a human population. Global warming, eutrophication of the oceans, deforestation, and destruction of the planet's biodiversity are symptomatic of unmitigated hazard brought on by biophysical disruption.

In this chapter I define the nonrecovery of human systems from disaster events as *punctuated entropy* and apply the concept to the case of the *Exxon Valdez* oil spill. This technological disaster is one of only four such catastrophes (the others are Three Mile Island, Chernobyl, and Bhopal) for which long-term data exist on the impacts to culture, community, and economy. It thus provides an invaluable opportunity to examine the ongoing effects of a catastrophe that has laid bare the core human-environment relationship that is now so threatened by the contemporary abuses of our global village.

In the context of this volume on anthropology of disasters, we can place this case study along a continuum of time and adaptation. Michael Moseley's chapter on the effects of drought on coastal civilizations of Peru is punctuated entropy writ large. In Moseley's example, forces of political ecology interact with long-term environmental change to dictate patterns of settlement, expansion, and depopulation. The combined disasters of drought, earthquakes, and landslides shifted the balance of power in the region and also shifted the centers of population growth from the highlands to coastal areas and back again. Adaptations occur as rational responses to shifts in precipitation and population, with more dramatic punctuated changes associated with disasters bringing equally rapid changes in human settlement patterns. Working in an archaeological context, Moseley can be a detached observer of human consequences of disastrous long-term changes, thus providing us with an appreciation of the relevance of temporal scale in the study of the cultural consequences of disasters.

While Moseley tracks changes in the archaeology of disasters across centuries, J. Terrence McCabe views adaptations among pastoralists in East Africa across the span of yearly drought and seasonal cycles. His perspective places us in the field as firsthand observers of present-time populational adaptations to cyclic drought hazards. However, unlike the case study of technological disaster and its aftermath presented here, the vulnerability created by drought is part of a natural repeating cycle that lies within the intergenerational memory of Turkana pastoralists. Moreover, the demonstrated culture of response and recovery from hazard is part of the adaptive tool kit of these pastoralists, whereby natural events associated with drought are treated as part of the normal functioning of ecosystems (i.e., as "normative disasters").

The Turkana pastoralists' ability to survive repeated drought gives them the power to mitigate their own vulnerability to hazardous conditions, with the certainty that droughts, even though debilitating, are seasonal and cyclic, and will end. Sharon Stephens's work on the vulnerabilities created by radiation hazards in the post-Chernobyl environment reflects the extreme of uncertainty from an unending threat. Control over the mitigation of the hazards rests not in the hands of at-risk populations, but rather within a "club" of experts—the

International Commission for Radiological Protection (ICRP) and other agencies that together make up the "radiation protection community" or, as perceived by the public, the "nuclear establishment" (Caufield 1989:167).

Unfortunately, these scientific experts do not speak the same cultural language as those who are at risk: the public. Decisions they make affect people's long-term vulnerability to radiation, but their decisions give no control to those at risk. Rather, they set standards of radiation exposure that are politically inflected and tend to feed into people's fears and psychological problems in coping with radiation hazards. There is no opportunity to adapt to such hazards, which creates a persistent and high "dread factor" connected to public conceptions of risk. Part of the issue of dread comes not from the degree of actual hazard of nuclear plants under normative operating conditions but from the public sense of risk and the stress such uncertainty generates. In responding to this dread, the public is treated by the radiation protection community as an undifferentiated group to be kept at a distance and managed by public relations experts, with no distinctions made regarding age, gender, ethnicity, or class. In contrast, many members of the public are specifically concerned about risks to men, women, and children as individuals. Questions as to who decides what level of risk is socially acceptable, and how that averaged risk may impact groups such as children, speak to the lack of control by the public of its vulnerability to long-term risks from radiation hazards and disasters.

The most emically focused and individualistic of these contributions is Susanna Hoffman's. Combining the role of both victim and anthropologist, she gives us a perspective on what it is like to lose and regain control, to suffer complete loss and rediscover self after a disaster—the Oakland firestorm that destroyed her home, her personal belongings, and her social and psychological past. The temporal context is the day of the event and the ensuing weeks, as Hoffman and her fellow victims cope with the disaster aftermath and work toward recovery. By going with her on this personal journey, we view the changing adaptive context of individuals and neighbors becoming recovery groups, at times pitted against outside aid agencies and frustrated by the inability of mitigators to understand the character of their loss and needs for recovery.

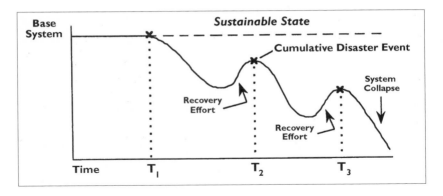

FIGURE 8.1

Punctuated entropy as it affects the adaptive flexibility of a human ecosystem.

Within this framework of time and adaptation is the case of the *Exxon Valdez* oil spill. The study context here is over five years of community-level attempts at adaptation, attempts overwhelmed, I argue, by punctuated entropy.

THE PUNCTUATED ENTROPY PARADIGM

Punctuated entropy is defined as a permanent decline in the adaptive flexibility of a human cultural system to the environment brought on by the cumulative impact of periodic disaster events. It predicts and explains the nonrecovery of human systems after a disaster. The accumulation of impact means that the opportunity for recovery is compromised by repeated disruptions to the human system (fig. 8.1).

The system consists of built and biophysical environments and their dynamic interaction. The biophysical environment includes such elements as the air, soil, vegetation, and water that provide the natural setting for human communities. For noncumulative events such as chronic ecological problems of drought, earthquakes, or floods, societies possess adaptive flexibility, also described as "equilibration" (Torry 1978a). Equilibration—adjustment to changed environmental conditions in the face of new sociotechnological exigencies—is well documented in the ethnographic literature (Dirks 1980; Torry 1978a; Waddell 1975; Brookfield and Brown 1967; Lee 1969; Spencer 1959).

In cases of punctuated entropy, adaptive flexibility is lost due to the severity and cumulative impact of the disaster events. As punctuated entropy takes hold, traditional adaptive strategies fail, the social fabric is deconstructed, and existing patterns of culture disintegrate or are severely modified or replaced by altered systems. In the long term, there is no cultural solution to the ensuing disruption, and system collapse ensues.

Disasters are conceptualized here as either technological or natural. Natural disasters arise from the biophysical environment, and most documented cases of successful adaptation are in response to natural disasters. Technological disasters arise from failures of technology resulting from either human error or system breakdown. Adaptive responses to this class of disaster are not integrated into the tool kits of most human cultures.

Cumulative natural disasters can also induce punctuated entropy, and may include serial earthquakes followed by landslides or tsunamis, extended droughts followed by sandstorms (see Moseley, this volume), or repeated severe flooding events (Piers et al. 1994:27). Technological disasters can have cumulative effects known as "secondary disasters" (Erickson 1976), which include cultural, social, and economic impacts that persist long after the event and that negatively alter or destroy affected communities (Freudenberg and Jones 1991; Dyer 1993; Hirsch 1997; Rodin et al. 1997).

Social stratification and the politics of environmental control can also result in punctuated entropy effects for politically and environmentally marginalized populations. In a socially stratified polity, exploitation of marginal populations following repeated natural disruptions can depress adaptability for those dispossessed of their resource base. Zaman (1988) describes how repeated flooding can induce the downward spiral of punctuated entropy for marginal peasants living on the floodplain. Land lost to flooding by politically marginal groups is bought out by the elite, making recovery for flood victims a difficult if not impossible task. In his study of the political ecology of northeastern Tanzania, Giblin (1992) illustrates a similar phenomenon wherein relations of production between patrons and clients determined whether precolonial farmers succeeded in controlling disease, accumulating livestock and food reserves, and preventing drought from causing famine.

While politically, socially, and economically more powerful groups may resist cumulative natural disasters such as repeated severe flooding, poverty creates vulnerability:

> On the eve of Bangladesh's massive floods in August 1988, this relatively powerless group [landless squatters] was living in an economically marginal situation but close to the city, on low-lying land prone to flooding. Their economic and political marginality meant they had few assets in reserve. It also meant that their children were unusually malnourished and chronically ill. This channeled the dynamic pressure arising out of landlessness and economic marginalization into a particular form of vulnerability: lack of resistance to diarrheal disease and hunger following the flooding in 1988. Factors involving power, access, location, livelihood, and biology mutually determined a situation of particular unsafe conditions and enhanced vulnerability. (Piers et al. 1994:27)

Another consequence of punctuated entropy is the acceleration of negative systemic change, thus increasing risk to life, health, and social, cultural, and economic sustainability. Negative consequences to the human condition include amplification of perceptions of risk and declining capacity of society to effectively adapt to the rapid changes in human-environment interactions.

Punctuated entropy is most apparent when the natural resource base is compromised, external recovery assistance is misdirected or withheld, and the postdisaster political economy of the region hinders restoration of traditional patterns of human-environment interaction. Punctuated entropy is counteracted most effectively when the natural resource base is uncompromised, external agencies aid community recovery, and the political economics of the region does not unconsciously or purposefully hinder the recovery process.

COMMUNITY MODELS, RISK, AND PUNCTUATED ENTROPY

Since the community is the unit of impact to be examined, a review of relevant paradigms of community will lay the foundation for applying punctuated entropy to the *Exxon Valdez* disaster. A community paradigm found to provide an explanation for the consequences of the oil spill on the human ecosystem of Prince William Sound is the Natural Resource Community (NRC), defined as a population of individuals living in a bounded area whose primary cultural existence depends on the utilization of renewable natural resources (Dyer et al. 1992).

Social and cultural characteristics of the NRC are based on the recognition of limits to nature, embracing values of sustainable resource use and avoiding risks that would jeopardize a pattern of life intimately dependent on the renewable cycles of nature. This model of community has application to traditional societies worldwide— those peasant and tribal people who are the primary subjects of anthropological endeavors. Thus, conclusions derived from this study have application wherever small-scale communities with localized agricultural, fishing, or subsistence-based economies are faced with intrusive industrial technologies and the risks and hazards they bring. Threats posed by technological hazards prompt strong risk-aversion strategies and behaviors best understood in the cultural context of community. The cultural context of the NRC community (Dyer 1993) can be characterized as follows:

1. Residents of NRCs are strongly linked to their resource base by traditions that integrate them into the natural order.

2. To the extent that cultural activities may destroy renewable resources, NRC residents practice folk management of resources to maintain their sustainability.

3. Because natural resources are utilized and renewed within bounded areas, they are viewed as limited and limiting in the variety of opportunities they provide their human stewards.

4. Progress is resisted to the extent that it threatens the sustainability of core traditions and the natural resource base on which they are structured.

The human-nature relationship of the NRC model can be conceptually linked to the ecological-symbolic approach (Kroll-Smith and Couch 1991), which recognizes the existence of culturally based responses to environmental disruptions (Dyer 1993). Its basic tenets are that people exist in exchange relationships with their built, modified, and biophysical environments, and that disruptions in the ordered relationship between individuals, groups, and communities are labeled and responded to as hazards and disasters (Kroll-Smith and Couch 1991). Critical to the maintenance of the human-nature relationship proposed by Kroll-Smith and Couch and central to the NRC paradigm is a social structure based on kinship and cooperative sharing of extracted resources. Dynes (1976:24) asserts that these core features are inadequate to the task of withstanding severe disasters: "Such societies possess such a delicate relationship with the environment that when it is disturbed the whole social and cultural structure is threatened."

Torry (1978b) counters Dynes's assertion by reviewing the adaptive strategies of a cross section of traditional societies suffering system disruptions. In all his cases, core traditions based on kinship and sharing adapt and persist in the face of calamity. Disintegration of the core results only from the kind of disasters wrought by cumulative events such as repeated or prolonged drought followed by severe famine (Dirks 1980). The punctuated entropy paradigm predicts that the increasing number of severe and cumulative disasters in the contemporary world will lead to the loss of core traditions and cultural patterns, such that social networks and cooperative relationships will break down, and communities and the traditions that hold them together will become extinct.

Natural Resource Communities are by definition dependent on renewable biological resources. Fixed, nonrenewable resources such as natural gas and oil are thus not included; they represent the primary nonrenewable resources for Dominant Social Paradigm (DSP) communities, the core extractive community model of the industrial world (Dyer 1993). An outcome of the DSP model that also conflicts with NRCs is the increasing risk associated with an extractive strategy unconstrained by concerns for environmental degradation. This Euro-Christian ideal of dominance over nature, manifested as global capitalism and driven by first-world technology, pushes communities toward a world economy at the expense of cultural diversity, environmental sustainability, and social justice (Greider 1997). In this process the perils for developing countries and traditional (tribal and peasant) societies come both from without and within as new technologies are adopted by central governments in an effort to "get ahead," while multinational corporations take advantage of cheap labor markets and weak or nonexistent environmental regulations in the global export of hazards and risk. The fundaments (Catton and Dunlap 1980) of the DSP paradigm are:

1. People are fundamentally different from all other creatures on earth over which they have domination.

2. People are masters of their destiny; they can choose their goals and learn to do whatever is necessary to achieve them.

3. The world is vast, and thus provides unlimited opportunities for humans.

4. The history of humanity is one of progress, for every problem has a solution, and this progress need never cease.

DSP strategies of resource extraction create an environment that promulgates conditions for disaster such that "with the passage of new generations, the cultural identity of severely impacted communities may be lost and the process of cultural extinction complete" (Curtis 1992:68). Douglas and Wildavsky (1982:21) describe the unmitigated risk of uncontrolled change promoted by the DSP strategy as "irreversible risk": "Irreversible changes are explosive and unstable, each deviation growing larger until the environment is so altered it can never return to its original state."

Irreversible changes of the DSP strategy are also a reflection of the mostly unchallenged use of natural resources through technological manipulation, the outcome being a "risk society" (Beck 1992) that imposes its doctrine of technological dominance on the global community with little regard for future sustainability. NRC residents in Prince William Sound were aware of the risks to culture and community a decade prior to the *Exxon Valdez* spill. Over a decade later, they have yet to recover from the secondary disasters spawned by this event.

THE DISASTER

On March 24, 1989, the *Exxon Valdez* tanker collided with Blight Reef in the Valdez Narrows, resulting in the worst oil spill in US history (fig. 8.2). Over 11 million gallons of North Slope crude poured into the waters of Prince William Sound, devastating the ecosystem and creating a disaster for local communities and residents who had built their lives

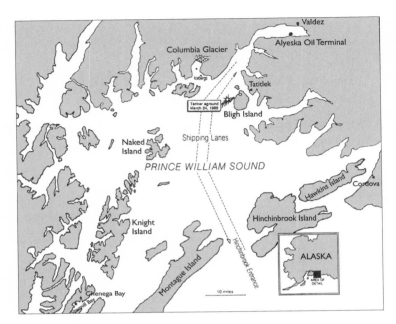

FIGURE 8.2

Prince William Sound, Alaska, site of the Exxon Valdez *oil spill.*

and culture around extracting the renewable natural resources of the region. Cumulative impacts of this event persist as "secondary disasters" (Dyer 1993; Picou, Gill, and Cohen 1997) whose ongoing impacts have permanently altered the adaptive flexibility and character of regional commercial fishing and subsistence communities.

Prince William Sound and the adjoining Copper River Delta estuary are one of the most biodiverse regions in North America. For millennia this biodiversity has maintained Native Tlingit, Chugach Eskimo, Eyak, and other cultures inhabiting the shores and rivers of the region (Davis 1984). Facing accelerated culture change from development interests, contemporary communities continue to subsist along thousands of miles of Alaskan coastline. Resources exploited include seabird eggs, beaver, seals, whales, sea otters, fish, shellfish, kelp, seal, moose, deer, bear, and a variety of berries, roots, and other plant resources. Seven species of *anadromous salmonids,* shrimp, black cod, halibut, herring, and other fish species have provided the basis for a rich subsistence culture and a multimillion-dollar commercial fishery.

Native communities in the region include Tatitlek, Chenega Bay, Nanwalek, Port Graham, Akhiok, Karluk, Uizinkie, Old Harbor, and Larsen Bay. Major towns in the sound include Cordova, Whitier, Valdez, and Kodiak. Many of the Native Alaskans in the region live in the towns but maintain kin and resource-sharing networks with Native villages. Sharing subsistence resources is a tradition that survived centuries of human abuses at the hands of external commercial interests. During the domination of Alaska by Russian fur traders in the eighteenth and nineteenth centuries, Native populations were forced into slave labor arrangements to hunt marine mammals for the European fur market. The Russian Orthodox Church was a mitigating factor in this process, and intermarriage between Russians and Native Alaskans was common (Davis 1984). Many Natives carry Russian surnames, and some can even trace their Russian ancestry back to the aristocracy. Before Alaska was purchased by the United States, depopulation from disease, outmigration, and even enslavement was ongoing. Native populations faced cultural and linguistic extinction, as in the case of the Eyak of Cordova. The last resident speaker of Eyak, Sophie Borodkin, died in 1994 at the age of eighty-nine. Even as Russian traders and immigrants imposed their religion, economy, and material culture on Native communities, they adopted their subsistence strategies, and by this process assumed syncretic lifestyles that mirrored the cultural patterns of their Native hosts.

Alaska became the forty-ninth state in 1967, and gold mining, lumber companies, and a growing salmon canning industry opened up the new frontier. In the late 1800s, Natives served as a cheap source of labor for the Alaskan canning industry, and at the turn of the century also provided labor for mining, construction, and road building. Despite this exploitation, support and respect for Native lifeways resulted in the Native Allotment Act of 1906, which allowed individual Alaskan Natives to claim 160 acres of land. This act was supplanted in 1971 by the Alaska Natives Claims Act (ANCSA). ANCSA has had a significant, and mostly negative, impact on Native communities, which were reorganized as corporations under the new law. Corporate organizational structure did not fit well with the subsistence lifestyles of traditional Native villages, and by 1990, twenty-three out of twenty-five of the existing ANCSA corporations were bankrupt (Jorgensen 1990).

ANCSA also led to dependence relationships between the state and Native villages, many of which did not cope well under their status as "welfare corporations." Such welfare status promoted vulnerability and maladaptations, including unstable marital relationships, chronic alcoholism, and persistent poverty. Countering this was the renewable and renewing subsistence lifestyle, the cultural glue that holds the community together and represents the best hope for social and cultural reproduction of the Native lifestyle:

> Down through the ages we have come to understand nature's comings and goings. We are attuned to her subconsciously. There is no way around nature. We do not try to conquer nature. We live by her rules and act accordingly. Our instinct to survive keeps time with her seasons. When nature's time for fish arrives, we fish; when she says hunt, we hunt. When she says, "It's berry picking time," we pick berries joyously. (Active 1992:2)

Yet, after 1992, subsistence culture was undermined by a sunset clause in ANCSA that allowed outside corporations access to Native resources. Such arrangements potentially result in minimal compensation to Native corporations eager to get anything they can for resources previously held as common corporate property. This accelerating process is contributing to poorly managed cutting of timber, mining exploration, and other activities that are transforming the natural landscape of Alaska.

The negative social and cultural changes promoted by ANCS prompted a resistance movement based on the desire of Alaska Natives to retribalize and sever their relationship with the corporate model (Berger 1985). Despite this movement, the model remained intact, and its persistence coincided with the intrusive and transforming development of Alaskan oil and gas resources. The *Exxon Valdez* oil spill was symptomatic of this transformation process.

The communities most severely impacted by the oil spill are Chenega Bay and Tatitlek, whose local ecosystems experienced significant loss of natural resources from oil pollution. Although it escaped the oil, Cordova, the primary fishing community, also suffered significant and ongoing impacts. Unlike residents of traditional Native villages, the 2,100 residents of Cordova comprise a diverse mix of old and new immigrants, whose lifestyles revolved around commercial fishing. An important component of the town's fishing strategy is the Prince William Sound Aquaculture Corporation (PWSAC). The PWSAC aquaculture of pink salmon supplements wild stock harvests, allowing increased catch effort and profits. The economy of Cordova also includes various fishing support businesses such as gear and electronic supply shops, grocery stores, bars, restaurants, and a smaller segment of scientific, civic, and environmental groups that together form this environmentally aware Natural Resource Community.

Cordova exists on the site of the historic Eyak Village, which persists as a "village within a town," with Native members of the Eyak Corporation scattered throughout various neighborhoods. Natives maintain important kin and sharing networks with the nearby villages of Tatitlek and Chenega Bay, and specific disaster effects in one Native community have social, cultural, and economic ripple effects in others. These communities—Chenega Bay, Cordova, and Tatitlek—are the focus of this case study of the effects of the *Exxon Valdez* oil spill. My goal here is to assess that disaster as a case of punctuated entropy, compare it with similar disaster events, and place it within a wider context of anthropological discourse on culture change. Because of the central importance of natural resource extraction to community livelihood, the loss of natural resources and the cultural consequences of loss are of primary concern.

Disaster outcomes that qualify the oil spill as a case of punctuated entropy are (1) the natural resource base is compromised, (2) outside recovery assistance is misdirected or withheld, and (3) the postdisaster political ecology of the region hinders restoration of traditional patterns of human-environment interaction.

COMPROMISE OF THE NATURAL RESOURCE BASE

When the *Exxon Valdez* ran aground on Bligh Reef on March 24, 1989, and spilled over ten million gallons of North Slope crude oil into Prince William Sound, it polluted one of the most pristine environments in the United States. A map of Prince William Sound shows the location of the spill in relation to the study communities of Chenega Bay, Cordova, and Tatitlek (see fig. 8.2). Commercial fishing, subsistence, recreation, and tourism, including sport fishing and hunting, have been lost or reduced in the years since the spill.

The initial biological impacts of the spill were made worse by the timing of the event. March is a period when phytoplankton and zooplankton, the basis of the food chain in the sound, begin their initial bloom. Disruption of reproductive cycles of fish, shellfish, and other marine organisms occurred, and benthic communities of urchins, kelp, and other shallow water species were devastated. Seabirds and marine animals were also heavily hit by oil. Between 260,000 and 560,000 seabirds were estimated lost, along with 5,500 sea otters, 144 eagles, and deer and other wildlife (Lord 1991). The 1989 fishing season for salmon, the primary economic resource, was closed due to oil in the water. Studies later showed that salmon eggs laid in oiled streams suffered 70 percent greater mortality than those in non-oiled streams. Additionally, herring eggs, a traditional subsistence food, showed 90 percent abnormalities in oiled areas compared to 6 percent in non-oiled areas.

As of 1996, some of these natural resources had shown recovery, but most are slow to recover or remain depressed. Only one species, the bald eagle, was considered "recovered" in 1996, while intertidal and subtidal communities, pink salmon, sockeye salmon, mussels, and common murres were "recovering" (Exxon Valdez Oil Spill Trustee Council 1996a). Among the animals labelled "not recovered" were three species of cormorants, harbor seals, and Pacific herring, sea otters, harlequin ducks, and killer whales. Recovery for other species, such as clams, rockfish, cutthroat trout, and the common loon, were "unknown." Surface and subsurface patches of oil still remain in many places. About 1.4 million gallons are estimated to remain in the mud, sand, and sediment in the Gulf of Alaska and Prince William Sound (Clark 2001).

Benthic organisms, such as urchins, starfish, and clams, suffered high mortality from both oiling and cleanup efforts. Scouring of beaches with hot water to remove the oil killed many benthic organisms through thermal pollution. Clams, an important subsistence food, have been slow to recover, and most shellfish beds in waters off of Tatitlek and Chenega Bay remain contaminated and unfit for human consumption.

The herring population, a major cash fishery and source of herring roe for subsistence, completely collapsed in 1993 and shows no sign of recovery. Pink salmon runs failed in 1992 and 1993 and were depressed in 1994, while sockeye have not recovered to their pre-spill numbers. Although the runs of hatchery salmon are recovered or recovering, wild stocks are still down from years prior to the spill. Evidence exists that potentially lethal doses of oil are still leaching into Prince William Sound streambeds where wild stocks of salmon spawn, and aquatic birds and marine mammals continue to show signs of exposure (Clark 2001). Killer whales, seabirds, and deer and seal populations have also not recovered from the spill. Harbor seals, an important subsistence resource, have declined about 6 percent per year (Exxon Valdez Oil Spill Trustee Council 1996a).

As two Native residents of Chenega Bay said of their resources:

> Seals are scarce. When you go out on a boat, you seldom see seals or sea lions like before. Man, the water is just dead. Along the eighteen miles of Knight Island where we used to harvest, I didn't see even one. Now we have to go thirty miles by boat to find seals. We used to get them less than two miles away from the village." (Fall and Utermohle 1995:IV-9)

> I still hunger for clams, shrimp, crab, octopus, gumboots. Nothing in this world will replace them. To be finally living in my ancestors' area and be able to teach my kids, but now it's all gone. We still try, but you can't replace them. (Fall and Utermohle 1995:IV-16)

Any disaster that substantially disrupted the commercial harvest of marine resources in a Natural Resource Community would predictably result in an increased reliance on subsistence harvesting. Subsistence harvesting acts as an economic buffer in the event of economic disruption, allowing time for households to regain their economic equilibrium. A survey of Alaska Natives in Cordova indicated that by 1991 over half of all respondents could no longer obtain previously consumed subsistence foods (Picou and Gill 1995). This significant decline in subsistence viability is contributing to long-term pernicious effects on the NRCs of Prince William Sound. Thus, the documented ongoing compromise of the natural resource base of Prince William Sound by the

Exxon Valdez oil spill disaster fullfills condition (1) of the punctuated entropy model.

Also "not recovered" are the NRC residents of Cordova, Chenega Bay, and Tatitlek, whose reliance on the natural resource base was disrupted by the spill:

> Living in a place like this ties you into a cyclic view of life because your daily work is tied directly from where your food and water and survival comes from. You have to be tied into the cycles of nature. For Natives, a lot of their daily work is getting food and I don't want to say that it's better than the way other people live. It's just when you have an oil spill maybe you and I can get by fine. I don't have to go fishing. Pay me some money and I'll go find something else. But if you live in some of these villages, and you're not used to using money so much to get your food, and all your culture is completely interwoven with the natural system—an oil spill is real trouble. (Key respondent, Cordova, quoted in Dyer 1993)

Nonrecovery of culture and communities parallels the nonrecovery of the natural resource base. No predictions have been made on when the ecosystem as a whole will recover to its predisaster condition, but it is certain that permanent damage has been done to the human-environment connection. The cultural and community impact of nonrecovery from natural resource loss is further compounded by a series of ongoing secondary disasters (points T-2 and T-3 in fig. 8.1), including the misdirection and withholding of external assistance.

MISDIRECTION AND WITHHOLDING OF EXTERNAL ASSISTANCE

The premise of this section, taken as condition (2) of three driving processes in the punctuated entropy paradigm, is that nonrecovery is linked to input of culturally misdirected (inappropriate) exogenous capital into economically fragile communities. This capital disrupts patterns of traditional adaptation and recovery from disaster, including social networks that provide needed psychological support and sharing of resources (Davis 1984; Dyer 1993; Picou, Gill, and Cohen 1997; Rodin et al. 1997). It further added to disruption of the natural resource base from ecologically destructive oil cleaning and removal practices. While the capital infusion was directed at cleaning the environment, the social and cultural needs of communities received inadequate support, resulting in the depression of adaptive flexibility and the occurrence of "secondary disasters" (points T_2 and T_3 of fig. 8.1).

The initial response of the Exxon Corporation to the spill was to engage in a massive cleanup campaign. The VECO Corporation, a regular provider of special services to the Alaska petroleum industry, hired locals for cleanup at wages of more than $16 an hour (Cohen 1997). For Natives, this often meant abandoning or missing cycles of traditional subsistence and village ritual. Employed as captains, rock scrubbers, beach cleaners, boat washers, and animal caretakers, they had to leave their families for months at a time. The cessation of commercial fishing, the workers' extended absence from home, and the stress associated with the cleanup began a process of family, cultural, and community disruption that continues today.

Further community disruption was caused by the thousands of outsiders seeking employment opportunities in the cleanup. At the height of the summer of 1989, some 11,000 workers were on the spill cleanup payroll (Cohen 1997). Exxon officials moved into the communities of Prince William Sound with millions of dollars in cleanup equipment, paid up to $2,000 a day to rent fishing boats, and drafted residents and transient workers throughout the region to participate in the grand gesture. As one Exxon official declared, in a tone of extreme confidence, "Just watch and see what we are going to do."

The cleanup effort, part of a regional $2.5 billion post-spill infusion of capital by Exxon, was heavily criticized. The hot water used to remove beach oil proved deadly to nearshore intertidal organisms. Cleanup workers trampled ecologically sensitive beaches, and news reports alleged that cleanup workers in some areas were looting cultural artifacts from previously secret sites of spiritual significance to Alaskan Natives (Cohen 1997). Such "cultural pollution" added to the trauma of Native communities already in shock from the devastation of their subsistence resource base. The intrusive presence of a "cleanup army" stressed the cultural patterns and cooperative networks so useful in the harvesting of salmon and subsistence activities. With fishing activities suspended in 1989, residents faced a choice to participate in an economic boon or wait it out and hope for a good fishing season in 1990.

The "money spill" that followed from the cleanup created an artificial economy with corrosive effects on the social networks of communities, particularly the Native communities. Cash from cleanup earnings provided short-term "improvements" in their material culture. At the same time, the sudden presence of readily available cash was socially destructive, fueling social instability by allowing for unmitigated access to drugs, alcohol, and firearms. Natives were ill-prepared to manage either the money or its social consequences:

> In village X, a brother of a local resident always brought in a seal to be shared by the village. He would land in his seaplane and leave the seal on the beach for them to pick up. We flew over X about a week after he dropped off the seal last summer (1989). It was still on the beach where he had left it—rotting. Everyone was so drunk because of the spill crisis they hadn't bothered with it. (Cordova resident, quoted in Dyer 1993)

Residents who traditionally generated social capital by sharing resources from commercial fishing and subsistence were engaged in an activity for which they gained no traditional prestige but an inordinate amount of cash. As Morton Fried (1967:66) has observed, the prestige associated with natural resource harvesting amounts to privilege of access and is a form of ownership, where "ownership...really means that the man who fulfills the social requirements of 'owner' is one to whom prestige will accrue as the distribution proceeds."

Prestige prevails in societies where people are chronically reliant on products that others labored to obtain, and whose procurement was backed by strong positive inducements (Ingold 1988). Prestige in subsistence cultures is tied more to respect for traditional patterns of intercommunity sharing between extended families than to individual success at accruing economic capital. Kruse (1991) notes that exposure to cash income is not sufficient to alter patterns of subsistence use. Besides prestige, the subsistence lifestyle also nurtures well-being by providing "psychic income" (Neale 1971) that outweighs the economic capital lost by participating in a culture of nature.

When the oil spill altered this culture of nature, psychic income and prestige were lost, sharing broke down, and those who most benefited from working on the cleanup or renting out their vessels were identified by others as "Exxon whores." Sudden wealth for some created anomalous relationships between friends, neighbors, and working partners:

> I've known X for years, and he was never worth very much as a fisherman. He was a good neighbor, and we used to help each other out when something needed fixing, or some work on the boat needed an extra hand. But since he made that money on the spill, he doesn't even talk to me anymore. They're building a new house even in Whiteshed, and I guess they'll be moving out altogether. (Key respondent, Cordova, quoted in Dyer 1993)

Subsistence sharing, a strong tradition in past years (Stratton 1989), has been compromised by the disaster event. Sharing is a core tradition of Native community and culture in Prince William Sound, but has deteriorated with time (Fall and Utermohle 1990) as the Native culture of nature is marginalized by intrusive patterns of DSP economy. Sharing commonly ensures a distribution of resources in seasonally harsh environments and reifies labor and kin ties. Sharing of labor is another adaptive strategy, and another tradition compromised by the spill:

> Before the spill, we [fishermen's wives] used to get together and help each other out with childcare, and just support each other. We would get together and visit—have tea, or drink a bit. It was nice when your husbands were out fishing. After the spill, it just seemed like everybody was too busy trying to make money, or find out what was going on. Nobody felt like getting together to just socialize. Some of our husbands were making real good money, but others weren't doing so good. It made it hard to talk to each other. And we just never really have gotten back together. Some of us just don't talk to each other at all anymore. (Fishermen's wife, Cordova)

Another telling impact was wrought by household participation in the cleanup. Native workers on cleanup crews complained of perceived mistreatment and abuse from crew chiefs. They felt the working environment was antithetical to their traditions of cooperative work. For example, one married couple, who left their children with relatives to work on the spill, reported:

> We wanted to work to clean up our water, but they took away our enthusiasm. One rule they had was "No talking." This made it very hard on us. When we work, it is a shared experience. We weren't even allowed to socialize after work. This really bothered us, this hurt our marriage. (Key respondent, 1992, Cordova)

Wives complained of husbands returning traumatized and withdrawn because of what they saw out on the water (HUD worker, Eyak Village). Parent-child relationships did not escape the disruption. Many children in Cordova, accustomed to home care and nurturing from parents, found themselves estranged from their parents in child-care centers. When parents participating in the cleanup did return, the household routine was less than normal:

> People didn't have family lives during the first period [of the cleanup] because they worked so many hours a day. And in most cases it was a man and a woman and they were so tired when they got home that they went straight to bed. They were up and gone early in the morning...there was no social life. There was no place to go. You didn't want your kids playing on the beaches. (Field notes, July 1991, Cordova)

In an example of withholding assistance, parents in Tatitlek choosing to work on the cleanup completely lacked child-care support (Rodin et al. 1997). The community requested a grant of $40,000 from Exxon to be used to provide child care for cleanup workers. Despite support from the North Pacific Rim, a social service organization dedicated to the assistance of regional villages, Exxon ignored the proposal. This prompted the village administrator to remark, "It was pretty incredible that Exxon would spend $80,000 to save a sea otter but they weren't willing to spend any money on children" (Impact Assessment, Inc., 1990:81).

Some escaped from the trauma of the disaster by squandering their spill earnings on drugs and alcohol (Rodin et al. 1997). Increases in the rates of domestic violence and violations of the law, as well as substantially increased demand on mental health services, stressed support workers and communities alike (Dyer 1993):

> People who worked on the spill are still having problems. When a social service person comes in from the outside, they're either in love with the place, or gone in six weeks. And when they fall in love with the place, it's a love affair like you wouldn't believe. These people were damaged by the spill, just like everybody else. They tried to cope, their workload went up, but it was like the hurt helping the hurt. It was very difficult for them. And we would not accept at all a stranger coming in from Fairbanks, or Juneau, or Nome, to sit there and say: "Yes, I know how you feel." No you don't know how I feel, because you were not there. You did not go through the scare, the trauma, the fright, and the financial disaster. There was nothing a social worker from anywhere else can say to help us. We have got to heal from within.

Healing has been hard to achieve. Visits with mental health workers four years after the event confirm the persistence of postdisaster stress. Subsequent efforts to help mitigate stress have included "talking circles" to allow people to share feelings and provide support for those who continue to struggle with the spill aftermath (personal communication, social worker, Cordova, 1997).

Picou and Gill (1997:226) measured the persistence of stress among commercial fishers in Cordova, and their conclusions are consistent with nonrecovery as predicted by punctuated entropy:

> Without mitigated human restoration, the persistent threat, uncertainty, and lack of ecological and economic resolution resulting from the spill will continue to produce patterns of chronic stress. In summary, the restoration of renewable resources must be accompanied by the restoration of the quality of life in communities negatively affected by the *Exxon Valdez* oil spill.

A CORROSIVE POSTDISASTER POLITICAL ECOLOGY

Cordova, Chenega Bay, and Tatitlek were bombarded with outsiders in the postdisaster environment. The political reaction to the spill event included the expensive cleanup, most of which occurred in the two summers (1989 and 1990) after the spill. Residents also engaged in years of community meetings, legal deliberations, and state and federal hearings. They continue to live with uncertainty as to when, if ever, their fishing and subsistence lifestyles will return to normal. The mechanism identified to restore victims of this technological disaster was litigatory restitution. Restitution was seen as the solution to recover lost subsistence and fishing resources. In order to achieve it, hordes of lawyers locked up the communities, fishermen, and Natives in a prolonged legal process that hindered social healing.

For many Natives, being legally isolated from the outside meant losing regular contact and communication with social networks and supporting organizations that were core to the cooperative and therapeutic basis of subsistence culture. For example, a longtime director of the Subsistence Division of Alaska Fish and Game went to Tatitlek to talk to an elder about shellfish pollution, asking for help in making a safety video. Despite many years of trusted association, the elder refused to communicate with him, saying that any questions would first "have to be cleared through my lawyer" (key respondent, Alaska Department of Fish and Game, Anchorage).

While a code of legal silence descended on Chenega Bay and Tatitlek and intruded into the communities and lives of spill victims, the media focused on a battle between environmental concerns and industry that virtually ignored the needs and NRC worldview of Native Alaskans. Instead of spurring a reexamination of the development process, the preponderance of press coverage favored government and industry officials (Daley and O'Neill 1997). Understanding the impact of the technological disaster on Native communities was not a priority of the media culture of response. Rather, the disaster was promoted as an *inevitable* technological accident, part of the price for maintaining an oil-based economy:

> The disaster narrative overtly moved the discourse away from the political arena and into the politically inaccessible realm of technological inevitability. Many of the media-contested disputes between industry and state officials were *post hoc* assessments of what kind of oil spill contingency plans had been

considered acceptable for various hypothetical spills. (Daley and O'Neill 1997:246)

The years following the spill saw the litigatory process winding its way toward the goal of "restoration." Restoration, as agreed upon by Exxon and the federal government, in no way meant restoration of community, culture, social networks, or physical and mental health of disaster victims. Instead, it was restricted to settlement of "damages to publicly owned natural resources affected by the spill" (Piper 1993:261). Also excluded were various claims from private parties, the most prominent being Alaska Natives and Alaska Native corporations, owners of nearly all the private land in the spill area.

Among the most corrosive secondary disasters contributing to the punctuated entropy process were court decisions to deny compensation for impacts to community and way of life (Hirsch 1997). There is simply no value recognition for the cultural markers that define Native communities under the Western legal system. If we accept the premise that the NRC model holds for most of the village world of developing cultures, the potential for lasting social and cultural damage—secondary disasters—in the face of exported technological hazards is enormous.

An important lesson for anthropologists is that the legal system of Western society is poorly designed to accommodate cultural diversity and associated human needs in the face of technological disaster. Twelve years after the spill and seven years after a trial culminating in $5 billion in punitive damages, legal battles for compensation are still being waged.

While this legal dance continues, the social and cultural fabric of the communities remains largely unrestored. One social worker, having spent several weeks in one village, expressed exasperation at the lack of adequate social and mental health services for communities he described as "completely dysfunctional." Chronic alcoholism, domestic violence, sexual abuse of children, and all other social ills have been magnified by the loss of subsistence resources and the unending corrosive legal process.

Depopulation through suicide and outmigration threaten the sustainability of these communities, and no legal moves have been made to mitigate these outcomes. Meanwhile, a 1992 sunset clause in the 1972 legislation establishing the Native corporation system in Alaska opens up vast areas of Native corporate holdings to oil and mineral development. Selling out to outside investors may be a last-gasp response for these communities suffering the brunt of a severe case of postdisaster punctuated entropy.

CONCLUSIONS

The case has been made that the *Exxon Valdez* oil spill is a technological disaster arising from a process of punctuated entropy for severely impacted commercial fishing and subsistence-based communities of Prince William Sound. This has occurred because (1) the natural resource base has been compromised, (2) external assistance has been misdirected or withheld, and (3) the postdisaster political ecology of the region has hindered restoration of traditional patterns of human-environment interaction.

There may be no way at this point to reorder the symbolic ecological relationship that has been so completely altered in the impacted NRCs. The end point of this punctuated entropy process can be conceived of as "cultural chaos," in which neither the rules for normal behavior nor the rules for coping with the unexpected—the cultural "emergency system" (Corlin 1975)—apply. Successfully mitigating the punctuated entropy process engulfing the victims of the *Exxon Valdez* oil spill may be an exercise in futility. The present worldview on technological disaster, as reflected in the case of the *Exxon Valdez* oil spill, tends to minimize differences rather than respect them. This allows for expansion of development processes with little regard for cultural or environmental sustainability (Greider 1997).

In the absence of innovative, culturally sensitive forms of mitigation and validation of the NRC paradigm by the DSP cultural brokers, there is cause for pessimism. Innovation, to be successful, must validate the human, cultural, and social capital that gives diversity to the social patchwork of our global village. Such capital includes skills, knowledge, social networks, and means of sustainable utilization of renewable natural resources (Freudenberg and Gramling 1992). As the natural resource base from which cultures reproduce themselves is destroyed, the loss of adaptive flexibility can result in the emergence of "corrosive communities" with little opportunity for recovery.

Preserving communal cohesion and combating community corrosion in the face of technological change has been realized elsewhere (Wybrow 1986). In cases of disaster by forced eviction from technologically intrusive structures (e.g., large dam projects), recovery is possible (Torry 1978). This requires that opportunities for adaptation of previous cultural systems are present in the new environment.

What have we learned as a society from this technological disaster, other than how a powerful legal system can deny or delay justice until the victims of the event are reduced to a nonrecoverable state of cultural and spiritual despair? If the NRC model represents a culturally appropriate one for sustainable communities, then we should seek to emulate and conserve such communities rather than marginalize them into nonexistence. And what roles can anthropologists play in this drama, given the lack of impact they have had on similar disaster outcomes?

These questions may speak to the very survival of the human species. Global warming, coastal eutrophication, desertification, depletion of the ozone layer, deforestation, and worsening impacts from flood, drought, and other catastrophes all reflect a decrease in the adaptive flexibility and environmental sustainability of human systems. It is time for anthropologists to go beyond the study of disasters as simply another intellectual exercise in the study of culture. It is critical to bring the holistic dynamism of the discipline to combat punctuated entropy by creating culturally appropriate innovations to disaster preparedness, response, and mitigation. If punctuated entropy is a real phenomenon, as proposed here, then its potential pervasiveness is a warning to humankind to listen carefully to the voices of vulnerability; for, as Pogo once said, "We have seen the enemy, and he is us."

9

Modeling Protracted Drought, Collateral Natural Disaster, and Human Responses in the Andes

Michael E. Moseley

This essay models the economic and demographic ramifications of protracted drought and concurrent natural disasters in the arid Andean Cordillera. I write from a geoarchaeological perspective that is diachronic, or long term. This temporal viewpoint does not capture the short-term immediacies of disastrous tragedies and human suffering vividly portrayed by other contributors to this volume. But a time-depth perspective does elucidate a very wide range of hazardous processes that occur on many different time scales, including some that modern populations and their national planners are neither aware of nor immune to. Droughts that endure for a century or more are among the latter. Arduous to mitigate, these protracted disasters occasion great change in biotic and human communities over multiple generations. Consequently, when rainfall eventually recovers and landscapes are recolonized, life generally differs from its former state.

Attenuated droughts are recurrent disasters in the geoarchaeological record. If global warming alters rainfall patterns as predicted, then, as happened in the past, some regions of the world will experience below-normal precipitation that lasts for many years. If rainfall declines

10 percent or more in regions that are now semiarid or more particularly arid, afflicted populations will also become more vulnerable to disruption by other disasters. Increased vulnerability is due to the fact that a natural disaster is broadly analogous to a natural disease. When a healthy population is affected by a single disaster or a single disease, it normally recovers. However, when a population is hit first by one disorder and then by a second or third, recovery becomes tenuous, and the probability of collapse increases. From this viewpoint, protracted drought is particularly similar to AIDS, whose victims over time suffer increasing inability to resist other illnesses. Likewise, populations stressed by long drought experience diminished capabilities to recuperate from other concurrent disasters of natural or human origin.

Individual and collateral natural hazards are common in the Andes, and I first summarize their origins, agrarian symptoms, and characteristics. I then focus upon an attenuated drought between A.D. 1100 and 1500. This long dry spell reached its nadir early in the fourteenth century, when rainfall was 10 to 15 percent below long-term norms. The geopolitical landscape changed because millions of people moved in pursuit of diminishing moisture supplies. Dryness affected the two fundamental forms of agriculture that the world continues to rely upon: rainfall farming, in which precipitation directly wets soil that sustains crops, and runoff farming, such as irrigation, in which rain residue moves from where it fell before wetting agricultural soil elsewhere. Drought exerts differential stress upon rainfall and runoff farming. Populations that depend upon the latter suffer much greater strain than those that rely upon the former. This is because soils, like sponges, absorb fixed amounts of rainfall and must reach saturation before residue precipitation is shed as runoff. Consequently, the loss of runoff can more than double the loss of rainfall during drought in arid and semiarid regions of the globe where soil absorption values are high.

In the Central Andean Cordillera, rainfall sustains mountain agropastoralism, and runoff supports irrigation agriculture on the desert coast. The attenuated dry period that began in A.D. 1100 affected both regions, but in distinct ways. I explore this variation with a model of differential drought stress. Failed responses to stress include cases of social and political collapse, several of which are summarized. Numerous successful responses mitigating drought are my primary

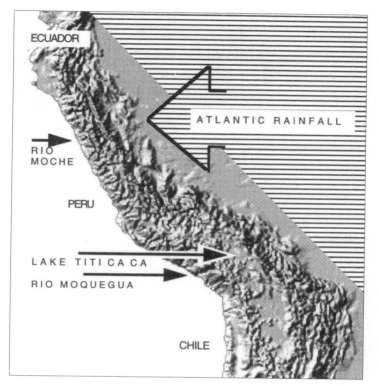

FIGURE 9.1

The Central Andean Cordillera.

concern. A comparison of human adjustments on the coast and in the highlands reveals that deserts and mountains offer markedly different response options to drought. Clearly, people have more options where it is wetter than where it is dryer. A brief review of Inca policies suggests certain precedents for state and national mitigation of protracted dryness. I conclude with some implications of past events for the present and future.

ENVIRONMENTAL SETTING

Forming the mountain spine of continental South America, the Andean landscape is one of global extremes. It is the world's longest mountain chain and is second only to the Himalayas in elevation. The central Cordillera consists of two parallel mountain ranges (fig. 9.1).

The higher eastern and more modest western ranges bracket lower intermontane basins that drain into the Amazon, except in the far south, where they are landlocked. Biotic diversity is exceptional. With eighty-four representatives of the world's one hundred and four life zones, Peru has the largest number of ecological life zones per unit area on earth (Tossi 1960; Earls 1996). Biotic diversity is distributed very asymmetrically along altitudinal, latitudinal, and longitudinal axes. As in all towering ranges, ecological zones are stratified by altitude, and far fewer species of plants and animals live at high elevations than at low ones. Each stratified ecological zone is multifaceted, with fractured habitats cracked by rugged topography.

Towering mountain peaks of the central Cordillera split and divide the continental climate into wet Atlantic and dry Pacific regimes. Normally, all rainfall in the central uplands is derived from the Atlantic Ocean thousands of kilometers away. There is a marked longitudinal gradient in precipitation, from wet in southern Ecuador to dry in northern Chile. Fronting on the moist Amazon basin, the high eastern Andean escarpment receives abundant precipitation. But by catching moisture-laden clouds, the lofty mountain wall filters their passage and creates rain shadows and decreased precipitation to the west. Consequently, biodiversity is greatest along the Atlantic flanks of the Cordillera. The eastern escarpment is very steep, with exceptionally precipitous slopes that are very difficult or impossible to farm. Because the Atlantic watershed breaks through the eastern range and reaches deep into the intermontane basins, it receives and discharges approximately 90 percent of all Andean rainfall. Rainfall is seasonal, and mountain basins have relatively modest slopes amenable to both rainfall and runoff farming. Cultivation is combined with herding in high altitude grasslands to support agropastoralism. Because there is more arable land and pasture in the sierra than along the eastern or western escarpments, the largest pre-Hispanic populations in the Andes resided in the sierra uplands, where millions of indigenous people still live today.

Biodiversity is limited along the arid Pacific watershed because this region receives and discharges only 10 percent of central Andean precipitation. Whereas rainfall farming is possible at high elevations, below altitudes of 2,500 meters the sierra is arid, and below 1,000 meters the coast is hyperarid between northern Peru and central Chile.

Seasonal runoff feeds more than sixty short rivers that descend the western escarpment along steep parallel courses. Although most carry water only part of the year, they support canal irrigation in the dry sierra and in coastal valleys where flat land is relatively abundant. Desert valley agriculture is intensive and has long supported densely packed populations.

Northern river valleys have better water supplies than southern ones due to the latitudinal gradient to rainfall. The Andes are low, narrow, tropical, and wet in Ecuador to the north. To the south the eastern and western ranges and the sierra uplands become progressively higher, wider, and dryer, culminating in a towering 800-kilometer-long, landlocked mountain basin. Lake Titicaca occupies the northern end, where limited precipitation and abundant land support very large agropastoral populations. The rest of the mountain basin, however, is extremely dry, and human habitation is sparse.

ENERGETICS OF CHANGE

The frequency of Andean natural hazards and disasters is well above global norms. Paradigms of plate tectonics and ocean/atmosphere interaction characterize the central Cordillera as an exceptionally dynamic region subject to many forms of stressful environmental change. Change is propelled by energy from two independent sources. One emanates from within the earth and generates crustal movement and mountain building. This energy produces volcanic eruptions and violent earthquakes (see Garcia, this volume). Because the Cordillera is still actively growing, it is subject to ongoing tectonic creep and recurrent seismic shocks. Solar energy is the second source of power that changes natural conditions. Conveyed by marine and meteorological currents, this energy generates hazards such as El Niño–Southern Oscillation (ENSO) events and droughts. Because much of the central Cordillera is arid to hyperarid, it is highly sensitive to climatic perturbations of regional and global scope.

The two power sources contributing to environmental change produce natural hazards that are both frequent and variable in nature. Disasters of tectonic and ocean-atmosphere origin transpire independently of one another. Generally, crises strike different places at different times. The time that elapses between one disaster and another is extremely important. It allows afflicted populations to respond and recover during intervening eras of relative stability. In the Andes, however, natural disasters also transpire concurrently or in close succession. Collateral natural disasters are significant because the combined effects of concurrent crises can exert severe synergistic stress on biotic and human communities. As with disease, when a population is struck by one disaster and then again by a second or third concurrent affliction, survival becomes tenuous.

PERCEPTIONS OF TIME, CHANGE, AND LOSS

Environmental change that impacts negatively upon people transpires on many spatial and temporal scales. Some transformations are slow and subtle, others sudden and spectacular. Sudden disasters that forcefully affect people are readily detectable because they are dramatic. Examples generated by nature include earthquakes (see Garcia, this volume) and droughts (see McCabe, this volume). Examples generated by humans include the Oakland firestorm, the *Exxon Valdez* oil spill, and the Bhopal gas release examined respectively by Hoffman, Dyer, and Rajan (this volume). These are all forms of calamity that people perceive quickly and react to, and indeed, the term "natural disaster" generally implies this type of sudden, dramatic crises.

Disasters can also be far more subtle and pernicious. The insidious side of attenuated catastrophe is illustrated by Button's (this volume) examination of the highly publicized case of surreptitious chemical dumping in Massachusetts, which entailed toxic contamination of Woburn's municipal water supply and high incidents of cancer deaths among consumers of the water. This toxic tragedy is symptomatic of a broad class of disasters that are difficult to perceive, identify causally, diagnose medically, or prove legally. This is because the health, reproduction, and longevity of afflicted populations diminish gradually and sporadically over many years, with few evident common denominators. When loss is gradual, subtle, and difficult to quantify, its origin can remain elusive.

Nature regularly outdoes the insidious likes of the Woburn tragedy on grander scales. Therefore, it is useful to distinguish between swift and attenuated disasters. Both inflict great loss, but when loss is slow and extends over decades or centuries its cumulative impact is difficult to comprehend, and the causal agencies are often unrecognized (Moseley and Feldman 1982a). Human perceptions of protracted change can be rather elastic. A short drought is recognized as an unnatural condition, but one that endures for centuries becomes the natural state of things. Protracted hazards should not be dismissed as "out of sight, out of mind," because their cumulative tolls can match or exceed those of short-term emergencies. Furthermore, their long duration increases the probability of temporal overlap with swift disasters. The latter are relatively common in the Andes. In historic times strong ENSO events have occurred twice or more per century, and large magnitude earthquakes have been even more frequent. A drought that endures for a hundred years or more will likely overlap with collateral natural catastrophes of El Niño and tectonic origin.

SYMPTOMS OF CHANGE

Attenuated hazards and their negative impact upon humans are detectable in certain proxy or indirect records of past conditions. The time depth of many proxy records places natural disaster in a long-term perspective that has weaknesses as well as strengths. The impact of an ancient disaster upon sociopolitical organization can be difficult to assess. In the Andes, prehistoric polities are identified by "corporate" styles of art and architecture associated with elites and the ruling class. Although corporate styles reflect overarching organization, it is often unclear if this organization was centralized, confederated, cohesive, or structured as recursive hierarchies (Moseley 1992). Ancient corporate styles are known to have changed and to have disappeared in the wake of severe catastrophes, but what this means in terms of sociopolitical transformation is open to interpretation. Comparisons of ancient and modern catastrophes are also tenuous when it comes to property loss. Destruction of housing and loss of chattel figure into studies of modern disasters, whereas studies of ancient disasters must gauge property in different ways. Another shortcoming pertains to disaster-induced fatalities, which are generally evasive in the archaeological record. This inhibits comparison with contemporary disasters, which are frequently ranked by their deadliness.

On the other hand, reliance on long-term records has the strength of placing natural hazards in an evolutionary perspective. Disaster-induced fatalities are certainly tragic, but viewed in remote time they are not of lasting consequence when reproduction among surviving populations leads to demographic recovery. Similarly, temporary loss of chattel and housing is an ephemeral problem. Disaster studies traditionally have presumed that people recover from natural calamities. This is generally the norm, and over the millennia Andean populations have recuperated from multitudes of natural disasters. However, recovery is by no means the rule, and to believe so is dangerously short-sighted. Long-term records of past conditions demonstrate that profound evolutionary repercussions arise from natural changes that unalterably destroy economic infrastructure and impair means of making a living. Similar to habitat loss, this type of devastation curtails social production, reproduction, and survival.

It is noteworthy that evidence of human habitat loss has long been widespread and abundant, but Western society has never recognized it as such. Every year the international press recounts numerous discoveries of prehistoric monuments, sites, and cities that have been found around the world in what is today desert or jungle wilderness. While marveling at these archaeological finds, few people ever wonder why bygone populations achieved greatness in what are now wastelands. Obviously, ancient cities did not arise or prosper in ecological barrens.

Andean populations have traditionally supported themselves by cultivating arable land. If subsistence farmers do not willingly give up productive terrain, large-scale permanent desertion of farmland is more readily attributable to changes in land than to changes in farmers. Loss of agrarian habitat is a physical condition writ boldly over the Andean landscape, where abandoned planting surfaces comprise the largest and most widespread of all archaeological phenomena on the continent. Reaching from Colombia and Venezuela down the Cordillera for thousands of kilometers into Chile and Argentina, there are millions of hectares of abandoned farmland. In some regions of the Cordillera, 30 to 100 percent more terrain was formerly cultivated at one time or another. In Peru alone, the total amount of forsaken land may well exceed 40 percent of that in present production (Clement and Moseley 1991).

Pervasive long-term abandonment of arable land is symptomatic of change and a phenomenon termed "agrarian collapse" (Denevan

1987). There are many anecdotal cultural explanations for this situation, and farmers certainly make the ultimate decision about terrain that will or will not be cultivated. But the simplest, most encompassing reason for land loss is a natural one: Farming cannot remain stable or sustainable in changing physical environments. When environments are more dynamic than the technologies used to exploit them, the exploitation fails. Studies of abandoned land suggest agriculture was expanded at many different times and in many different places when local conditions favorable to the reclamation of new lands were anticipated by past populations. When expectations were not met, or when environmental conditions changed, the agrarian regression ensued either temporarily or permanently. This age-old process continues today. Billion-dollar agricultural reclamation works are designed and erected on the basis of twentieth-century design expectations. Because of global warning, however, very different rainfall, runoff, and farming realities will likely ensue during the twenty-first century.

TYPES OF NATURAL HAZARDS

As the numbers and types of proxy records elucidating past conditions have grown, there has also been growth in the roster of natural hazards known or suspected to have afflicted Andean populations. Deleterious tectonic agencies include volcanic eruptions, earthquakes of 7 or greater on the Richter scale, and earthquake-induced landslides, as well as tectonic creep and uplift. Negative hydrological processes involve water table lowering and subsidence, river down-cutting, and sea-level fluctuation. Stressful climatic perturbations range from temperature fluctuations at high altitudes through severe and prolonged ENSO conditions to protracted drought.

In the central Andes, collateral natural disasters are often generated by the most frequent hazards. For the Cordillera as a whole, large-magnitude earthquakes have occurred on the average of once every three years during historic times (Keefer 1994). Strong to very strong El Niño events have occurred two or three times per century (Quinn, Neal, and de Mayolo 1987). Strong earthquakes that strike the steep mountain range produce billions of cubic meters of landslide debris and loose material. Along the arid Pacific watershed, earthquake debris will lie in loose repose for years due to the normal lack of rainfall at elevations below about 2,500 meters. Eventually, the material is entrained by runoff from strong El Niño rainfall. Once it is picked up, the debris results in prodigious sediment loads that exacerbate the erosional and depositional impact of ENSO-induced flash floods.

The synergistic consequences of strong El Niños that follow large earthquakes include a third hazard. Debris swept off the landscape and disgorged into the sea is reworked by long shore currents and deposited on beaches, resulting in beach progradation and growth. Strong winds off the sea move the new beach sediment inland, forming dunes and sand seas that inundate cultural landscapes for decades before moving on to achieve final repose on the mountain escarpment (Moseley et al. 1992). Collateral earthquake, ENSO, and dune incursion disasters are examples of so-called convergent catastrophes. These complex cataclysms can result from variable combinations of natural hazards, including those that are frequent and swift as well as those that are attenuated but less common, such as protracted droughts. Convergent catastrophes are potent because they exert compound stress on biotic and human populations that can be difficult to recover from.

DROUGHT EVENTS

In the mid-1980s, ice cores extracted from the Quelccaya glacial cap in the central Andes provided a 1,500-year proxy record of past climatic conditions (Thompson et al. 1985). Initial analysis documented a marked 25 to 30 percent precipitation decrease from A.D. 562 to 594, notable for its rapid onset and exceptional severity (Schaaf 1988; Shimada et al. 1991). Subsequent analysis of the ice cores also revealed a protracted precipitation downturn between A.D. 1100 and 1500 that reached 10 to 15 percent below normal rainfall during its nadir (Ortloff and Kolata 1993; Thompson et al. 1986). Rainfall conditions reversed themselves in the central Cordillera with the advent of the Little Ice Age, a global climatic oscillation that brought cool conditions to many regions of the Northern Hemisphere. Andean ice cores date the local onset of the Little Ice Age to A.D. 1500, after which rainfall gradually rose above normal by 20 to 25 percent before returning to long-term averages around A.D. 1700.

Recently, limnological cores from Lake Titicaca have provided a 3,500-year record of lake-level variation induced by precipitation variation. These cores implicate early Holocene aridity, followed by moister conditions with mid-Holocene lake filling around 1500 B.C. This was followed by drought-induced lake-level low stands at about 900 to 800 B.C., 400 to 200 B.C., A.D. 1 to 300, and A.D. 1100 to 1450 (Abbott et al. 1997; Binford et al. 1997). The rainfall regime of the central Cordillera is such that these droughts were very likely felt over much of the mountain range. Independent corroboration should come from ice cores recently extracted in northern Peru, where the glacial record of past climatic conditions extends back to late Pleistocene time frames (Thompson et al. 1995). If concordance characterizes the two different proxy records, then protracted droughts will clearly have been recurrent sources of episodic stress on Andean populations.

Significantly, the Titicaca lake cores and the Quelccaya ice cores are concordant in their documentation of late drought beginning around A.D. 1100 and lasting approximately 400 years. This downturn in precipitation appears to be the Andean expression of worldwide perturbations in rainfall and temperature known in Europe as the "medieval warm period" or "medieval optimum." Its best-studied New World expression is the so-called Pueblo drought in the American Southwest. Corollary shifts in precipitation are documented to the west (Jones et al. 1999) and along the Pacific coast (Raab and Larson 1997), where there is also evidence of elevated sea surface temperatures (Arnold 1997). Extreme and persistent drought in California during the last millennium is also mirrored in Patagonia in the Southern Hemisphere (Stine 1994). Given these hemispheric and global correlations, there is no basis for doubting the lake and ice core documentation of Andean drought during medieval times. The challenge is to understand its cultural consequences.

The long duration of the A.D. 1100 Andean dry period is important because it allowed coping strategies to develop over many centuries. Consequently, drought responses can be elicited from the archaeological record and then assessed in terms of adaptive viability. This has been done successfully for the coeval climatic downturn in the Southwest, where the Pueblo drought was first detected some seventy years ago (Douglass 1929). However, analyzing the consequences of episodic desiccation is a new mission for Andean studies. Ortloff and Kolata (1993) offer a pioneering study that classifies the drought vulnerability of different types of water systems. Their investigation also reviews the downside of drought and the negative agrarian consequences of the A.D. 1100 perturbation for the Tiwanaku and Chimor polities and the coastal Chiribaya culture. After modeling drought as exerting differential stress on rainfall and runoff farming, I address the upside of drought and positive human responses to problems of mitigating water deprivation.

DIFFERENTIAL DROUGHT STRESS

To model drought in the central Cordillera is to oversimplify a very complex condition. Precipitation is not uniform, but varies along latitudinal and longitudinal axes. Mountaintops and glacier peaks receive much more moisture than their lower slopes. Eastern mountain faces receive more precipitation than do western slopes. Thus, variation is the norm on both macro and micro scales. Currently, the Andean drought that began in A.D. 1100 is calibrated only in two high-altitude areas some 170 kilometers apart: the Quelccaya ice cap, situated high in the Atlantic watershed, and Lake Titicaca, situated in the arid basin between the eastern and western watersheds. Both the glacial and lake cores implicate precipitation declines on the order of 10 to 15 percent. How these declines affected annual wet- and dry-season rainfall distribution patterns is not clear, nor are implications clear for the longitudinal and latitudinal gradients in annual precipitation. I suspect dryness was relatively greater along the arid Pacific watershed than along the moister Atlantic escarpment. However, the drought must be modeled as a uniform precipitation decline until more climatic data are available.

In arid Andean regions, drought depresses both plant productivity and plant variability, so that farmland that normally supports three or four crop types sustains but one or two, with lesser yields. Rangeland suffers similar effects, and animals have fewer types of forage and less abundant fodder during times of below-normal precipitation. As a consequence, herds and humans must move over greater than normal distances to procure food (see McCabe, this volume). Agriculture is affected by desiccation, but not in a uniform manner. Drought depresses crop productivity and crop variability differentially for rainfall and runoff farming. The latter suffers more than the former, because hydrological relationships between rainfall and runoff are nonlinear. The chief reason is that the soil absorbs moisture and acts like a natural sponge that must reach a fixed saturation point before shedding water (Poveda and Mesa n.d.; Vorosmarty et al. 1989). Once the soil sheds runoff, surface flow is lost to evaporation and seepage through a series of linear relationships.

Differential drought stress and the hydrological relationships between rainfall, soil, runoff, and flow loss can be illustrated in the Rio Moquegua basin, which lies on the Pacific watershed to the west of Lake Titicaca. The river system is 139 kilometers in length, with headwaters reaching slightly beyond 5100 meters above sea level and a drainage basin of 3,480 square kilometers. The average soil absorption value is 260 millimeters of moisture (ONERN 1976, 1985). The earth must take up this amount of rainfall to reach saturation and then shed excess moisture as runoff. As in other Pacific drainages, precipitation is negligible along the Moquegua coast, but in the interior it gradually increases with increasing altitude. However, the quantity of rainwater exceeds soil retention values only in the upper 19 percent of the basin above 3,900 meters in elevation. Between 3,900 and 4,500 meters, average annual rainfall is about 360 millimeters, of which 260 millimeters are taken up by the earth and 100 millimeters are shed as runoff. In this zone a 10-percent, or 36-millimeter, decline in precipitation drops rainfall to 324 millimeters, but it drops runoff by 36 percent, from 100 millimeters to 64 millimeters. Because the soil always absorbs the same amount of moisture, a 15-percent decline in precipitation results in a 54-percent decline in runoff.

In the elevation zone between 4,500 and 4,900 meters, rainfall averages 480 millimeters, and a 10- or 15-percent precipitation reduction results in a runoff reduction of 21.8 or 32.7 percent. Thus, the asymmetrical disparity between rainfall and runoff reductions diminishes as precipitation increases. Comprising less than 3 percent of the Moquegua basin, the zone of alpine tundra above 4,900 meters receives more than 500 millimeters of annual precipitation, principally in the form of snow and ice (ONERN 1976). The runoff contribution is not known because an unknown amount of this moisture is retained in glaciers and snowfields. Nonetheless, for the upper river basin as a whole, rainfall declines of 10 to 15 percent result in runoff reductions of 25 to 40 percent or more. Significantly, the asymmetrical relationship between rainfall and runoff also works in reverse. Increased precipitation rapidly saturates the soil, which then discards water and amplifies runoff. This was particularly dramatic during the first two centuries of the Little Ice Age, when precipitation rose by 20 to 25 percent and runoff by 72 to 90 percent.

Differential drought stress is exacerbated by the fact that once rainfall saturates the soil and moisture is released, surface runoff is lost to evaporation and seepage. Due to these factors the Rio Moquegua loses some 4 percent of its flow per kilometer in the arid sierra at elevations around 2,250 meters. Other than spring floods, the river channel does not normally carry surface flow at elevations below 1,200 meters. Farming in the coastal section of the drainage at elevations below 350 meters depends mainly upon springs fed by subsurface runoff from high in the river basin. The relationship between highland rainfall and coastal spring flow is highly asymmetrical because subsurface flow crosses porous geological strata. Like soil, porous deposits absorb fixed amounts of moisture before shedding subsurface runoff. The amount of moisture taken up underground is difficult to measure, but there are indirect implications that coastal spring flow may have dropped by 80 percent during the A.D. 1100 drought (Ortloff and Kolata 1993).

In summary, linear and nonlinear hydrological relationships result in drought exerting differential stress on rainfall farming and runoff farming. The calculations developed for the Moquegua basin are approximations for one river system. Nonetheless, they model asymmetrical relationships characteristic of rainfall and runoff throughout the central Cordillera and in many other regions of the world. This background is important for understanding how ancient Andean people sought to mitigate protracted drought on the coast and in the highlands.

DESERT STRESS AND RESPONSE

In the central Andes, distinctions between coastal and highland populations and societies can be traced back to the dawn of civilization. The differences between the two are due partly to adaptations to different environmental conditions and different agricultural conditions. Rainfall farming is hydrologically more stable and water efficient than is runoff farming, but the latter has greater economic allure because it produces higher yields on average. Hence, there tends to be substantial investment of resources in irrigation reclamation during episodes of normal or above-normal precipitation, when runoff is average or abundant. Desert is farmed, populations grow, and cities thrive, be they in ancient Peru or the American Southwest. These developments are not sustainable when there are long declines in precipitation, because runoff declines in a disproportional manner. Consequently, over the millennia, irrigation agriculture and its dependent populations have repeatedly pulsed outward over arid landscapes and then contracted inward in concordance with long-term oscillations in rainfall and runoff. This push-pull process is reflected in the ruins of agrarian works that blanket arid Andean landscapes. Significantly, such landscapes disclose not only expansion during good times but Herculean efforts to alleviate bad times.

The Quelccaya ice cores (Thompson 1985) and the Titicaca lake cores (Abbott et al. 1997) indicate that rainfall was above long-term norms between about A.D. 775 and A.D. 1000. With above-average runoff, coastal irrigation systems could expand and populations could grow beyond long-term norms. Hydrological, economic, and demographic boom times went bust during the A.D. 1100 to 1500 dry period. If mountain rainfall dwindled by 10 to 15 percent, then runoff reaching the coast retracted by at least twice as much as the drought peaked during the fourteenth century. Decline in the flow of coastal rivers produced a proportional decline in the productivity of irrigation agriculture. When runoff is scarce, it is hydrologically inefficient to irrigate fields at the far ends of canal systems because they require long-distance transport of water, which, in turn, exacerbates moisture loss due to evaporation and seepage. Consequently, as drought advanced, distant planting surfaces were abandoned, and canal systems shrank in size. The contraction of irrigation during the medieval drought was certainly a prevalent condition that has local documentation in studies of ancient canals and fields in the Moquegua and Moche drainages (Ortloff and Kolata 1991).

Drought relief was pursued by a number of means. Coastal economies had significant maritime components. It is not clear to what degree changes in meteorological conditions that induced dry times may have changed marine currents affecting Andean fishery. Nonetheless, it is reasonable to assume that fishing was intensified as farming suffered shortfalls from depressed runoff and rainfall. Beyond this, coastal populations had very limited ways to compensate for water scarcity and agricultural shortfalls. Reconstructing canals to make water delivery more efficient and stone-lining channels to limit seepage were undertaken without notable success in the lower Moche Valley (Ortloff and Kolata 1991), if not elsewhere. Diversifying plant foods to include drought-tolerant domesticates and wild species transpired in the lower Moquegua Valley (Dendy 1991), if not elsewhere. Extending horticulture to coastal lomas areas was another limited option. Lomas are patchy communities of wild vegetation sustained by winter fogs off the ocean (Dillon, Tago, and Leiva 1999), and they were sites of circumscribed plant tending in ethnohistorical times (Rostworowski 1981).

The most dramatic attempts to mitigate irrigation losses entailed the utilization of groundwater and subsurface runoff. Today this is done mechanically by pumping water, which often depletes local aquifers. Hand-dug sunken gardens were used during the A.D. 1100 dry episode (cf. Moseley and Feldman 1984b). To create sunken gardens, prodigious labor was expended on excavating artificial planting surfaces down to where natural soil moisture could sustain crop growth. This required moving vast quantities of earth, and the effort was tenable only in high water table areas where moisture occurred within about four meters of the ground surface. Such areas were limited and generally restricted to low-lying localities near the shoreline and, in northern and central Peru, areas near the mouths of rivers. Hence, as irrigation in the valley interiors contracted due to depressed river runoff, farming atrophied and shifted downstream toward ocean-side areas with relatively accessible subsurface runoff.

Over the course of many dry centuries, thousands of sunken gardens were dug wherever feasible, and many valleys are still scarred by large mounds of earth ringing flat-bottomed pits. Accessible supplies of subsurface runoff were limited, and groundwater was inaccessible in many entrenched southern valleys characterized by steep gradients and bedrock shorelines. Consequently, sunken garden farming provided only minor compensation for the downturn in irrigation agriculture. Because there were few means to effectively mitigate drought in the desert, food was in short supply. To varying degrees nutritional stress is reflected in the relatively high incidence of childhood anemia, osseous lesions, long bone bowing, and other maladies reported for late prehistoric mortuary populations that relied upon irrigation agriculture (e.g. Burges 1991, 1992; Williams 1990; Verano 1987). If runoff to the desert dropped by more than 20 percent, as is highly probable, concomitant demographic declines would be expected among agrarian populations along the entire arid coast. Systematic site and settlement pattern surveys provide proxy records of ancient population dynamics, and studies in northern and southern desert valleys (Willey 1953; Wilson 1988; Owen 1993a, 1993b) point to significant demographic declines. Such demographic reductions and redistributions are common corollaries of severe or protracted drought elsewhere in the world (see McCabe, this volume).

Hydrological conditions conducive to agrarian and demographic recuperation did not return to the littoral valleys until desiccation waned and the Little Ice Age ushered in above-normal rainfall and runoff. By then, the highland Inca forces had conquered the drought-depressed coast. Shortly thereafter desert populations were decimated by the convergent catastrophes of Old World pandemics and Spanish subjugation, which permanently altered economic and social conditions of the region.

CONVERGENT CATASTROPHES

Collateral disasters involving earthquakes and El Niños certainly transpired during the four centuries of drought, and two documented cases warrant brief review. When the medieval drought began in southern Peru, a local culture called Chiribaya occupied the Moquegua drainage (Lozada 1998). This society focused principally on coastal fishing and spring-fed farming but also extended into the lower arid sierra, where seasonal river flow supported irrigation. Vulnerability to drought was very high due to agrarian dependency upon surface and subsurface runoff from very distant rainfall high in the Moquegua basin, and agricultural productivity was severely depressed by A.D. 1300 as the medieval episode of desiccation neared its peak. The stressed population experienced a major collateral natural disaster around A.D.1360, when an exceptionally severe El Niño flooded settlements, destroyed irrigation systems, and decimated the cultural landscape, largely obliterating the Chiribaya culture (Moseley et al. 1992; Satterlee

1993). Demographic recuperation was minimal; postdisaster population levels in the lower drainage remained some 80 percent below their
pre-drought and pre-flood levels for more than a century and a half
(Owen 1993a, 1993b). Marginal demographic and economic recovery
from the convergent catastrophes is attributable to the continued
drought. Calculations for one Chiribaya irrigation system suggest its
spring water supplies dropped by at least 80 percent in the A.D. 1320s
(Ortloff and Kolata 1993). Thus, the collateral ENSO disaster struck a
population with minimal resources for recovery, and agrarian recuperation did not transpire until the Little Ice Age, when the region was in
Spanish hands.

In the Moche Valley of northern Peru at least 30 percent more terrain was farmed in the past than in the 1970s (Moseley and Deeds
1982). The ruined canals and fields of this drainage chronicle an outward expansion of irrigation agriculture around a millennium ago,
when runoff and rainfall were at or above long-term norms (Ortloff
and Kolata 1993). These ancient works bear widespread evidence of
flood destruction by an A.D. 1100 ENSO event that disrupted many
northern valleys (Moseley and Cordy-Collins 1990). At the time the
Moche Valley was the seat of a powerful state, Chimor, which com-
manded large labor resources, and the local irrigation system was
entirely reconstructed. This costly undertaking proceeded upon the
presumption that previous climatic conditions would prevail following
the destructive ENSO event, but this was not the case. The rebuilt
canals carried little, then no water. Large tracts of land were lost to
farming as river runoff dwindled, and reclamation efforts shifted to low
areas, where sunken gardens could access groundwater. Historically, it
is noteworthy that in the 1990s agriculture has expanded back into formerly farmed areas due to a massive, multi-valley irrigation project that
draws water from a distant desert river with abundant flow. This project
was designed with no knowledge of why earlier, larger agrarian systems
collapsed in the first place (Moseley et al. 1991). Rather, it proceeds on
the presumption that climatic conditions of the twentieth century will
prevail in the twenty-first. Thus, history may well repeat itself.

HIGHLAND STRESS AND RESPONSE

A compelling argument has been made that the A.D. 1100 drought induced the collapse of the Tiwanaku polity centered around Lake Titicaca (Binford et al. 1998). The argument holds that the economic well-being of Tiwanaku was anchored by "ridge field" farming in extensive low-lying areas along the lake margins, where high water table conditions prevailed. Planting transpired atop linear ridges of earth about 1 to 1.5 meters high, 2 to 3 meters wide, and more than 10 meters long. Built in parallel rows, each ridge was separated from the next by a depressed trough of similar dimensions that held slow-moving runoff or standing water, which was essential to the high productivity and practicability of ridge field farming. Warmed during the day, the water released heat at night that mitigated frost. Also, algae and aquatic debris from the troughs was collected to fertilize the planting surfaces (Kolata 1993). As high lake and runoff levels declined after A.D. 1100, ridged fields lost water and viability. By the time the lake fell 12 meters or more to its drought-induced low stand, more than 50,000 hectares of ridged fields were abandoned, Tiwanaku had collapsed, and much of the population had dispersed (Albarracin and Mathews 1990).

Sunken gardens were tenable in limited regions of the landlocked Titicaca basin but were not an option in most sierra basins with steep drainages descending to the Atlantic or Pacific. Along the western escarpment there were few means to compensate food loss in the dry sierra below 2,200 meters in elevation. Here slopes are sheer, groundwater is deep, and natural vegetation is sparse. In this region of the Moquegua basin, at least, irrigation and populations dependent upon it dwindled significantly during the medieval dry period.

Unlike the coastal valleys, where farming shifted downstream to low elevations in pursuit of subsurface water, sierra farming shifted upstream to higher elevations in pursuit of surface water. This was because pre-drought quantities of rainfall, moist soil, runoff, and pasture still existed. But these conditions prevailed only at altitudes of 100 to 300 meters or more above previous elevations.

There are and were many constraints on the uphill pursuit of scarce rainfall and soil moisture. Progressively fewer types of crops can grow at successively higher altitudes, and very few domesticates are productive near the elevational limits of farming. The frequency of frost, hail, violent weather, and soil erosion increases with elevation, while soil quality decreases. Furthermore, glacial moraines indicate that during the A.D. 1100 drought, mountain temperatures cooled some 0.6 degrees Celsius (Seltzer 1991). By about A.D. 1300 colder, dryer climatic conditions forced a 70-meter downward shift in the altitudinal distribution of natural vegetation zones, pushing them below where they are today (Seltzer and Hastorf 1990). Thus, as highland people moved agriculture and pastoralism into higher, wetter altitudes, nature lowered the high-elevation temperatures at which plants, pasture, and crops could grow.

Nonetheless there were vast areas of pasture and marginally arable mountain land at high elevations in the Andes, most of it characterized by precipitous slopes because topographic roughness increases with altitude. To respond to drought, farming had to move from gentle to steep, often declivitous, inclines. Prodigious labor was expended on the construction of agricultural terraces over many generations in order to reclaim upland mountain slopes. Cultivating steep gradients exacerbates erosion, and terracing was essential for controlling the loss of poorly developed mountain soils. In the Titicaca basin and elsewhere, terracing was particularly important near the altitudinal limits of agriculture, where violent storms are a norm. Along the Pacific watershed and elsewhere, terracing was combined with canal irrigation to reclaim broken sierra headwaters where high elevation streams still carried runoff. In addition to moving farming higher, terracing was widely used to move farming eastward into the craggy Atlantic watershed. Even during drought, this region was relatively better watered than the rest of the central Cordillera. Here terracing allowed farming to expand into less extreme elevations where more types of crops could grow. Over the course of many dry centuries millions of terraces were built to reclaim vast rugged areas of the Andean uplands and the eastern escarpment.

Whereas agrarian productivity and dependent populations along the lower Pacific watershed declined by 20 percent or more, drought was a major catalyst for economic and demographic radiation into the upper and eastern highlands. By about A.D. 1450 more people resided at high altitudes and along the eastern slopes than at any other time. This did not last, however, since mountain safe havens during drought are generally not the best places to live under normal or above-normal rainfall conditions. Terraces are expensive to build and maintain, and they are very vulnerable to earthquakes and landslides—frequent

Andean hazards. Many more crops can grow at moderate altitudes, where weather hazards are less severe, than at high altitudes. Under normal conditions sierra runoff farming produces higher yields than does sierra rainfall farming. Hence, as drought waned and rainfall waxed to above normal during the Little Ice Age, farmers reverted to lower, warmer settings. The reversal was both voluntary at the folk level and coercive at the state level. To augment agrarian tax revenues, the Inca imperium often forcibly resettled high-altitude communities to lower terrain that had turned more productive with increased rainfall, soil moisture, and runoff (e.g. Hastorff 1993). Although precipitation rose above normal, demographic decimation in the wake of European disease left new Spanish overlords with more arable land than people to farm it. Because above-normal rainfall and runoff persisted until about A.D. 1700, remnants of the indigenous population could be forcibly relocated to still lower elevations. Relocation facilitated political control, religious conversion, and cultivation of Old World cultigens intolerant of extreme altitudes. If the drought had not broken, neither Inca nor Castilian resettlement policies would have been tenable.

To summarize, during the last millennium farming and the millions of people it supports have moved up and then down the slopes of the high Andes in concordance with long-term oscillations in rainfall and runoff. This poignant story of climate change and human response is written boldly over the mountain landscape in ubiquitous terraces and other ruins of past agrarian endeavors. The ruins also tell earlier, similar stories, because protracted drought occurred many times before.

ADAPTATION TO PROTRACTED DROUGHT

The A.D. 1100 dry period was the latest of many centenary droughts in the Andes. The recurrence of these protracted crises raises the probability that indigenous populations reacted to episodic desiccation in patterned ways based on prior experiences, and that some responses may be predictable. A very high degree of subsistence mobility characterizes highland agropastoral adaptations because they are based upon the exploitation of multiple, dispersed ecological zones stratified by altitude (Murra 1975). Annual hazards associated with short growing seasons and poorly developed mountain soils include erosion, erratic

and untimely precipitation, temperature fluctuations, frost, hail, nema-
todes, mice, and other pests. Remediation requires rapid transmission
of information so that agropastoral activities can be reprogrammed on
short notice (Earls 1996). It also requires preserving, storing, and stockpiling food reserves because poor harvests are frequent (Orlove and
Guillet 1985). Protracted declines in rainfall exacerbate many conditions that underlie human adaptations to the central Andes because
drought depresses biotic productivity and botanical variability and
increases the distances between valued commodities. In the American
Southwest, similarly, documented responses to medieval drought
included increased subsistence mobility, heightened information flow,
and elaboration of subsistence storage, as well as demographic redistri-
bution and decline (Cordell 2000).

Unlike the Southwest, the central Cordillera was home to very large
populations with very long traditions of complex organization, culminating with the Inca imperium. Severe or protracted droughts
impinged on these traditions at least four times before the medieval dry
spell. These recurring catastrophes toppled states and societies, but others arose in their wake. It is reasonable to suspect that these were learning experiences, and that certain Inca policies are most intelligible as
adaptations to drought. Inca political formation was a slow process that
began shortly after A.D. 1000 with the gradual consolidation of local eth-
nic groups (Bauer 1992). Because the nascent state arose and grew principally during four centuries of drought, contending with aridity was
inescapable. After A.D. 1400, the Inca adapted distinctive "corporate"
styles of art, architecture, and construction that commemorated many
imperial policies on a monumental scale both in the capital region and
in provinces that were or would be politically incorporated. One procedure employed corvée labor for large-scale agrarian reclamation of previously unfarmed or underutilized land. Initially much of the terrain was
at high, rugged elevations and along the eastern escarpment, where terracing was required for reclamation. Surmounting vast flights of verdant
terraces, the tourist attraction of Machu Picchu remains a monumental
expression of state commitments to opening drought-resistant lands.
Imperial reclamation projects were, however, large-scale elaborations
of drought responses pursued at the folk level throughout the highlands. Later, as the drought broke, corvée labor was used to reopen

farming in lower, warmer elevations, where conquered communities were often resettled.

Imperial revenues included agricultural staples grown on state lands, and the Inca concern with storing and stockpiling is unsurpassed in the annals of ancient civilization. Corporate-style storage vessels, called *aryballos,* were a hallmark of the state ceramics. Monumental construction and prominent display of warehouses were equally distinctive. These were generally one-room buildings constructed of masonry that surpassed the quality of commoners' houses. Erected in long rows, hundreds and in some cases thousands of warehouses were strategically positioned on high hills (LeVine 1992). Benefiting from cool temperatures that conserved food supplies, the lofty placement of storehouses made them visible from great distances, as if the state were broadcasting its preparedness. The stores were generally used for governmental purposes but could also mitigate food shortages among the common populace (Rowe 1946).

In addition to elaborate warehouses, large-scale investments were also made to build a pan-Andean highway system that stretched some 30,000 to 40,000 kilometers in length. Thus, state commitments to the movement of people and produce were no less than investments in elaborate warehousing. Facilitating the flow of information was vital to the well-being of the nation. Although a "pony express" was not tenable, young men were stationed as runners at established relay stations and sped data and messages encoded on cords between the capital and its political provinces.

In overview, Andean folk reactions to highland drought included opening new land with better moisture supplies, heightened storage of scarce food supplies, increased travel to secure distant resources, and greater information flow and exchange. In addition to relocating people on more productive terrain, these responses were played out on national scales by the Inca state and constitute state-level drought response policies that remain viable today.

CONCLUSION

Natural processes of ocean/atmosphere and tectonic origin are only as hazardous as people make them. Modern population growth has made them ever more catastrophic, to the point where fatalities from natural disasters now exceed those from war. Loss of life, property, and development potential to natural calamities is mounting annually. Much of the increase is attributable to human agencies, such as migration into disaster-prone areas (Board on Natural Disasters 1999). Natural agencies are also involved because some types of events, such as El Niños, have increased in frequency since the 1950s, and other changes are expected to accompany global warming.

To understand the future impact of natural processes it is imperative to comprehend their past, and the Andean Cordillera has a significant role to play in this quest. The Andes are a natural laboratory for investigating ocean/atmosphere and tectonic hazards and their human consequences, since conditions here have analogies in many other areas of the world, for at least four reasons. First, a large majority of the world's life zones are represented in the central Cordillera. Second, the tectonically active range has wet and dry watersheds and thus river systems similar to drainages in many other continents. Third, many proxy records of past conditions exist in the Andes. Those related to climate include, but are not limited to, lake sediments, glacial moraines, and mountain ice caps. Some, such as the latter, are very sensitive to climatic change. In an ominous sign of the warmer times, Cordillera ice caps as well as ice deposits elsewhere are now melting for the first time in thousands of years (Thompson et al. 1994; Thompson, Davis, and Mosley-Thompson 1994). Fourth, as a pristine center of ancient civilization, Andean populations and polities offer a long record of successful and unsuccessful response to multifaceted environmental change.

Although drought is a new topic of inquiry for Andean studies, a number of preliminary observations have contemporary implications. The past century of relatively benign weather has obfuscated awareness of attenuated dry periods and their often catastrophic repercussions. Yet these climatic oscillations have been recurrent natural phenomena since Holocene times and are very likely to revisit humanity, a likelihood that is enhanced by global warming. Since hydrological relationships between rainfall and runoff are nonlinear, drought exerts disproportionally greater stress on runoff farming than on rainfall farming. Due to relatively greater yields, the world economy has made much larger investments in expanding irrigation agriculture than it has in improving rainfall farming. In the Americas these investments have fostered marked population growth in arid regions of the Pacific watershed and along the western coast. Because these areas are susceptible to frequent seismic and El Niño events, more people are now vulnerable to natural hazards. Furthermore, these regions have become increasingly dependent upon hydroelectric power supplies. Consequently, rainfall and more particularly runoff now provision exceptionally large populations with potable water, food, and energy. These provisions are distributed through complex infrastructures to consumers primarily concentrated in metropolitan areas, and the infrastructures are highly vulnerable to damage and disruption triggered by minor as well as major events.

Widespread dependence upon runoff for drinking water, irrigation agriculture, and hydroelectricity makes severe or protracted droughts extremely hazardous. The populations most susceptible to drought disruption are those in arid and semiarid regions where alternative water resources are least available. Here stress from decreased rainfall and runoff will be felt first and most severely. A particularly negative aspect of drought that endures for decades or centuries is that it heightens susceptibility to disruption from collateral disasters such as earthquakes and El Niño events. Past collateral catastrophes have included natural events as well as foreign conquests. The latter occurs because attenuated drought reconfigures political economies and geopolitical realities.

The geoarchaeological perspective of this chapter invites several closing comments on human recovery from natural disasters. If recovery is understood to mean a return to former conditions or generally similar conditions following a crisis, then this has been a long-term norm. For millennia people have been plagued by natural disasters, but relatively few register in the archaeological record, and those that do are predominantly very large catastrophes. This norm is now changing because disaster-induced human casualties and property losses are now mounting annually, and the dynamics of recuperation have assumed new dimensions. In 1998 Hurricane Mitch, for example, was so devastating to Honduras and El Salvador that there can be no return to predisaster conditions. High birth rates will replace disaster casualties, but social and economic circumstances will not be the same again because national development experienced a profound disjuncture. What will follow is social and economic reconfiguration, not the recovery of prior conditions. Similar disjunctures characterize severe drought that endures for decades or centuries. Depressed rainfall and runoff exert selective stress on biotic communities, which adapt by becoming more xerophytic. The same stress alters human adaptations on a time scale that negates a return to bygone norms. Therefore, by the time rainfall eventually reverts to previous levels, life has reconfigured itself to flourish in new ways.

Note

I am indebted to Peter Waylen for pointing out that differential drought stress evident in the archaeological record is the product of nonlinear hydrological relationships between rainfall and runoff due principally to soil moisture absorption. I thank many investigators who have studied the Moche, Moquegua, and Titicaca basins for generously sharing their research results.

10

Impact of and Response to Drought among Turkana Pastoralists

Implications for Anthropological Theory and Hazards Research

J. Terrence McCabe

I have been conducting fieldwork among pastoral peoples in East Africa for the last eighteen years. The principal focus of my research has been how people manage natural resources and cope with environmental stress and how policy (development, famine relief, and conservation) has impacted traditional systems of natural resource use. From the very beginning the importance of understanding the role of drought in pastoral subsistence and social organization was apparent to me. I therefore want to begin this paper with a recollection from my first days of fieldwork among the Turkana.[1]

The year was 1980, and I had just begun my fieldwork in the southern part of the Turkana district in northwestern Kenya, one of the driest and most inhospitable places in eastern Africa. This work was the initial phase of what became the South Turkana Ecosystems Project, one of the largest ecosystems oriented projects ever undertaken that incorporated humans into the analysis. I had made initial contacts with a number of Turkana families. A herd-owner named Angorot, with whom I later became good friends, offered to kill a goat for me. At the time Angorot was a fairly wealthy man, with livestock holdings of over 950 small stock, 107 head of cattle, and 68 camels. Instead of slaughtering one of his own goats, he walked down the dry wash to a friend's *awi* (homestead) and "borrowed" a goat to kill. When I asked him why he borrowed a goat rather than kill one of his own, he replied that he did not have one that was fat enough. Even though I was new to the field situation, it certainly looked to me as if there were many "fat" goats in the flock, and I strongly suspected that a lot more was going on there than Angorot was saying. For all of us who do fieldwork, of course, this is a rather familiar, if disconcerting, situation.

After being in the field for about a year, I began to learn that behavior such as that described above can best be understood as an attempt to create or strengthen social ties that can be utilized to gain access to labor or livestock. Livestock losses result from raids, disease, and especially from drought. Although the timing of droughts is impossible to predict, Turkana know that they will occur and that their survival depends upon their ability to cope with them.

Among the Turkana, many aspects of day-to-day behavior and social organization are impossible to understand until one appreciates the real and potential impact of drought on these pastoral people. I began to concentrate my research on the response to and impact of drought, and on the process by which Turkana families recover from drought. In addition, I examined the factors that contributed to vulnerability to drought stress on the one hand, and to resistance to drought stress on the other. In this chapter I describe some of the results of this long-term study, both from an individual or family perspective and also at the level of the group, in this case the Turkana section. In the first section I discuss the theoretical importance of understanding the impact of natural hazards for anthropology with a special focus on drought. I then present a brief overview of Turkana subsistence patterns, climate, and the impact of drought on the pastoral economy. In the third section I examine the process by which Turkana respond to drought and the process by which families recover from the losses associated with drought. In section four, I briefly present the results of a study that investigated issues related to drought vulnerability, and summarize the case study and present conclusions in the final section.

THEORETICAL OVERVIEW

This discussion of drought among the Turkana brings together three distinct but interrelated theoretical perspectives. The first is the call made by Vayda and McCay (1975:293) for ecological anthropologists to focus their attention on "environmental problems and how people respond to them." The second is the view that in the arid and semiarid areas of Africa, drought must be viewed as part of the normal functioning of the ecosystem, not something unusual or external to it (Glantz 1987). The third is that arid land ecosystems are persistent but nonequilibrial systems (Ellis and Swift 1988).

A Hazards Approach

In their article "New Directions in Ecological Anthropology," Vayda and McCay (1975) outlined a series of critiques to the "new ecological functionalism" that was popular in the late 1960s and 1970s. This body of literature utilized the ecosystem, and the role of humans in it, as a frame of reference and was epitomized by Rappaport's *Pigs for the Ancestors* (1968). Vayda and McCay felt that the ecosystem approach was too static and dependent upon homeostasis to be useful in studying how humans adapt to different environments. They also felt that the analytical focus of ecological anthropology should be not on the system but on the individual, as that is the locus of natural selection. Building upon Holling's (1973) notion of resistance and resilience, they advocated an approach that focused on how individuals respond to hazards as the central problematic for ecological anthropology. Although the role that hazards play in the long-term viability of particular societies has been an important subject of research among geographers and sociologists, few ecological anthropologists, with the exception of archaeologists, adopted a "hazards" approach in their own research (e.g. Moseley and Richardson 1992, Kolata 1993).

Hazards as a Normal Occurrence

One of the more recent approaches in hazards research is to consider natural hazards part of the normal functioning of ecosystems. García-Acosta (this volume) emphasizes the importance of this perspective and cites Torry (1979) as pioneering this view of hazards. With specific reference to drought in Africa, Glantz (1987) proposed that development efforts take drought into account as an expected event, and that for development projects to be successful they must be designed with the ability to cope with the stresses associated with drought.

> [M]any concerned with the study of drought have been left with the uneasy feeling that drought is still generally viewed as either an idiosyncratic occurrence, a transient event, or a temporary climatic aberration. Evidence shows that such views are misleading and that in some areas, meteorological drought is a recurring but aperiodic phenomenon, it is part of climate and not apart from it. (Glantz 1987:38)

Arid Land Ecosystems at "Disequilibrium"

Arid land ecosystems are currently understood to be nonequilibrial systems; thus, many of the homeostatic mechanisms that influence the relationship of various components of the ecosystem to one another do not operate in this type of environment. For most of this century African rangelands were considered equilibrial systems. This assumes that "conditions outside the system of interest are relatively stable over time, allowing internal processes of the system to play out or equilibrate, and regulate system structure and dynamics" (Ellis, Cougenhour, and Swift 1993:6). A tight coupling is assumed to exist between the amount and type of vegetation and the number of herbivores foraging on it. Once the numbers of herbivores exceeded the "carrying capacity" of the rangeland, the ecosystem would begin to degrade. This has been the theoretical underpinning for more than fifty years of livestock development projects as well as for forced destocking projects undertaken to preserve the environmental health of the African rangelands.

In an article published in 1988, ecologists on the South Turkana Ecosystem Project stated that climate was the driving force in explaining the dynamic nature of the Turkana ecosystem, and that there was only a weak linkage between the herbivore population and the plant community (Ellis and Swift 1988). Their position is summarized in the following quotation:

> The results of our work in Ngisonyoka Turkana...reveal anything but an equilibrial ecosystem. Here in the arid northwest

corner of Kenya, pastoralists are locked in a constant battle
against the vagaries of nature and the depredations of neighboring tribesmen...However, despite the dynamic nature of the
ecosystem, there is little evidence of degradation or of imminent system failure. Instead this ecosystem and its pastoral
inhabitants are relatively stable in response to the major stresses
on the system, e.g. frequent and severe droughts. (Ellis and
Swift 1988:453)

All three theoretical approaches will be relevant in the case study
that follows. How Turkana cope with the stresses associated with
drought answers the call first made by Vayda and McCay. However, I
argue that an examination of drought impact and response does not
need to abandon an ecosystem approach as advocated by Vayda and
McCay. The work of Glantz, and that of Ellis and Swift, clearly demonstrates that drought is an integral part of the ecological system and
indeed may be the most important element determining the nonequilibrial nature of that system.

CLIMATE AND DROUGHT IN TURKANA

The Turkana number approximately 200,000 people living in the
low-lying rangelands of northwestern Kenya. Their homeland is bor-
dered by West Pokot district to the south, the Rift Valley escarpment
and Uganda to the west, the Sudanese border to the north, and Lake
Turkana to the east (see fig. 10.1). They live primarily off the products
of their livestock, although some sections of the Turkana also engage in
small-scale cultivation.

The climate of Turkana district is hot and dry. In fact, it is one of
the driest areas of eastern Africa to support pastoralism. An analysis of
sixty years of rainfall records for Lodwar, the district capital, showed an
average of 180 millimeters and a three-year running mean varying
between a low of approximately 100 millimeters per year and a high of
about 270 millimeters per year (Ellis, Cougenhour, and Swift 1993).
However, the major perturbation that the Turkana have to contend
with is not the aridity itself, but the high degree of variability in the precipitation pattern and the frequent occurrence of drought. Ellis and
Swift (1988:454) have calculated that "rainfall has dropped 33 percent

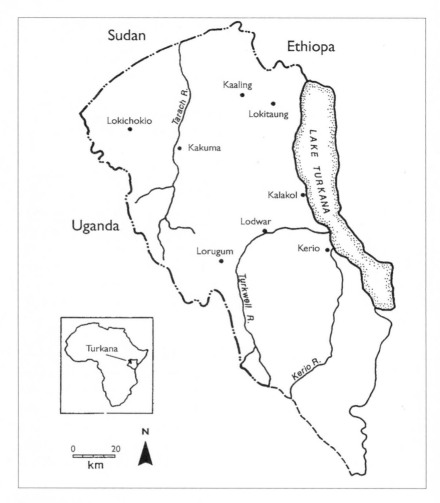

FIGURE 10.1

Turkana district.

or more below the long-term average 13 times in the last 50 years, i.e. once every 3 to 4 years, and at least 4 of these have been multi-year droughts." The rainfall records on which these calculations were based are presented in figure 10.2.

In arid land ecosystems there is a fairly direct relationship between precipitation and the primary productivity of the vegetation. Because growing or standing vegetation is the source of all forage resources avail-

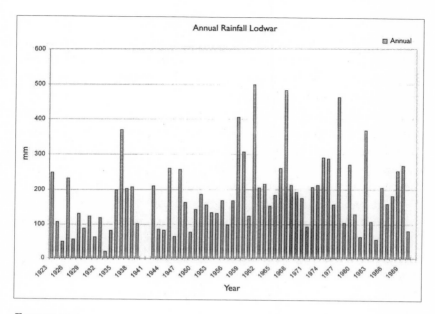

FIGURE 10.2

Annual rainfall, Lodwar.

able to livestock, a decrease in precipitation will have a strong influence on livestock health and condition. Ellis and Swift have estimated that during a single year-long drought, plant biomass would be one-half or less that of a nondrought year; in multiyear droughts, the plant biomass may be one-third to one-quarter that of a non-drought year.

During the ten years that I carried out intensive fieldwork among the Turkana, I experienced two severe drought episodes. The first occurred between 1979 and 1981, when I was conducting in-depth fieldwork with four Turkana families. By the end of the drought, each family had lost between 60 to 90 percent of its livestock. The other drought occurred from 1984 to 1985, while I was conducting a study (with ecologists and a nutritionist) on the impact and response to drought among four different sections of the Turkana. This fieldwork was not as detailed, but demonstrated the differences among Turkana sections toward drought impact and response. During this drought Turkana herd owners lost more than 50 percent of their livestock. Losses in livestock holdings of 50 percent or more among herds managed by traditional pastoralists resulting from drought have been reported fairly frequently in the literature (Hogg 1982, Roth 1996). Although it may seem counterintuitive, the nutritional state of the people may not decline much during a drought, because they will eat the animals that have died. During the recovery phase, however, people may be quite severely stressed. This is due to a lack of milk, because during the drought female animals will have often suffered spontaneous abortions or will not have become pregnant. In addition, herd owners are often unwilling to slaughter or sell livestock, as it is critical that herd numbers recover to pre-drought levels.

Although two significant droughts occurred among the Turkana in the decade of the 1980s, droughts of this magnitude commonly occur once every ten years, with less severe episodes occurring every three to four years. What this means is that for the Turkana to survive, they must have a subsistence system and a system of social organization that can cope with these stresses. Coping mechanisms entail responding to drought stress while it is happening and recovering from the losses once it has ended. The importance of both understanding what happens during a disaster and documenting the process of recovery is emphasized by García-Acosta (this volume). Too often emphasis is given to disaster itself, not the critically important recovery process. Below I outline how both of these coping mechanisms work, after which I discuss the differences in drought impact and vulnerability among the different sections of the Turkana.

DROUGHT RESPONSE AND THE PROCESS OF RECOVERY

Drought is unlike many other natural hazards in that it begins subtly, almost imperceptibly. In an environment characterized by climatic variability, the failure of the rains to begin when they "usually" do may mean a few more days, weeks, or months of the dry season, or it may mean that a catastrophic drought has commenced. For the Turkana, it means that the strategies that they employ to cope with the stresses of the dry season must continue, at least for a while. Drought is referred to as *akamu*—a longer and more severe dry season. However, each season is named among the Turkana, and the severity of the drought will often be reflected in the name that they give the dry season. For example, the 1984/85 drought was referred to as *akamu Ngibocheros* by the Ngisonyoka (the Turkana section where I conducted most of my work), alluding to the fact that the dry season was so bad that many herd-owners from the Ngibocheros section migrated south into Ngisonyoka territory searching for forage for their livestock. This was an extremely rare event and attested to the fact that it was a very stressful period for the Ngibocheros.

In the next section I describe an "idealized" version of the annual round so that the reader will have a clear understanding of the strategies that I am referring to. I use the land use pattern typical of the Ngisonyoka, the section of the Turkana that I am most familiar with. I want to stress here that Turkana herd owners differ from one another and that each year varies from one year to another, but commonalities do emerge, and one can abstract an "idealized" model.

THE ANNUAL ROUND[2]

Following the rains, the Ngisonyoka typically gather in the sandy plains known as the Toma. This area receives less rainfall than the higher elevations to the south, but during this period there is enough forage available for all livestock species. All members of the family are usually at the homestead or *awi*, and families join together in large neighborhood associations called *adakar*. An adakar may include hundreds of families and thousands of livestock. As the dry season sets in, the adakars begin to break up as there is not sufficient forage for all livestock in a restricted area. Three to five families will usually travel together, sharing herding tasks and, to some extent, food. These big awis, or *awi apolon*, may remain together for the dry season, or individual families may go their separate ways. The choice depends on each individual herd owner's preference.

As the dry season intensifies, a herd owner will typically begin to divide his livestock into species-specific and production-specific herds, if he has the labor to do so. The first animals to leave the awi are the cattle, which are moved to highland areas to take advantage of the grass that remains there. During this time the awi itself changes location frequently while moving in a southward direction. The reason for the southern migration pattern is that there is a south-to-north rainfall gradient, with the southern part of Ngisonyoka territory receiving substantially more precipitation than the northern part. Movement is often constrained by the presence of tribal enemies, who raid to steal livestock and to kill Turkana. For the Ngisonyoka, these enemies are the Pokot, who live in the plains just south of the district boundary.

The next strategy to be employed is to divide herds into milking and nonmilking animals. The milking herds of camels and small stock typically remain with the awi, while the nonmilking herds are separated and managed by young men, usually sons or brothers of the herd owner. These "satellite" herds will typically remain separate from the awi for the remainder of the dry season. During the dry season, herd owners often sell animals to purchase grain. They will, of course, sell animals at other times to buy clothes, sandals, and other items. They do not alter their migratory orbit to be near trading centers but will send a family member with an animal into a town to sell it.

During severe dry seasons, a herd owner may have to reduce the number of people depending upon the livestock for food. Nearly all Turkana families have some dependent individuals living with them. Often these are female relatives whose husbands have died or have become impoverished, and their children. Sometimes these people will be forced to leave one family and temporarily move in with a wealthier relative. At other times these people have to leave the pastoral sector altogether and relocate in a town or trading center, where they make a living by begging, brewing beer to sell, or getting temporary employment.

The pastoral diet changes during the dry seasons. As milk yields decline, Turkana bleed animals, consume wild foods, and, as mentioned above, sell animals in order to purchase grains. In "normal" dry seasons the animals sold are steers or old, nonreproductive females. If a family is poor, they may have to sell reproductive females, but this indicates severe stress.

Throughout the dry season, the awi and all satellite herds remain on the move. For the Ngisonyoka this usually means pushing into the wetter but more dangerous rangelands in the south of their territory. The risks include raiding and livestock disease. The denser bush in the south harbors ticks and tsetse flies, both vectors of serious livestock disease. Once the rains begin, the Ngisonyoka begin their northward journey back to their wet season area, the Toma. This pattern is illustrated in figure 10.3.

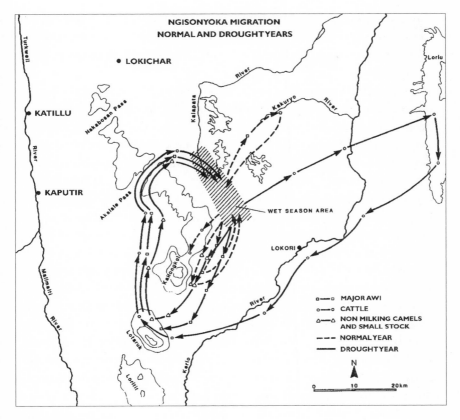

FIGURE 10.3

Ngisonyoka migration, normal and drought years.

DROUGHT

If the rains fail, the strategies utilized to cope with dry season stress continue. The farther the Ngisonyoka push south, the more they are exposed to the dangers associated with raiding, and the more their livestock may be exposed to disease. It is often very difficult, if not impossible, to distinguish livestock losses that result from drought as opposed to disease. Animals weakened by nutritional stress may succumb to diseases like contagious bovine pleuropneumonia, and that may be the direct cause of death. As enemies attempt to recover from drought, they often engage in large-scale raiding. Again, the actual cause of the loss of livestock may be raiding, but an underlying factor will be drought. This combination of "disasters" is referred to as "convergent catastrophes" by Moseley (this volume), and applies equally well to drought, disease, and raiding as it does to the natural events mentioned by Moseley.

At the first stages of drought, herd owners often increase the numbers of animals sold. As a drought progresses, the price for livestock drops (sometimes dramatically), and the price of grain goes up. As the drought intensifies, reproductive animals begin to be offered for sale, as many families will have sold all the males and older females. At a certain point, however, herd owners no longer consider it sensible to sell starving animals; they receive very little for them, and it is possible that they will recover. If they die, their skins can be sold for almost as much money as live animals would have brought.

During a severe drought (such as the one that occurred from 1979 to 1981), whole families begin to move into town, often locating themselves close to a mission in the hope of getting relief food or some small employment. If famine relief camps have been established, many of these now-destitute families may move there. If no other options are available, individuals or families will leave Turkana district and the pastoral sector and seek relief food or employment down country in Kenya. A summary of these choices and the system level impacts of these decisions are presented in table 10.1.

Although there is serious hardship associated with the choices necessitated by drought, the important questions are (1) Have people died from starvation? and (2) Were the herds able to recover? During the 1979–81 drought, no Ngisonyoka that I know of died, and most were able to recover. They did not have access to famine relief camps. In northern Turkana tens of thousands of people migrated into famine relief camps. They did not die, but it was much more difficult for them to recover from drought, as explained below.

DROUGHT RECOVERY

The ability of livestock to recover from drought often takes three, four, or more years. Recovery involves both the reproductive capacity of the livestock and the ability of particular herd owners to draw on their network of social relations for help. During the first year after a drought the livestock population generally remains fairly stable. People

TABLE 10
Drought Stress Syndrome and Pastoral Response

Climatic Condition	Drought Stress Syndrome	Pastoral Strategies	System-Level Effects
Dry season begins	Reduction in forage quantity and quality	Move to dry season range	Livestock production maintained
Dry season intensifies	Reduction in livestock production	Subdivide herds Increase mobility Alter human diet	Livestock production drops; no other change in system function
Dry season continues	Further reduction in livestock production	Same as above, plus: Sell small stock to buy grain Bleed animals	Livestock production down Small-stock numbers reduced Human nutrition adequate Pastoral system intact
Dry season continues	Livestock condition depressed Production very low	Same as above, plus: Slaughter animals for food Dependents move from poorer families to wealthier ones	Small stock reduced Large stock weakened Human nutrition decreases Pastoral system intact
Dry season conditions turn to drought conditions	Livestock condition poor Mortality sets in	Eat dead animals Gather wild food Beg for food Some family members begin to leave pastoral sector	Herd size reduced Human nutrition depressed Pastoral system maintained
Drought intensifies	Wholesale livestock mortality Human malnutrition	Whole families leave pastoral sector Many people seek famine relief	Human survival threatened Pastoral system destroyed Relief-dependent population

Source: Adapted from Ellis et al. 1987.

try to refrain from selling animals, if they can, but most reproductive females will have either aborted or not become pregnant, so there is little herd growth. As previously mentioned, this first year may a period of extreme hardship; without calves, the livestock will not produce milk, and because herd owners are very reluctant to sell animals there may be very little food available for the family.

During the second year there is typically a very high fertility rate, and livestock numbers begin to increase. By the third, fourth, or fifth year, many families will have recouped their losses. But this will only happen if they have enough animals to form the basis of their household herd, and in many cases, livestock holdings will be too low for the family to remain in the pastoral sector.

The Turkana system of social organization also allows them to cope with these stresses at the family level. Each herd owner is the center of a system of social relationships that he has built up over his lifetime. Kinship provides the opportunity to become involved in a social network, although it does not require that one do so. A man's social network usually includes close male relatives, in-laws, and stock associates or friends. These networks are reinforced through the transfer of livestock. I began this chapter with a description of Angerot "borrowing" a goat from a much poorer man and noted that this was a means by which Angorot was strengthening his social ties. I once interviewed Angorot concerning livestock owed to him and livestock he owed to others. In each case there were about sixty outstanding debts. He could pay them off anytime and achieve "a balanced budget," but to do so is the antithesis of how the Turkana system of social organization works.

When a family needs livestock because of losses associated with drought, disease, or raiding, a herd owner will utilize his social network gain access to livestock, labor, or food. Not everyone will be affected same way during a drought. Wealthy men will have distributed rds in different areas, and those who come out of a drought animals will recover more quickly. Many of their animals will d through these social networks over the course of the

accumulate livestock following losses are through the s or by raiding neighboring groups. Bridewealth in highest recorded for pastoral peoples. A typical

TABLE 10.1

Drought Stress Syndrome and Pastoral Response

Climatic Condition	Drought Stress Syndrome	Pastoral Strategies	System-Level Effects
Dry season begins	Reduction in forage quantity and quality	Move to dry season range	Livestock production maintained
Dry season intensifies	Reduction in livestock production	Subdivide herds Increase mobility Alter human diet	Livestock production drops; no other change in system function
Dry season continues	Further reduction in livestock production	Same as above, plus: Sell small stock to buy grain Bleed animals	Livestock production down Small-stock numbers reduced Human nutrition adequate Pastoral system intact
Dry season continues	Livestock condition depressed Production very low	Same as above, plus: Slaughter animals for food Dependents move from poorer families to wealthier ones	Small stock reduced Large stock weakened Human nutrition decreases Pastoral system intact
Dry season conditions turn to drought conditions	Livestock condition poor Mortality sets in	Eat dead animals Gather wild food Beg for food Some family members begin to leave pastoral sector	Herd size reduced Human nutrition depressed Pastoral system maintained
Drought intensifies	Wholesale livestock mortality Human malnutrition	Whole families leave pastoral sector Many people seek famine relief	Human survival threatened Pastoral system destroyed Relief-dependent population

Source: Adapted from Ellis et al. 1987.

try to refrain from selling animals, if they can, but most reproductive females will have either aborted or not become pregnant, so there is little herd growth. As previously mentioned, this first year may be a period of extreme hardship; without calves, the livestock will not produce milk, and because herd owners are very reluctant to sell animals, there may be very little food available for the family.

During the second year there is typically a very high fertility rate, and livestock numbers begin to increase. By the third, fourth, or fifth year, many families will have recouped their losses. But this will only happen if they have enough animals to form the basis of their household herd, and in many cases, livestock holdings will be too low for the family to remain in the pastoral sector.

The Turkana system of social organization also allows them to cope with these stresses at the family level. Each herd owner is the center of a system of social relationships that he has built up over his lifetime. Kinship provides the opportunity to become involved in a social network, although it does not require that one do so. A man's social network usually includes close male relatives, in-laws, and stock associates or friends. These networks are reinforced through the transfer of livestock. I began this chapter with a description of Angerot "borrowing" a goat from a much poorer man and noted that this was a means by which Angorot was strengthening his social ties. I once interviewed Angorot concerning livestock owed to him and livestock he owed to others. In each case there were about sixty outstanding debts. He could pay them off anytime and achieve "a balanced budget," but to do so is the antithesis of how the Turkana system of social organization works.

When a family needs livestock because of losses associated with drought, disease, or raiding, a herd owner will utilize his social network to gain access to livestock, labor, or food. Not everyone will be affected in the same way during a drought. Wealthy men will have distributed their herds in different areas, and those who come out of a drought with many animals will recover more quickly. Many of their animals will get distributed through these social networks over the course of the recovery period.

Other ways to accumulate livestock following losses are through the marriage of daughters or by raiding neighboring groups. Bridewealth in Turkana is among the highest recorded for pastoral peoples. A typical bridewealth payment includes ten to thirty cattle, ten to thirty camels, and one to two hundred small stock. A family that has lost livestock but has daughters of marriageable age can quickly recover from losses as the girls get married.

Men who have become destitute following a drought can and do raid pastoral groups neighboring the Turkana. Raiding is a quick way to rebuild herds and has become increasingly deadly with the introduction of automatic weapons. Surrounding pastoralists also have access to modern weapons, and during and following droughts, the danger of raids and counter-raids is very real.

Of course, not all Turkana recover from drought. After each drought there occurs a permanent loss of people who migrate out of Turkana district. However, for the most part the Turkana have adapted to drought through a flexible system of livestock management and through their social organization and system of social relations.

FAMINE RELIEF

During 1984–85, I examined the impact of famine relief camps on the traditional system of coping with drought among the Turkana. A detailed description of this study can be found in McCabe 1990, but I think that it is useful here to summarize some of the more important findings. The famine relief camps had major impacts on herd management and grazing orbits. At first, the Turkana placed older people and those not critical to livestock management in the camps. However, a change in policy necessitated that the whole family be present if any individual members were to receive food. Many Turkana changed their herding patterns so that they would be in proximity to the famine camps. Livestock that were already nutritionally stressed were thus forced to forage on heavily used and often overgrazed rangelands, resulting in further stress and often death. Poor families became truly destitute, with little hope for recovery.

One of the main reasons why recovery was so difficult was that those families that had migrated into the famine camps found that their pastoral friends and neighbors were less willing to give them livestock to recover from drought. Many successful Turkana felt that residents of the famine camps had spurned the traditional system and would not make good exchange partners. In addition, the number of

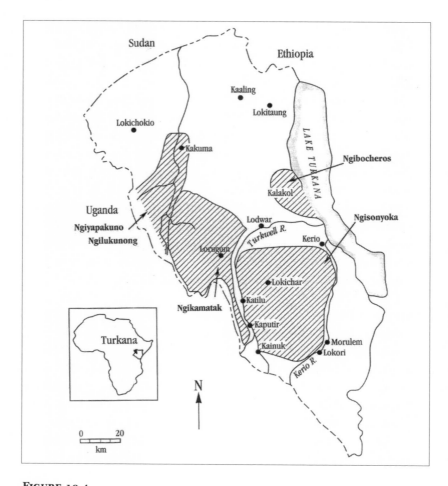

FIGURE 10.4

Turkana sections included in the drought study.

animals included in the bridewealth for their daughters dropped dramatically. The famine residents were treated in the same way as destitute pastoralists who migrated to the banks of the Turkwell to adopt cultivation. Bridewealth payments for young women from these families are often made in honey, and only a few animals are transferred.

The net result of the famine relief camps was that, although they were able to feed many people who otherwise might have had a hard time surviving, at least within the pastoral sector, the traditional system of mutual aid was shattered. However, many Turkana were able to successfully cope with the drought, and drought vulnerability was not equally shared across all sections of the Turkana.

DROUGHT VULNERABILITY

Another aspect of the 1986 study mentioned above was an examination of the impact and response to drought among four sections of the Turkana (Ellis et al. 1987). My colleagues and I focused on the 1984–85 drought but also collected information concerning the period 1980–85. We chose three other groups in addition to the Ngisonyoka for this study: the Ngikamatak, the Ngibocheros, and the Ngiyapakuno and Ngilukumong pastoralists and agro-pastoralists who lived along the Tarach River (see fig. 10.4). These groups varied with respect to the size of the area exploited, the topography and vegetal associations of their home areas, the degree of sedentarization, and their dependence on livestock for subsistence.

We collected data on household size and livestock holdings; size, topographic characteristics, type of vegetation, and biomass of dry and wet season rangelands; and degree of mobility, human diet, and livestock mortality for each of the seasons from 1980 to 1985. During this stressful period, herd owners in each section fared differently from those in other sections, with the Ngisonyoka, the Ngikamatak, and the pastoralists living along the Tarach having better nutrition and suffering less livestock loss than the Ngibocheros and the agro-pastoralists living along the Tarach. It is obviously impossible to summarize all the results of this project here, but I feel that it will be instructive to discuss our conclusions as they relate to factors that led to drought resistance and drought vulnerability. One of the obvious commonalities among those who suffered the most during this time period was that they were less mobile than the other groups. This can be illustrated by comparing the mobility pattern of the Ngibocheros (fig. 10.7) with that of the pastoralists living along the Tarach. In contrast, figures 10.5 and 10.6 show the movement pattern of the Tarach pastoralists in normal and drought years. Even in "normal" years the Tarach pastoralists move above the Rift Valley escarpment during the dry season, and during drought periods they moved very long distances into the Didinga hills in the southern Sudan. It should be noted that this long-distance migration did not occur without significant opposition from the

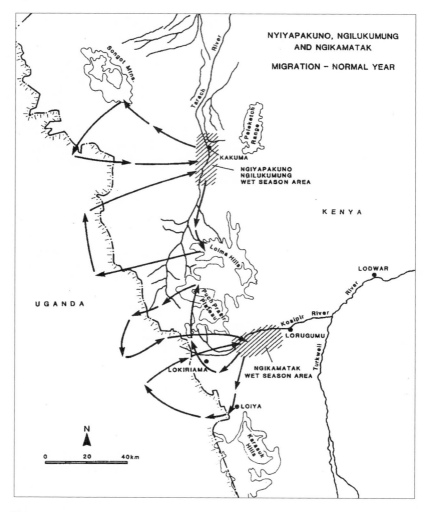

FIGURE 10.5

Ngiyapakuno, Ngilukumung, and Ngikamatak migration, normal year.

residents of the southern Sudan, but the Ngiyapakuno and Ngilukumong pastoralists pushed into these areas nevertheless. The Ngibocheros, on the other hand, chose to remain in their home area despite the environmental conditions. They utilize the gallery forest along the Turkwell River during the dry season and drought periods, but do not engage in extensive migrations.

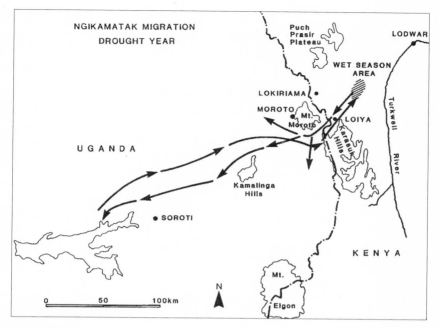

FIGURE 10.6

Ngikamatak migration, drought year.

A constricted migratory orbit was also characteristic of the agro-pastoral population. Among these people, labor demand constrained the ability of many families to separate herds for long periods of time, and the need to protect the farm necessitated that some family members remained sedentary for most of the year.

Another factor characteristic of the agro-pastoral population and the Ngibocheros was that the human population per unit of land was higher than in the other sections. Based on our overall evaluation, we constructed a table that summarized what factors we felt led to drought vulnerability and drought resistance (see table 10.2).

Although these conclusions may not be unexpected to those familiar with nomadic pastoralists, they do suggest that current trends in the development of Africa's rangelands are a cause for concern. The history of livestock development projects for East Africa shows a marked tendency to dissolve the traditional management system, based on communal rangelands, and to move to some form of privatization. Whether the

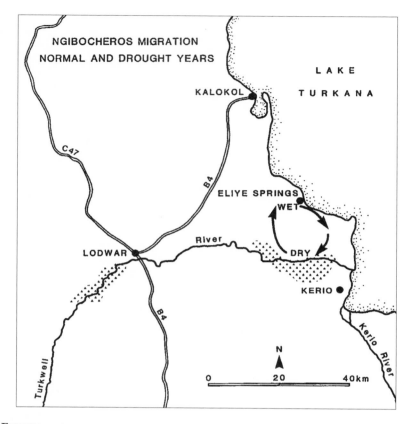

Figure 10.7

Ngibocheros migration, normal and drought years.

private holdings are in the form of individual ranches, group ranches, or grazing blocks, they reduce the size of the rangeland and make access to distant dry-season and drought-reserve pastures difficult, if not impossible. In addition, most livestock development projects stress the need for supplying meat to urban centers and thus concentrate on the raising of cattle rather than goats or camels. While this strategy may be beneficial for urban consumers, shifting livestock preference from drought-resilient animals to species that are more prone to suffer during droughts puts pastoral people increasingly at risk.

Pastoral rangelands have also been restricted through the creation of national parks and reserves. Although conservation policy has had

TABLE 10.2

Factors Leading to Drought Resistance and Drought Vulnerability

	Drought Resistance	Drought Vulnerability
Regional size	Large	Small
Vegetation biomass	High	Low
Range diversity	High	Low
Access to dry season range	Free access	Restricted access
Browsers vs. grazers	Browsers	Grazers
Livestock vs. cultivation	Livestock	Cultivation
Stocking rates	Low/moderate	High
Human density	Low	High
TLU[1]/person	High	Low

Source: Ellis et al. 1987.

[1]TLU = tropical livestock unit = 250 kg live weight.

significant impacts on the pastoral people of East Africa, the revenue generated by national parks usually goes to the national treasury, with little returning to the local communities. Some areas, such as Maasai Mara Game Reserve and Amboseli National Park in Kenya, have attempted to channel portions of gate receipts back to local residents, but so far the results of these attempts have been mixed.

Not connected to development per se are changes that are occurring in pastoral economies throughout Africa. Pastoral people who have traditionally depended on livestock for their subsistence are rapidly adopting agriculture. My own work has shown that over 80 percent of the Maasai in Ngorongono adopted agriculture when allowed to, and surveys in other parts of Tanzania have noted the same trend (McCabe 1997a, 1997b). Furthermore, the numbers of people in the arid and semiarid rangelands are increasing, but there is no indication that livestock populations are. Thus, the number of livestock per person is decreasing. In Ngorongoro, I noted the beginning of a breakdown in the traditional system of exchanging livestock, as the livestock population was no longer able to support the human population (McCabe 1992).

These changes suggest that African pastoral peoples, who have proven successful in coping with drought and recovering from drought stress, are becoming more vulnerable to drought. An important goal for many of those engaged in hazards research is to assist planners in making communities less vulnerable to hazards (Mileti 1997). In many of the arid rangelands throughout the world, sustainable, hazard-resilient communities that have existed for generations, and perhaps millennia, are being undermined. A growing human population and loss of grazing land has meant that the pastoralists of today are denser, more dependent upon cultivation, and less mobile than their ancestors. As our 1986 study demonstrated, these factors increase vulnerability to environmental hazards, such as drought.

CONCLUSIONS

The Turkana case study demonstrates that a hazards approach in anthropology can make important theoretical contributions and has significant practical applications. Vayda and McCay's call for ecological anthropologists to concentrate their research on how people adapt to environmental hazards was rarely heeded. Ecosystem studies continued to be conducted but fell out of favor as attacks against equilibrium-based studies became more vehement. The work by ecologists, such as Ellis and Swift, has demonstrated that ecosystem studies need not be based on equilibrium models, and that in addition to incorporating drought into their theoretical framework, the framework itself can be based on the impact of drought. The case study also demonstrates that the Turkana view drought as a normal part of the environment within which they live, the point advocated by Hewitt (1983) and Glantz (1987) in the 1980s and by García-Acosta (this volume).

The case study further demonstrates that development planners must take into account how indigenous peoples cope with environmental stress and how the projects they are involved with will impact coping strategies. The need to understand indigenous coping strategies may be as vital for stress-prone communities in the United States as it is for East African pastoralists. One goal in the process of building hazard-resilient communities should be an examination of traditional coping strategies and how project design can build upon and help strengthen what is already there.

This case study also illustrates many of the issues highlighted by other authors in the volume. Oliver-Smith notes that disasters are multidimensional and that it is important to view disasters as a process. Certainly such is the case if one is to understand how Turkana pastoralists cope with drought. García-Acosta mentions that disasters can be "revealers," again, a point particularly relevant for the Turkana. One cannot understand many aspects of Turkana social organization until one understands the role that hazards such as drought play, and the full meaning of many aspects of their social organization are not "revealed" until one examines the whole process of drought and recovery. Moseley places special emphasis on the idea of "convergent catastrophes." As previously mentioned, drought, disease, and raiding fit clearly into this conceptual framework. Finally, Dyer uses the concept of "punctuated entropy" to examine how societies become progressively more vulnerable to disasters. Although he is concerned with natural hazards, I think that the role of development has had a similar impact on many pastoral peoples in the world today.

We are only beginning to scratch the surface in understanding the importance of disaster research for anthropology. It can be used as a tool in examining daily life and aspects of social organization. It can lead to theory building for anthropology, much in the way it has for the ecology of arid land ecosystems. It brings together anthropologists from many different backgrounds and theoretical persuasions (as evidenced in this volume) to address a common problem. All this suggests that those who have been advocating this approach for years will finally see their aspirations realized as the field of disaster research in anthropology emerges into the mainstream of anthropological work.

Notes

1. The subject of this chapter is the impact of, and response to, drought among Turkana pastoralists in northwestern Kenya. A number of the participants at the School of American Research seminar were concerned with

drought, and this paper complements chapters written by Moseley and García-Acosta in this regard. The process by which populations adapt to environmental stresses was also a major concern of the seminar participants, and in this context this paper fits well with chapters by Dyer, Moseley, and Oliver-Smith. There are also a number of cross-cutting themes of particular importance to the authors contributing to this book, and where appropriate I will refer the reader to these chapters. Examples of such themes are differential vulnerability to disasters by certain segments of the population and the consideration of a disaster as a "process" rather than an event.

2. A more thorough description of an "idealized" annual round may be found in McCabe and Ellis (1987).

11

Missing Expertise, Categorical Politics, and Chronic Disasters

The Case of Bhopal

S. Ravi Rajan

Anthony Oliver-Smith and Susanna Hoffman began their introduction to this volume by stating, "The conjunction of a human population and a potentially destructive agent does not inevitably produce a disaster." Their essay, and the case studies that follow it, argue instead that "a disaster becomes unavoidable in the context of a historically produced pattern of vulnerability."[1] In making such an argument, the various chapters of this book have identified patterns involving infrastructure and organization, the political economies of production and distribution, and societal outlooks to hazard and risk, across a range of disasters and cultural contexts. This chapter, which continues to explore this recurrent theme, focuses on two phenomena that have, in different ways, appeared in the preceding chapters. They are perhaps best described as "missing expertise" and "categorical politics."[2]

The idea of "missing expertise" concerns civil administrations and other institutions of the state. It refers to the phenomenon wherein the production of the potential for risk is not matched by a concomitant creation of expertise and institutions with the wherewithal to help mitigate a crisis, should one ensue. Many of the cases discussed in this book, including those that dealt with Chernobyl, Woburn, and Valdez, have tacitly, if not explicitly, identified some aspect of missing expertise. The first object in this chapter is to construct a heuristic taxonomy of the different aspects of this phenomenon.

The phrase "categorical politics" concerns the civil society, and in particular, activist organizations. It refers to forms of political intervention that are driven solely by framing social problems via some overarching structural analysis, and that either ignore or dismiss phenomena that are not visible through their theoretical lens.

The central argument in this chapter is that the combination of missing expertise in the state and the preponderance of categorical politics among the civil society often produces a pattern of vulnerability that results in perpetrating chronic disasters. The case is made with reference to the world's worst chemical disaster to date, involving the U.S. multinational company Union Carbide in Bhopal, India, in December 1984.[3] The first part of this chapter explores the different types of missing expertise in the state by analyzing the efficacy of the governmental relief and rehabilitation schemes. The second half examines the responses of social activists and anthropologists with the view to elaborating upon the problems associated with categorical politics.

THE STATE AND THE PROBLEM OF MISSING EXPERTISE

Anthropological studies of disasters have identified a number of types of administrative expertise requisite for effective disaster mitigation (Oliver-Smith 1996). For purely heuristic reasons, it is useful to classify them under three categories—contingent, conceptual, and ethnographic. Each of these types of expertise was lacking, in varying degrees, in Bhopal. The purpose of this section is to examine the nature of such missing expertise.

Contingent Expertise

Contingent expertise refers to an administration's preparedness to respond immediately and effectively to a potential hazard. It is concerned, therefore, with the conscious adaptive mechanisms and institutions built by governments prior to cataclysmic events. Such institutions include warning systems, evacuation procedures, and other measures that help mitigate the societal impact of the disaster in the immediate aftermath.

By all accounts, contingent expertise in Bhopal was conspicuous by its absence. The state government, for example, was unable to evacuate the population from the scene of the gas leak, despite a policy decision to do so after the accident had been confirmed. Again, there was no attempt by the government, on the night of the disaster, to communicate effectively with the people by, for example, informing them, through the radio or other means, about how to respond to the gas leak. For example, a simple announcement suggesting that people cover their faces with wet cloth could have prevented considerable injury. Moreover, it took forty hours for the government to set up the first coordination meeting of secretaries and heads of departments to develop an effective relief strategy. In the meantime, more than two thousand animal carcasses littered the streets and houses and posed a severe public health threat (CSE 1985:218).

The absence of effective contingency planning by the state bureaucracy to tackle a scenario such as the gas leak of December 1984 meant that there was no agency or scheme that had the training or the wherewithal to do the job. The Indian army, which was deployed by the state to evacuate the stricken area on the night of the disaster, made a heroic attempt but was overpowered by the sheer enormity of the task and the absence of a rehearsed method to cope with it. The same is true for a variety of other agencies and individuals involved in relief efforts in the immediate aftermath, including medical professionals and voluntary service agencies (CSE 1985:209).

In discussing the absence of contingent expertise, it is instructive to compare the Bhopal case with governmental responses to more conventional disasters, such as famines, floods, and cyclones. In a number of examples state governments were able to respond reasonably efficiently, primarily because there was a prior systemic recognition of potential threats and a concomitant erection of reactive mechanisms, in addition to effective training at various levels of the governmental bureaucracy. Such recognition and institution building, in turn, was a consequence of the politicization of vulnerability, and consequent societal mobilization.[4]

The absence of contingent expertise is most evident in two specific types of contexts. One of these involves novel hazards, such as industrial and technological accidents; Bhopal is a prime example. The other context is where the scale of the disaster is immense. The Orissa cyclone of 1999 and the Gujarat earthquake of 2001 are infamous examples. In both novel accidents and large-scale calamities, the absence of contingent expertise is a consequence of the scope of the hazard exceeding existing state capacity to cope with it. Crucially, in each of these two types of cases, three critical features present in the successful adaptive systems set up to meet the threat of low-scale conventional disasters are missing. The first of these is hazard awareness. The administration in Bhopal, for example, did not know the full potential of the threat posed by the Union Carbide pesticides factory. Likewise, the Orissa state government did not have prior knowledge that a storm of such intensity could strike. Again, the administrations in Gujarat and Uttar Pradesh were unaware of the underlying seismic threat. In each case, the respective governments failed to scope out potential hazards and generate systematic data on possible threats.

The second missing feature involves efforts, on the basis of such awareness, to minimize either the onset of the threat or its impact when a cataclysmic event occurs. Effective monitoring of the plant in Bhopal, building early warning systems and shelters in Orissa, and enforcing building codes in Uttar Pradesh and Gujarat, are examples in this regard. The third missing feature is the absence of the infrastructure needed to effectively respond to a disaster, should one ensue. Such infrastructure includes the deployment of appropriate technological systems, the provision of adequate training to designated staff, and effective risk communication procedures in the wake of a hazardous event.[5]

The experience of erecting functional institutions to deal with conventional disasters of low intensity indicates that there is no a priori reason why novel and large-scale disasters cannot equally be subject to effective contingent planning. Missing expertise, in such contexts, therefore reflects a general absence of societal and cultural prioritization of the need to build such expertise. Such absences speak to a wider problem in India, which concerns the cultures of risk and the political economy of hazard in society as a whole. In this sense, the Bhopal gas disaster is indeed a canary in the mine, pointing to a more entrenched and perhaps intractable set of social factors that underlie how risk and vulnerability are framed and tackled.

Conceptual Expertise

Most disasters manifest as sudden, catastrophic events. Although devastating by nature, their period of intensity is short. Many disasters, however, metamorphose into chronic events, affecting communities over months and, in some cases, years and decades. Chronic disasters, by their very nature, demand a wide range of expertise, over and beyond the contingent. One type is best described as "conceptual expertise," the kind needed to devise long-term rehabilitation strategies and to trouble-shoot them in practice.

The absence of this type of expertise in Bhopal was evident in the manner in which the state government approached the task of social and economic rehabilitation. The first attempts to address the immense problem involved tested strategies conventionally used in responding to natural disasters, such as ex gratia payments to the victims' families to help tide them through the immediate crisis, and the distribution of clothes, food, blankets, and other material goods (CSE 1985:222). When it became clear that such piecemeal methods were not going to suffice because of the lingering, chronic character of the disaster, the administration realized that it was faced with the fundamental challenge of devising an innovative economic rehabilitation strategy. As M. N. Buch, a retired civil servant and an important contributor to the plan for New Bhopal, then argued, such a program had to address two central issues. It had to be economically feasible, while at the same time being ergonomically viable for the physically injured survivors.[6]

By the first anniversary of the gas disaster, the state administration faced mounting public pressure to launch an effective rehabilitation program. In a bid to address this pressing problem and to cope with a public relations crisis, the government proposed a rehabilitation strategy that, in essence, combined three standard regional development programs already underway elsewhere in the state. The first of these consisted of an attempt to attract private companies to "develop commercial, services and industrial sectors" and "clean services industries" such as "servicing, repairs, electronics, etc.," in a bid to plug the "void in the economic life of this part of the city." The second component was to "train people so that they can acquire new skills and get employment in works not involving hard labour" and, further, to employ those people who could not compete in the open market in "small public sector units or units run by services organizations." The government's third scheme involved helping people in "setting up their own businesses." To this end, it decided to bring to the gas-affected parts of Bhopal an urban poverty alleviation plan already in force in other regions of the state of Madhya Pradesh, the Special Training and Employment Program for the Urban Poor (STEP-UP), itself a derivative of the Integrated Rural Development Program (IRDP), the governmental poverty-elimination scheme for rural areas across India. STEP-UP envisaged small loans to help individuals start businesses in the retail and service sectors. The government would serve as a guarantor and a provider of training in skills where needed (Rajan 1988).

These three schemes were conceived in the absence of adequate socioeconomic and other relevant data on the survivors. Moreover, they were launched without systematic feasibility studies (Rajan 1999). The programs consequently began to unravel almost from the outset. The attempt at attracting firms failed; although some big industrial companies had offered to help, they did not keep their initial promises. According to one official, "Once we began negotiating, we found the terms of the private houses were too exploitative. They wanted subsidies, land, but were not willing to put much in. They were just looking for cheap labor."[7] The production facilities, too, collapsed for similar reasons. According to Ishwar Das, then commissioner of gas relief, "We had thought of developing Bhopal as an export center. But the idea has not clicked. It requires sophisticated machines, a much higher quality of garments produced, and a link-up with export houses. The private sector has not, however, pitched in. Governmental agencies such as the railways which had been approached have already got other agencies supplying their needs."[8] The government had overestimated the potential of these centers, which closed down within a year of being launched due to sheer economic inviability. The fate of the third governmental scheme, STEP-UP, was no different. A transplant from another policy context, it had not been designed for the situation in Bhopal after the accident, where an enormous number of victims were concentrated in a small geographical area. Consequently this program, too, unraveled.

The failure of conceptual expertise in Bhopal was also evident in the governmental medical rehabilitation program, which, like the socioeconomic program, suffered from a critical systemic disability to effectively mobilize expertise. A telling example was the Thyiocyanate controversy over how to diagnose and treat those who had been exposed to the poisonous gas during the leak.

Two schools of medical thought emerged. One of these, the so-called pulmonary pathology theory, postulated that "small amounts of cyanide...much larger than [those] which would normally produced in the body, [are] continuously contributed to the cyanogen pool of the gas victims from MIC (Methyl Isocyanate) molecules which are attached to alpha chains of hemoglobin molecules...Cyanide blocks the activity of a large number of enzymes but the most important from the point of view of its effects is the enzyme called cytochrome oxidase in all the cells, which controls oxygen utilization of the cells. This leads to under-utilization or non-utilization of oxygen at the cellular level producing chronic hypoxia which is responsible for the whole range of symptoms" (MFC 1985:10). It claimed, in short, that all of the mortality and the prevalent morbidity in the gas-hit population of Bhopal were exclusively due to "direct injury to lung tissues which over a period will lead to diffuse pulmonary fibrosis" (MFC 1985:6).

The second medical hypothesis, the "enlarged cyanogen pool theory," contended that MIC, being a highly reactive chemical, would have damaged those organs it had come directly in contact with, such as the lungs, eyes, and skin. However, in direct contradiction to the cyanogen pool theory, it argued that there was "no metabolic pathway that converts isocyanate into cyanide"(MFC 1985:8). The counter-theory it proposed was that of chronic cyanide poisoning of the victims due to an enlarged cyanogen pool, in addition to lung and eye damage (MFC 1985:6).

Existing evidence at that time supported both theories but did not establish either beyond doubt. The only way to resolve the controversy, under these circumstances, was to engage in long-term research projects on topics ranging from the toxicology of the MIC to the epidemiology of the gas-affected population. The premier Indian medical body, the Indian Council of Medical Research (ICMR), along with other agencies, committed itself to laying the groundwork for just such a program of research (CSE 1985:219–20).

For the gas victims, however, the intensity of their suffering demanded a more immediate response. The challenge for the medical rehabilitation establishment was to somehow devise a pragmatic strategy of treatment while being committed to long-term research. As several voluntary organizations of doctors, such as the Medico Friends Circle, pointed out, there was no reason why a strategy that pragmatically combined both theories could not be devised and implemented, pending revision after rigorous scientific research (MFC 1985). Rather than adopt such an approach, however, the proponents of the cyanogen pool and fibrosis theories in Bhopal began to fiercely contest one another's theories. These conflicts had multiple origins. At the outset, there were personality clashes and power struggles between some of the key doctors involved. Next, various doctors adopted an inflexible philosophy of science that demanded extremely strict criteria of scientific certainty as the basis of any treatment procedure. Each faction used ad hominem arguments to challenge its opponents. As a result, the medical establishment in Bhopal persisted in an inconclusive theoretical debate while neglecting the primary issue of the health of the gas victims. Meanwhile the ICMR, a prestigious national agency vested with power and resources, failed to intervene quickly and with the necessary credibility to bring the controversy to the kind of closure that would have enabled effective treatment while at the same time committing to the long-term research that could resolve the controversy (Sathyamala 1988; MFC 1985).

A common feature underlying both the economic and medical rehabilitation programs was that the state administration failed to diagnose the nature of the problem of rehabilitation methodically and then be pragmatic in designing appropriate responses. This lack was augmented by the inability of the government to troubleshoot the failure of its programs. Governmental officials themselves were often angry about the course of events. In the aftermath of an intense day of protests outside his office, for example, a young governmental official in charge of implementing the governmental program expressed his frustration that despite his hard work, there was little tangible benefit to the victims.[9] The wider issue raised by him and other officials was that national social science and policy institutions that they had contacted, such as the Tata Institute for Social Sciences and the Indian Institutes of Management, had failed to help either in designing the rehabilitation programs or troubleshooting their failure.

Unlike the case of contingent expertise, the absence of conceptual expertise needs to be addressed with much more than rehearsed responses. To begin with, it demands a dynamic and pragmatic approach to governance, especially one that builds institutions that expand the role of government beyond the traditional domains of preserving law and order and collecting taxes. Effecting such types of governance, in turn, demands investment in a wide range of training for civil officials. At the same time, the absence of conceptual expertise in Bhopal points to the need to augment the capacity of the social science and policy institutions. In contrast to its natural science and technological institutions, Indian social science has suffered from both an absence of defined mission and poor funding. As a result, there has been little systematic investment in building the kinds of conceptual expertise needed to address complex problems such as postdisaster rehabilitation. However, if the recent successes in the forestry and water sectors are indicators, such expertise can be built in a relatively short time, if there is concerted interest and funding (Saxena 1997; Poffenberger and McGean 1998). For this to happen, however, it is important first to recognize the absence of conceptual expertise as a critical issue worthy of national attention.

Ethnographic Expertise

If the socioeconomic and medical rehabilitation programs were conceived poorly, the character of the day-to-day interactions between the bureaucracy and the gas victims diminished what little chance they had of success. One arena where the impact of such interactions was particularly palpable was the process of getting the bureaucracy to formally acknowledge someone a victim so that he or she could benefit from the governmental rehabilitation schemes. For that to happen, a victim needed to procure the appropriate official certificate. This crucial piece of paper, however, was only given when a series of other documents, testifying to everything from proof of residence to exposure to the gas, were produced. As a tailor put it, "You may be badly affected, you may be coughing violently, you may show scars on your body, but if you don't have the necessary papers, you have no chance" (Rajan

1988:16). This was no trivial matter. In a survey conducted in mid-1985, it emerged that only 25 percent of the households reported having hospital admission certificates, and only 600 of a total surveyed population of 18,000 households reported having had blood tests or X-ray records (Rajan 1988:16). In the absence of such records it was next to impossible to claim the status of a victim without a bribe. Even where claimants possessed the requisite documentation, they had to negotiate a series of further hurdles. For example, they had to fill out a form applying to be recognized as a victim. The complexity of the form, and the accompanying hassles of document procurement, made it difficult for the average Bhopal survivor to satisfy the requirements of the claims process. Ultimately, this meant that the victim became totally dependent on expensive touts for an act as basic as filling out the claim.

Yet another set of examples illustrating the interaction of the victim and the bureaucracy were visible in the medical rehabilitation system. At the outset, the hospital as a physical space was one of the most inhospitable places imaginable, with long queues and waiting periods in crowded corridors and rooms. Moreover, patients had to endure hostile staff members, who, across the range from clerks to doctors, saw the extra numbers as further burden to their work. If the physical space reduced the patient to an insignificant entity in a big and impersonal medical machine, the verbal transactions between the hospital staff and the gas victims reflected the unequal power gradient between them. The language and tone of the staff were dismissive, often bordering on the contemptuous, echoing the clearly evident lines of class and, in some cases, gender and religion that separated them. Illiterate and poor, the gas-affected patient was in a definite sense a liminal entity, and significantly "different" enough as to be almost monstrous.[10] Equally important, by refusing to respond to treatment, the victim was a perpetual burden.

Given this wider hubris, the medical community in Bhopal invented a language to talk about, if not explain, the sheer monstrosity of the gas victim. Women's gynecological problems stemming from the effects of the gas inhalation, for example, were systematically denied and repeatedly attributed to factors such as "faking," "psychological," or "poverty and poor hygiene" (MFC 1985; Sathyamana 1988:30). Men's problems were attributed to "compensation neurosis" or to wider social factors, such as baseline diseases like tuberculosis

(Sathyamana 1988:30). Underlying such language was an institutional-ized "scientific" point of view that privileged one form of knowing over another. Subjective testimonies did not count. Indeed, the average interview between the doctor and the patient involved little in the way of conversation or an attempt to understand the physical and emo-tional pain of the victim. Instead, the patient was often treated as a car-rier of disease, which could be objectively measured and treated.

The government-run medical rehabilitation program, therefore, had neither a theory nor a praxis of healing. The gas victims, as a con-sequence, were often forced to go to private practitioners, many of whom had no formal certification and were referred to as quacks by the medical establishment. It is important to ask why so many gas victims patronized their practices. Talking to the practitioners provided impor-tant clues. The practitioners did not rely on medical theory as the basis of their cure, but on an instrumental matching of symptoms with what they knew of the products belonging to a range of medical systems, including homeopathic, unani, ayurvedic, and allopathic. Their objec-tive was less to advance medical theory than to find temporary cures and, in the process, advance their clientele. Undoubtedly, there are important ethical issues involved in such a practice, especially consider-ing the fact that these practitioners were for the most part college dropouts. It is noteworthy that at least some of them were good listen-ers and provided not just drugs but a space wherein the victims felt that their subjective testimonies did count and that they could express their pain in the vernacular (BGIA 1986).

These examples serve to illustrate the third category of missing expertise, best described as "ethnographic." Such expertise refers to an ability to gain a contextual and grounded understanding and to act on the basis of such experience. In Bhopal, the existence of ethnographic expertise could have engendered a radically redesigned claim form or a change in the nature of the doctor-patient interaction. Attention to small details such as these could have altered the lives of the victims in tangibly positive ways. Unlike contingent and conceptual forms of expertise, which, as issues of contention, periodically enter the public and political arena, ethnographic expertise has rarely made it into the pantheon of what is considered the criteria of good governance. Indeed, it is a specific insight provided by anthropological studies of disasters (Oliver-Smith 1996). Translating the idea of ethnographic expertise into an explicit set of practices, however, requires the development of innovations and iterative experimental alliances between anthropologists and bureaucracies. For this to happen, it is critical for anthropologists to stake their expertise and be willing to break the barrier between the pure and the applied, the descriptive and the prescriptive modes of thinking. Unfortunately, as the next section will describe, this did not happen in Bhopal, which says something about the discipline at large.

MISSING EXPERTISE AND THE "NO-RISK" HYPOTHESIS

The phenomenon of missing expertise, characterized by the absence of contingent, conceptual, and ethnographic expertise, bears some family resemblances to the "no-risk" thesis advanced by Paine in this volume. In Bhopal, as in the cases discussed by Paine, there was a cultural context and logic that resulted in a cognitive repression of risk.

At the outset, it can be argued that the state and central governments in Bhopal were, like the Basque separatists described by Paine, "aggressively purposive" in embracing danger for "its cleansing and fortifying properties." In the case of Bhopal, these had to do with the calculus of nation building, wherein costs and benefits were weighted and certain dangers embraced in the "national interest." Missing expertise and risk repression, here, were important residues of societal decisions, tacit or implicit, of "acceptable risk."

The theory of missing expertise is similar to the "no-risk" hypothesis in at least one further respect. In Bhopal, as well as in the cases described by Paine and Stephens (this volume), experts played a critical role in suppressing risk. They did this by discounting the perceptions and concerns of "lay" peoples, whom they characterized with phrases such as "uneducated" and "irrational." In the process, they demanded that "individuals stop thinking like individuals." Given a social hierarchy in which experts wield considerable power over the lives of lay peoples while insulated from any backlash by their systemic facelessness, victims and ordinary people had few places to turn to have their fears mollified or their subjective pain heard.

There is an important difference between the idea of missing expertise and the "no-risk" hypothesis. The latter, at least as formulated by Paine (this volume), is deterministic in the sense that it argues that "risk repression is the ultimate goal" and that "risk avoidance is a strategy towards that end." There is, however, no clear evidence that this was true in the Bhopal case. At worst, risk avoidance by experts was a contingent phenomenon having to do with factors such as preconceived biases and poor training. Such contingency makes the case for "missing expertise," as opposed to structured risk avoidance, as an explanation of the way the events transpired. Regardless of whether we choose the "missing expertise" or "no-risk" theories as the frameworks for analyzing the culture of catastrophe, it is critical to locate the social production of vulnerability in a wider, political frame. In Bhopal, the phenomenon of missing expertise cannot be adequately described without attending to the political and moral economy in which it is embedded.

There are at least three aspects to a politics of missing expertise. First are the fundamental, structural divisions in society, having to do with factors such as class, caste, gender, and religion, that separated one victim from another, and victims from the state administration and the community at large. As author Arundhati Roy has argued with respect to a different kind of Indian disaster, the Narmada dam, "There is no egalitarian social contact whatsoever between the two worlds...So when the bottom half of society simply shears off and falls away, it happens silently. It doesn't create the torsion, the upheaval, the blowout, the sheer structural damage that it might, had there been the equivalent of vertical bolts. This works perfectly for the supporters of these projects" (Ram 2001). Indeed, such deep-rooted divisions rule out either wider societal concern or empathy.

A related facet of the politics of missing expertise is the liminality of the victim and the sheer banality of poverty alleviation as a statist project. Indeed, if one contrasts the rehabilitation effort in Bhopal with most governmental poverty alleviation programs across India, the events following the disaster do not in fact appear pathological but quite normal. The Bhopal case merely mirrors the wider persistence of poverty despite numerous "poverty alleviation" programs.

Yet another aspect of the politics of missing expertise in Bhopal has to do with the capture of the state by a variety of vested interests. At the fore was the Union Carbide Company, which launched a systematic campaign of erasure that included manufacturing evidence to discount the enlarged cyanogen pool theory. Other societal forces that effected capture were the chemical industry at large, and the national and local politicians and their minions who stood to gain from the construction of the plant. Given a company culture that preferred to sacrifice safety for profit, these local actors produced a culture of corruption that both helped produce a "no-risk" culture as well as perpetrate the dynamic of missing expertise.[11] The subcultures of denial (no-risk) and absence or withdrawal (missing expertise) were, in essence, two sides of the same coin.

Undoubtedly the phenomenon of missing expertise is not adequately understood without locating it in factors such as social stratification, the political economy of the state and private capital, and the ambitions and aspirations of those groups who seek to capture the state for their own ends. At the same time, it is important not to conflate the problem of missing expertise with such wider, societal issues. Unless missing expertise, as an issue, gets politicized as a separate category, problems such as those that arose in Bhopal due to the absence of contingent, conceptual, and ethnographic expertise will be reproduced even in an egalitarian utopia. Conversely, it is important to recognize that efforts to build state capacity and expertise, as, for example, in the case of community forestry and irrigation, and cyclone warning and evacuation, have yielded important and socially beneficial results.

THE CIVIL SOCIETY AND CATEGORICAL POLITICS

The analysis of the politics of missing expertise in Bhopal is incomplete until one more important question is addressed. Why, despite democracy, a free press, a vibrant civil society, and the presence of a socially concerned (and often activist) academic community that included world-class anthropologists, did the phenomenon of missing expertise fail to be addressed, let alone resolved? One answer to this question lies in a distinction between categorical and pragmatic interventions. The distinction is best illustrated by examining two leading civic actors in Bhopal: the activist organization Zahreeli Gas Khand Sangharsh Morcha (roughly translated as the "Poisonous Gas-Event Struggle Front," hereafter called the Morcha), and a small group of anthropologists from the University of Delhi.

The Morcha
The Morcha was formed in response to the disaster and saw itself

primarily as a political movement. Its rank and file included many motivated gas victims and dedicated volunteers from smaller towns in Madhya Pradesh state, such as Indore, and from the city of Bhopal. It also included middle-class activists from cities like Delhi, Bombay, and Calcutta. The Morcha's perspective on the disaster stand is perhaps best summarized in the following article that was first published in the *Economic and Political Weekly* on the first anniversary of the gas leak:

> The Morcha contends that the gas victims have the legal right to free and comprehensive medical relief as well as economic rehabilitation and compensation; that the Union Carbide (UC) and the government are not only morally but legally obliged to provide such relief speedily but they alone possess adequate resources to do so; that the moral obligation of the Indian citizens is to see that this is done. The priority task to this end is to engage all efforts to persuade and pressurize the UC and the government to fulfill their obligation instead of frittering away time and energy in philanthropic operations sustained by funding from dubious sources...the Bhopal disaster is not identical with run-of-the mill natural calamities. Here the politics of secrecy, the politics of multinationals, legal liability, the absence of a democratic polity, federal culture in the state machinery, etc. have all contributed to build up a complex web of mystery, conspiracy, conflict and apathy. Hence the overriding priority of agitation and mass action. (Das 1985)

Underlying the Morcha's perspective was the notion that there could be only two types of responses to Bhopal. One was what it described as the "reformist," which essentially concentrated on providing relief without challenging wider political and structural issues. The other was the "revolutionary," which implied mass mobilization to force the state to provide people with what they were entitled to. In drawing such a distinction and adopting the latter approach, the Morcha believed that the class composition of the state would prevent it from providing effective rehabilitation and justice. Such a structural and categorical analysis was however founded upon one important assumption—that the government possessed the expertise to erect an effective rehabilitation program, or could mobilize such a program, if it had the political will. It is evident from the previous section that the government did not necessarily have the requisite political will. At the same time, the failure of its rehabilitation programs was equally a result of missing expertise. The Morcha's underlying structural analysis could have been tested had alternatives been proposed and the government challenged to implement them.

The Morcha initially stated that it would indeed adopt such an approach. In its early statements, it claimed that it would present "people's plans" as alternatives to the governmental schemes of relief and rehabilitation. It also committed to establishing a network of national and international organizations to debate and act on the "larger issues" raised by Bhopal (Das 1985). In practice, however, the thrust of the Morcha's program was on mobilizing the gas-affected people against the state government. It therefore organized large rallies and demonstrations against the government and the company, at which it addressed some of the people's most pressing material anxieties, and helped draft various petitions and demands that it made to the state government on behalf of the victims.

The Morcha's strategy, thus, was mobilization, based upon a categorical politics. It was successful, to an extent, in attracting the gas-affected victims to its rallies, but it failed to systematically address the issue of rehabilitation and the wider problem of growing social and economic destitution. Due to its obsession with demonstrating its doctrine, which discriminated sharply between revolutionary and reformist activities and deemed the issue of rehabilitation to be of the latter category, the Morcha refused to engage with the governmental rehabilitation program. It also failed to analyze the reasons for the government program's failure and suggest viable alternatives. By not recognizing that the breakdown of the governmental program of rehabilitation was due as much to the complex nature of the problem and to the related problem of missing expertise in the state as it was to factors such as class apathy, the Morcha's rhetoric became a self-fulfilling prophesy.

It is difficult to imagine what might have happened had the Morcha produced a set of blueprints for a rehabilitation program. Conceivably, the state bureaucracy might have ignored its alternative, but such thought is purely speculative. Moreover, it is important to recognize that, like the governmental bureaucracy, the Morcha could not mobilize expertise from the rest of the nation, despite its stated commitment to do so. While part of this failure was due to Morcha's overwhelmingly categorical politics, it is important to recognize that the kinds of expertise sought and required were not forthcoming. It is instructive here to contrast the response of the medical community, which did indeed provide a range of expertise, with the social scientific community, which did not.

Categorical political perspectives like those of the Morcha have a long and complex genealogy in India. Perhaps the most important of the political impulses that make groups like the Morcha normal, rather than exceptional, has its origins in the colonial period, when the state was considered illegitimate. Just as the nationalist activists saw the colonial state as imperial and exploitative, activists on the political left have traditionally seen the postcolonial state as serving specific class interests and especially as being anti-poor.

During the past two decades two new, related persuasions have emerged. The first is the perceived illegitimacy of the project of "development" and of the interests that it ostensibly serves. The second is the urgent need to preserve "tradition," including both cultures and natures that were seen as vanishing rapidly in the context of a modernizing nation. These new directions have varied sources, ranging from the Marxist to the Gandhian and various other traditions of Indian socialism. Because of this diversity, the individuals and groups in the Morcha coalition did not and could not possibly agree on such fundamental issues as the meaning of development, the role of science and technology, the place of nature, and the importance of tradition. Yet these activists were united by a wider concern: to get rid of the structures that produced the issues each was most passionate about. For most of them, the fundamental structure that needed to be replaced was the state and what it stood for, which, for different activists, meant something different. It is for this reason that a diverse and contradictory group like the Morcha, which simultaneously espoused Marxist, nationalist, internationalist, environmentalist, antidevelopmentalist, and protraditionalist ideologies, could come in to being and thrive.

Such an approach to politics has characterized other organizations and movements in India since the mid-1970s. In many instances, coalitions with comparable constituents have produced very effective results. Obvious examples are the various resistance movements against dams, of which the Narmada struggle is the most well known, and, more recently, campaigns such as those against the patenting of indigenous seeds or wider ones such as those against globalization.

These instances, however, differed in one important way from Bhopal: They were all determined in large measure by overarching structural factors such as class, capital, and power. Addressing the post-disaster problem in Bhopal, due to the sheer novelty of the disaster, demanded attention to the specific details underlying the problem of effective social and economic rehabilitation. While the Morcha's strategy of politicizing the big structural issues was successful inasmuch as it kept the issue of Bhopal in the limelight, what was missing was a politics that simultaneously offered and organized around concrete alternatives. As argued in the previous section, what made Bhopal unique and different was the novelty of the problem. Moreover, the absence of expertise in the state to create such alternatives was not reducible to the politics of the lack of political will. For these reasons, the Bhopal disaster dictated that categorical politics be supplanted by a pragmatic one. Indeed, given that the problem of missing expertise meant diminished choice in public policy, the challenge in Bhopal was a politics that could help create more choices. This, in turn, demanded a different kind of political organization, one that could balance protest with expertise and concern with empathy, as opposed to counterposing one with the other. As it turned out, the Morcha could not transcend its categorical politics, and in the end, when the accident began to fade in public memory, many of the Morcha activists went away to re-enact their politics elsewhere.

The Anthropologists

A group of anthropologists from the University of Delhi were an important presence in Bhopal. These scholars, who were also public intellectuals of national renown, played a critical role in opening up civic space in which activist groups such as the Morcha could operate. They provided political cover for activities that ranged from grassroots mobilization to civic protest by helping to legitimize the importance of such activities in a democracy. They were also instrumental in ensuring that the state police and administration did not unduly harass activists.[12] The anthropologists in Bhopal played another important role. They helped produce a rich and substantive interpretation of the disaster that helped to frame the public discourse on its meaning. This critique had at least three important components. At the outset, it drew attention to the politics of corporate power, the operation of multinational agencies, and the latent corruption in the Indian state system. Second, it opened up the question of the relevance of green revolution technologies and the wider issue of technological choice. It also theorized about the cultural politics of development and its conceptual and ideological underpinnings. Last but by no means least, it helped produce an innovative analysis of social suffering and its underlying causes, including factors such as the nature of bureaucracies and the assumptions in the social scientific calculations underlying public policy (Das 1995; Visvanathan 1988).

Beyond doubt, the contributions of the anthropologists were crucial and important, both in tangible, political terms, such as helping to maintain a civic space for protest and dissent, and in terms of their wider contribution to the disciplines of political ecology and cultural studies of science and development. At the same time, the anthropologists in Bhopal made no systematic attempt to engage with the bureaucracy pragmatically. It is important to note here that, as sensitive field anthropologists, they did have a well-developed sense of the nature of missing ethnographic expertise. For example, they were among the first to notice the politics underlying the claims process. Yet they failed to translate their ethnographically derived insights into concrete suggestions on how to improve the governmental rehabilitation program. They failed, in particular, to articulate a scenario of ethnographically enriched policy.

Perhaps most important, though, the anthropologists in Bhopal did not problematize or politicize the problem of missing expertise in a manner that could have helped catalyze social and administrative learning. Their academic and activist work was premised upon the idea that careful analysis of the character of the cultures of bureaucracies, the ideologies of development, and the structure of the state had potential to open up public discourse and civic action in ways amenable to the empowerment of marginal communities. In adopting such a perspective, however, they tacitly, though perhaps not deliberately,

conflated the problem of missing expertise in Bhopal, which they recognized, with the big structural questions they were concerned with as
cultural anthropologists confronting the issues of state and development in a country like India.

Moreover, they could not transcend their reflexive critique of the
hubris of experts and stake the relevance of their own expertise. The
combination of a theoretical stance that looked upon Bhopal as a phenomenon that manifested wider structural issues, as opposed to a disaster that posed specific and particular challenges for those involved in
rehabilitation, along with a reticence to enter the fray as experts in
their own right, meant that the anthropologists could neither identify
the specific areas of missing expertise nor help address the problem.
Again, like the bureaucracy and the state government, they were
unable to mobilize expertise to tackle some of the more intractable
aspects of the governmental rehabilitation program.

Given that the Indian anthropologists are in many respects a part
of a wider international disciplinary community, it is important to ask
the question of how much their activities in Bhopal resonate with those
within their discipline internationally. It is very useful here to discuss an
important and influential work in the anthropology of environment
and development, James Ferguson's *The Anti Politics Machine* (1990).
After presenting a sensitive and detailed ethnography of the character
of the state and a developmental project in Lesotho, South Africa,
Ferguson turns to the broader question of the relevance of anthropological expertise. In a short but lucid essay that offers much that is of
relevance to the Bhopal story, Ferguson (1990:283–84) writes,

> There is not one question —"What is to be done"—but hun-
> dreds...It seems, at the least, presumptuous to offer prescrip-
> tions here. The toiling miners and the abandoned old women
> know the tactics proper to their situation better than the expert
> does. Indeed the only general answer to the question, "What
> should they do?" is: "They are doing it"...For anyone who
> shares the political commitments I have been discussing, mak-
> ing "development" the form of one's intellectual political
> engagement would seem to imply the view that democracy,
> equality and empowerment are to be worked for and brought

about through the benevolent intervention of state agencies—
that these progressive changes are to be advanced through the
action of progressive planners acting on proper advise...Acting
on such a theory, it is all too easy to enter into complicity with a
state bureaucracy that, after all, in all but the most extraordinary situations, serves the dominant or hegemonic interests in
society—the very social forces, in most cases, that must be challenged if the impoverished and oppressed majority are to
improve their lot.

Such perspectives on the role of anthropology and of expertise are
undoubtedly well intentioned but not substantively different from the
kinds of categorical politics advanced, for example, by the Morcha in
Bhopal. It is important to emphasize that such forms of analysis are not
irrelevant but incomplete. It is indeed the case that, as Ferguson
(1990:279–80) puts it, "Since it is the powerlessness that ultimately
underlies the surface conditions of poverty, ill health and hunger, the
larger goal, therefore, ought to be empowerment." However, empowerment entails much more than radical slogans and protest marches. For
social scientists, it entails more than critique, cynical disdain for expertise, the rejection of state bureaucracies, or the celebration of the
agency of various categories of "local" actors. Rather, empowerment
poses the fundamental challenge of how to catalyze and engender societal adaptation to the existent and emergent risk societies. In the context of a rapidly changing world and the emergence of a world risk
society (Beck 1992, 1999), this question is of fundamental relevance
because traditional systems of adaptation to risk, such as those discussed by McCabe (this volume), are either being increasingly rendered irrelevant or, in cases of novel risks, such as Bhopal, are
nonexistent. The challenge of catalyzing adaptation therefore
demands a basic cognizance of the fact that missing expertise and categorical politics are important factors accounting for the patterns of vulnerability that constitute the world risk society today.

CONCLUSION

Disasters, as Oliver-Smith and Hoffman point out in their introduction, are like canaries in the mine for all humankind. The various

chapters of this book reiterate the fact that disasters do not just happen but are often acute manifestations of deep societal fault lines that bear remarkable family resemblances across cultures and contexts. What makes disasters stand out is their dramatic character. The acuteness and intensity of events such as cyclones, earthquakes, and chemical spills draw public attention in ways that pervasive poverty, chronic epidemics, and incipient environmental injustice do not. The prevalence of disasters in societies, however, is indicative of wider adaptive failures, especially the absence of a politics that draws attention to various forms of missing expertise. Moreover, such absences ultimately reflect on the assumptions and the practices of even the most enlightened forms of civic action and the most reflective of academic disciplines.

Notes

I would like to gratefully acknowledge the patience and help provided by Anthony Oliver-Smith and Susanna Hoffman during the course of previous drafts of this essay, which has, for many reasons, been personally difficult to write. I am also indebted to my seminar co-participants and to the gracious hospitality of the School of American Research.

1. The terms "disaster," "vulnerability," and "hazard" are used in this essay in the sense of the definitions in the introduction to this volume.

2. The terms "missing expertise" and "categorical politics" are ideal types developed for the purposes of this chapter and are characterized in the following two paragraphs.

3. The disaster involved a gas leak from a pesticides manufacturing plant owned and operated by the Union Carbide Company, a U.S.-based multinational, on the night of December 3, 1984. The accident occurred as a consequence of water leaking into a container of methyl isocyanate, setting off an exothermic reaction and the consequent production of large quantities of lethal gas. The disaster occurred in the wake of a series of previous accidents, some of which claimed lives, that pointed to poor design and maintenance. (For more on the accident and its prehistory see Chohan 1994; CSE 1985; Dembo, Morehouse, and Wykle 1990; and Morehouse and Subramanian 1986.) The official figure of the total number of people dead in Bhopal is seven thousand. More than half a million people continue to suffer in Bhopal today (Narayan 1999).

4. An excellent example is the history of famine in India; see Sen 1999.

Another good example of successful development of expertise is the case of the Surat plague; see Shah 1997.

5. See Parasuraman and Unnikrishnan 2000.

6. Interview with M. N. Buch, April 1986.

7. Interview with Iswhar Das, November 1986.

8. Ibid.

9. Interview with Pravesh Sharma, September 1986.

10. Note the similarity here with the cases described by Hoffman and Stephens in this volume.

11. See Chohan et al. 1984; Dembo, Morehouse, and Wykle 1990; Morehouse and Subramanian 1986; and Rajan 1999.

12. Among the most prominent anthropologists in this regard were Veena Das, Shiv Visvanathan, and J. P. S. Uberoi. Das and Uberoi were then professors at the Delhi School of Economics. Visvanathan was a professorial fellow at the Center for the Study of Developing Societies.

References

Abbott, M. B., M. W. Binford, M. Brenner, and K. R. Kelts
1997   A 3500 14C Yr High-Resolution Record of Water-Level Changes in Lake
Titicaca, Bolivia/Peru. *Quaternary Research* 47:169–80.

Active, John
1992   Spirituality Defines Subsistence. *Cordova Times,* April 8, 78(15):2.

Adler, Patricia, ed.
1992   *Fire in the Hills.* Berkeley: 2904 Avalon Ave.

Albarracin-Jordan, J., and J. E. Mathews
1990   *Asentamientos prehispanicos del valle de Tiwanaku.* La Paz, Bolivia:
Producciones Cima.

Aldana, Susana
1996   *¿Ocurrencias del tiempo? Fenómenos naturales y sociedad en el Perú colonial.* Vol. I.
Bogota: LA RED/Centro de Investigaciones y Estudios Superiores en
Antropología Social.

Alexander, David
1993   *Natural Disasters.* New York: Chapman and Hall.

Almog, Shmuel
1987   *Zionism and History: The Rise of a New Jewish Consciousness.* New York and
Jerusalem: St. Martin's Press and Magnes Press.

References

Aran, Gideon

1991   Jewish Zionist Fundamentalism: The Bloc of the Faithful (Gush Emunim). In *Fundamentalisms Observed*. M. E. Martin and R. S. Appelby, eds. Pp. 265–344. Chicago: University of Chicago Press.

Arnold, J. E.

1997   Bigger Boats, Crowded Creekbanks: Environmental Stresses in Perspective. *American Antiquity* 62:337–39.

Avineri, Shlomo

1981   Introduction: Zionism as a Revolution. In *The Making of Modern Zionism: The Intellectual Origins of the Jewish State*. Pp. 3–13. New York: Basic Books.

BGIA (Bhopal Group for Information and Action)

1986   *Bhopal, the Newsletter of the Bhopal Group for Information and Action.*

Bales, Richard

1997   Did the Cow Do It? *Illinois State Historical Society Journal* 90(1):2–24.

Basham, A. L.

1959   *The Wonder That Was India*. New York: Grove Press.

Bateson, Gregory

1972   *Steps to an Ecology of Mind*. New York: Ballantine Books.

Bauer, B.

1992   *The Development of the Inca State*. Austin: University of Texas Press.

Bauman, Zigmunt

1989   *Modernity and the Holocaust*. Ithaca: Cornell University Press.

Baverstock, K. F., and J. W. Stather, eds.

1989   *Low Dose Radiation: Biological Bases of Risk Assessment*. London/New York: Taylor and Francis.

Beck, Ulrich

1987   The Anthropological Shock: Chernobyl and the Contours of the Risk Society. *Berkeley Journal of Sociology* 32:153–65.

1992   *Risk Society: Towards a New Modernity*. London: Sage Publications.

1999   *World Risk Society*. Cambridge: Polity Press.

Belshaw, Cyril

1951   Social Consequence of the Mount Lamington Eruption. *Oceania* 21(4):241–51.

Ben-Ari, E.

1989   Masks and Soldiering: The Israeli Army and the Palestinian Uprising. *Cultural Anthropology* 4:372–89.

1998   *Mastering Soldiers: Conflict, Emotions and the Enemy in an Israeli Military Unit*. New York, Oxford: Berghahn Books.

Benthal, Jonathan

1993   *Disasters, Relief, and the Media*. London: Taurus.

Berger, Thomas R.

1985   *Village Journey: The Report of the Alaska Native Review Commission.* New York: Wang and Hill.

Biersack, Aletta

1999   Introduction: From the "New Ecology" to the New Ecologies. *American Anthropologist* 101(1):5–18.

Binford, Michael W., Alan L. Kolata, Mark Brenner, John W. Janusek, Matthew T. Seddon, Mark Abbott, and Jason H. Curtis

1997   Climate Variation and the Rise and Fall of an Andean Civilization. *Quaternary Research* 47:235–48.

Binkley, Marian

1994   *Voices from Off Shore: Narratives of Risk and Danger in the Nova Scotian Deep-Sea Fishery.* St. John's: ISER Books, Memorial University of Newfoundland.

Bird-David, Nurit

1993   Tribal Metaphorization of Human Nature Relatedness: A Comparative Analysis. In *Environmentalism: The View from Anthropology.* Kay Milton, ed. Pp. 112–25. London: Routledge.

Bjarnason, Thoroddur, and Thorolfur Thorlindsson

1993   In Defense of a Folk Model: The "Skipper Effect" in the Icelandic Cod Fishery. *American Anthropologist* 95(2):371–94.

Blaikie, Piers, Terry Cannon, Ian Davis, and Ben Wisner

1994   *At Risk: Natural Hazards, People's Vulnerability, and Disasters.* New York: Routledge.

Board on Natural Disasters [of the National Research Council]

1999   Mitigation Emerges as Major Strategy for Reducing Losses Caused by Natural Disasters. *Science* 284:1943–47.

Boas, Franz

1940   Mythology and Folktales of the North American Indians. In *Race, Language, and Culture.* F. Boaz, ed. Pp. 451–90. New York: Free Press.

Bode, Barbara

1989   *No Bells to Toll.* New York: Scribner.

Borah, Woodrow

   El siglo de la depresión en Nueva España. México, D.F.: Secretaria de Educación Pública.

Boyer, Richard E.

1975   *Gran inundación: Vida y sociedad en México (1629–1638).* México, D.F.: Secretaria de Educación Pública.

Braudel, Fernand

1986   *La historia y las ciencias sociales.* Madrid: Alianza Editorial.

Briggs, Charles, ed.

1996   *Disorderly Discourse: Narratives, Conflict, and Experience.* New York: Oxford University Press.

Brookfield, H. C., and Paula Brown

1967   *Struggle for Land.* New York: Oxford University Press.

Brown, Phil, and Edwin J. Mikkelsen

1990   *No Safe Place: Toxic Waste, Leukemia, and Community Action.* Berkeley: University of California Press.

Bruner, Jerome, Jacqueline Goodnow, and George Austin

1956   *A Study of Thinking.* New York: Wiley.

Bryant, Bunyan, ed.

1995   *Environmental Justice: Issues, Policies, and Solutions.* Washington, DC: Island Press.

Burges, Shelly

1991   Patterns of Anemia in Chiribaya: A Late Intermediate Population in Southern Peru. Paper presented at the American Anthropological Association 90th Annual Meeting, Chicago.

1992   Health at Algodonal: A Preliminary Report. Paper presented at the Society for American Archaeology 57th Annual Meeting, Pittsburgh.

Button, Gregory V.

1993   Social Conflict and the Formation of Emergent Groups in a Technological Disaster: The Exxon Valdez Oil Spill and the Response of Residents in the Area of Homer, Alaska. Ph.D. diss., Department of Anthropology, Brandeis University.

1995   "What You Don't Know Can't Hurt You": The Right to Know and the Shetlands Island Oil Spill. *Human Ecology* 23(2):241–57.

1999   The Negation of Disaster. In *The Angry Earth.* A. Oliver-Smith and S. Hoffman, eds. New York: Routledge.

CSE (Centre for Science and Environment)

The State of India's Environment 1984–85: The Second Citizen's Report. New Delhi: Centre for Science and Environment.

Camino Diez Canseco, Lupe

1996   Una aproximación a la concepción andina de los desastres a través de la Crónica de Guaman Poma, siglo XVII. Virginia García-Acosta, coord. *Historia y Desastres en America Latina* 1:139–64. Lima: LA RED/Centro de Investigaciones y Estudios Superiores en Antropología Social.

Campbell, John K.

1964   *Honour, Family and Patronage.* Oxford: Clarendon Press.

Campbell, Joseph

1949   *Hero with a Thousand Faces.* Princeton: Princeton University Press.

Campos, Isabel

1994   Cuando los dioses se enojan: El huracán de 1561. Vulnerabilidad ideológica y prevención en la sociedad Maya yucateca. Paper presented at the Seminario Internacional "Sociedad y Prevención de Desastres," Mexico, D.F., 1994. Consejo Mexicano de Ciencias Sociales/Universidad Nacional Autónoma de México/LA RED.

Caputo, María Graciela, Jorge Enrique Hardoy, and Hilda Herzer, eds.

1985   *Desastres naturales y sociedad en América latina.* Buenos Aires: Grupo Editor Latinoamericano.

Cassier, Ernst

1966   *The Philosophy of Symbolic Forms.* New Haven: Yale University Press.

Catton, W. R. Jr., and R. E. Dunlap

1980   A New Ecological Paradigm for Post-Exuberant Sociology. *American Behavioral Scientist* (24):15–47.

Caufield, Catherine

1989   *Multiple Exposures: Chronicles of the Radiation Age.* Chicago: University of Chicago Press.

Cerny, Susan S., and Anthony Bruce

1992   *The Berkeley Fire.* Berkeley: Berkeley Architectural Heritage Association.

Chávez Orozco, Luis

1953   *La crisis agrícola novohispana de 1784–85.* Mexico, D.F.: Banco Nacional de Crédito Agrícola y Ganadero.

Chevalier, François

1976   *La formación de los latifundios en México.* Mexico, D.F: Problemas Agrícolas e Industriales de México.

Chohan, T. R., et al.

1994   *Bhopal, the Inside Story: Carbide Workers Speak Out on the World's Worst Industrial Disaster.* New York: Apex Press.

Christensen, Terje, and Sharon Stephens, eds.

2000   *Children and Radiation: Scientific Questions and Political Challenges. Trondheim,* Norway: NOSEB.

Chugoku Newspaper.

1992   *Exposure: Victims of Radiation Speak Out.* K. McIvor, transl. Tokyo: Kodansha International.

Clark, David L.

1996   Monstrosity, Illegibility, Denegation: De Man, Nichol, and the Resistance to Postmodernism. In *Monster Theory.* J. Cohen, ed. Pp. 40–71. Minneapolis: University of Minnesota Press.

Clement, C. O., and M. E. Moseley

1991   The Spring-Fed Irrigation Systemeters of Carrizal, Peru: A Case Study of the Hypothesis of Agrarian Collapse. *Journal of Field Archaeology* 18:425–42.

Coe, Michael D.

1994   *Mexico: From the Olmecs to the Aztecs.* London: Thames and Hudson.

REFERENCES

Cohen, Jeffrey J.
1996   Monster Culture (Seven Theses). In *Monster Theory*. J. Cohen, ed. Pp. 3–25. Minneapolis: University of Minnesota Press.

Cohen, Jeffrey J., ed.
1996   *Monster Theory*. Minneapolis: University of Minnesota Press.

Cohen, Maurie J.
1997   Economic Impacts of the Exxon Valdez Oil Spill. In *The Exxon Valdez Disaster: Readings on a Modern Social Problem*. J. S. Picou, D. A. Gill, and M. J. Cohen, eds. Pp. 133–64. Dubuque, IA: Kendall/Hunt Publishing Co.

Cohen, S.
1988   Criminology and the Uprising. *Tikkun* 3(5):60–62, 95–96.

Cohn, Carol
1987   Sex and Death in the Rational World of Defense Intellectuals. *Signs* 12:687–718.

Collins, Jane
1992   Marxism Confronts the Environment. In *Understanding Economic Process*. Sutti Ortiz and Susan Lees, eds. Monographs in Economic Anthropology no. 10. Lanham, MD: University Press of America.

Cooney, Ellen
1992   After the Great Fire. In *Fire in the Hills*. P. Adler, ed. P. 9. Berkeley: 2904 Avalon Ave.

Cordell, Linda
2000   Aftermath of Chaos in the Pueblo Southwest. In *Environmental Disaster and the Archaeology of Human Response*. Garth Bawden and Richard Maitin Reycraft, eds. Pp. 179–94. Anthropological Papers no. 7. Albuquerque: Maxwell Museum of Anthropology.

Corlin, C.
1975   The Nation in Your Mind: Continuity and Change among Tibetan Refugees in Nepal. Ph.D. diss., Department of Social Anthropology, University of Gothenberg.

Cormack, Mike
1992   *Ideology*. Ann Arbor: University of Michigan Press.

Cromer, Gerald
1988   The Debate about Kahanism in Israeli Society, 1948–1988. In *Occasional Papers of the Harry Frank Guggenheim Foundation*. New York: Harry Frank Guggenheim Foundation.

Cronon, W.
1983   *Nature's Metropolis: Chicago and the Great West*. New York: W. W. Norton.

Curtis, Sue Ann
1992   Cultural Relativism and Risk-Assessment Strategies for Federal Projects. *Human Organization* 51(1):65–70.

Cutter, Susan

1996   Vulnerability to Environmental Hazards. *Progress in Human Geography* 20:4:529–39.

Daley, Patrick, and Dan O'Neill

1997   Sad Is Too Mild a Word: Press Coverage of the Exxon Valdez Oil Spill. In *The Exxon Valdez Disaster: Readings on a Modern Social Problem*. J. S. Picou, D.A. Gill, and M. J. Cohen, eds. Pp. 239–54. Dubuque, IA: Kendall/Hunt Publishing Co.

Darnton, Robert

1975   Writing News and Telling Stories. *Daedalus* 104(2):1.

Das, Sujit

1985   A Worse Aftermath. *Economic and Political Weekly,* December 14.

Das, Veena

1995   *Critical Events 1995: An Anthropological Perspective on Contemporary India.* Delhi: Oxford University Press.

Davis, Nancy Yaw

1984   Contemporary Pacific Eskimo. In *Handbook of North American Indians*, vol. 5. D. Dumas, ed. Pp. 198–204. Washington, DC: Smithsonian Institution.

Dembo, David, Ward Morehouse, and Lucinda Wykle

1990   *Abuse of Power, Social Performance of Multinational Corporations: The Case of Union Carbide.* New York: New Horizons Press.

Denevan, William M.

1987   Terrace Abandonment in the Colca Valley, Peru. In *Pre-Hispanic Agricultural Fields in the Andean Region.* W. M. Denevan, J. Mathewson, and G. Knapp, eds. Pp. 1–43. London: British Archaeological Review.

Dendy, J. H.

1991   A Descriptive Catalog and Preliminary Analysis of Botanical Remains from Archaeological Excavations at Chiribaya Alta, Lower Osmore Drainage, Peru. MA thesis, Anthropology Department, Washington University.

Derrida, Jacques

1974   *On Grammatology.* G. C. Spivak, transl. Baltimore: Johns Hopkins University Press.

Deshen, Shlomo

1970   On Religious Change: The Situational Analysis of Symbolic Action. *Comparative Studies of Society and History* 12:260–74.

Diamond, Stanley

1957   Kibbutz and Shtetl: The History of an Idea. *Social Problems* 5(2):71–99.

Dillon, M., M. Tago, and S. Leiva G.

1999   The Lomas Formations of Coastal Peru: Composition and Biographic History. Paper presented at the Field Museum of Natural History Symposium on El Niño, Chicago.

REFERENCES

DiPerna, Paula

1985 *Cluster Mystery: Epidemic and the Children of Woburn.* St. Louis: C. V. Mosby Company.

Dirks, Robert

1980 Social Responses During Severe Food Shortages and Famine. *Current Anthropology* 21(1):21–44.

Dombrowsky, Wolf R.

1987 Critical Theory in Sociological Disaster Research. In *Sociology of Disasters. Contribution of Sociology to Disaster Research.* R. R. Dynes, E. L. Quarantelli, and D. Wenger, eds. Pp. 331–56. Milan: Franco Angeli Libri.

Doughty, Paul

1999 Plan and Pattern in Reaction to Earthquake: Peru 1970–1998. In *The Angry Earth: Disaster in Anthropological Perspective.* A. Oliver-Smith and S. Hoffman, eds. Pp. 234–56. New York: Routledge.

Douglas, Mary

1966 *Purity and Danger.* New York: Praeger.

1970 *Natural Symbols.* New York: Pantheon.

1975 *Implicit Meanings: Essays in Anthropology.* London: Routledge.

1985 *Risk Acceptability According to the Social Sciences.* New York: Russell Sage.

1990 Risk as a Forensic Source. *Daedalus* 119(4):1–16.

1992 *Risk and Blame: Essays in Cultural Theory.* London: Routledge.

Douglas, Mary, and Aaron Wildavsky

1982 *Risk and Culture: An Essay on the Selection of Technological and Environmental Dangers.* Berkeley: University of California Press.

Douglass, A. E.

1929 The Secrets of the Southwest Solved by Talkative Tree-Rings. *National Geographic* 54:737–70.

Dyer, Christopher L.

1993 Tradition Loss as Secondary Disaster: The Long-Term Cultural Impacts of the Exxon Valdez Oil Spill. *Sociology Spectrum* 13:65–88.

1995 *Assessment of the Economic Development Administrations Post-Disaster Recovery Program after Hurricane Andrew.* Bethesda, MD: Aguirre International.

Dyer, Christopher L., Duane A. Gill, and John S. Picou.

1992 Social Disruption and the Valdez Oil Spill: Alaskan Natives in a Natural Resource Community. *Sociology Spectrum* 12:105–26.

Dynes, Russell

1976 The Comparative Study of Disaster: A Social Organizational Approach. *Mass Emergencies* 1(1):21–32.

Earls, John

1996   Rotative Rank Hierarchy and Recursive Organization: The Andean Peasant Community as a Viable System. *Journal of the Steward Anthropological Society* 24:297–320.

Edelstein, Michael

1988   *Contaminated Communities.* Boulder: Westview Press.

Eggington, Joyce

1980   *The Poisoning of Michigan.* New York: Norton and Company.

Ellis, James E., Michael Cougenhour, and David Swift

1993   Climate Variability, Ecosystem Stability, and the Implications for Range and Livestock Development. In *Range Ecology at Disequilibrium: New Models of Natural Variability and Pastoral Adaptation in Africa Savannas.* R. H. Behnke, I. Scoones, and C. Kerven, eds. Pp. 31–41. London: Overseas Development Institute.

Ellis, James E., Kathleen Galvin, J. Terrence McCabe, and David Swift

1987   *Pastoralism and Drought in Turkana District, Kenya.* Oslo and Nairobi: Norwegian Agency for International Development.

Ellis, James E. and David Swift

1988   Stability of African Pastoral Ecosystems: Alternative Paradigms and Implications for Development. *Journal of Range Management* 41(6):450–59.

Elon, Amos

1981   *The Israelis: Founders and Sons.* Jerusalem: Adam Publishers.

Erickson, Kai

1976   *Everything in Its Path: Destruction of Community in the Buffalo Creek Flood.* New York: Simon and Schuster.

1994   *A New Species of Trouble.* New York: Norton.

Escobar, Antonio

1997   Las sequías y sus impactos en las sociedades del México decimonónico, 1856–1900. In *Historia y desastres en América latina.* V. García-Acosta, ed. Pp. 219–257, vol. II. Lima: LA RED/Centro de Investigaciones y Estudios Superiores en Antropología Social.

n.d.   *Desastres agrícolas en México: Catálogo Histórico. vol. II, 1823–1900.* Mexico, D.F: Centro de Investigaciones y Estudios Superiores en Antropología Social.

Escobar, Arturo

1999   After Nature: Steps to an Antiessentialist Political Ecology. *Current Anthropology* 40(1):1–30.

Evens, Terence M. S.

1980   Stigma and Morality in a Kibbutz. In *A Composite Portrait of Israel.* E. Marx, ed. Pp. 179–210. London: Academic Press.

Even-Zohar, Itamar

1990   The Emergence of a Native Hebrew Culture in Palestine, 1882–1948. *Poetics Today* 11(1):175–91.

Exxon Valdez Oil Spill Trustee Council

1996   *Recovery of Injured Resources and Services: 1996 Status Report.* State of Alaska and National Oceanic and Atmospheric Administration.

Ezrahi, Aviezer

1997   *Rubber Bullets: Power and Conscience in Modern Israel.* New York: Farrar, Straus and Giroux.

Fackenheim, Emil L.

1987   Holocaust. In *Contemporary Jewish Religious Thought.* A. A. Cohen and P. Mendes-Flohr, eds. New York: Charles Scribner's Sons.

Fall, James A., and Charles J. Utermohle

1995   *An Investigation of the Sociocultural Consequences of Outer Continental Shelf Development in Alaska, Prince William Sound.* Anchorage: U.S. Department of the Interior.

Feld, Steven, and Keith H. Basso, eds.

1996   *Senses of Place.* Santa Fe: School of American Research Press.

Ferguson, James

1990   *The Anti Politics Machine.* Cambridge: Cambridge University Press.

Fernandez, Maria Augusta, ed.

1996   *Ciudades en riesgo: Degradación ambiental, riesgos urbanos, y desastres.* Bogotá: LA RED.

Firth, Raymond

1959   *Social Change in Tikopia.* London: Allen and Unwin.

Fiske, John

1989   *Reading the Popular.* New York: Unwin Hyman.

Flanders, Nicholas E.

1989   The Alaska Native Corporation as Conglomerate: The Problem of Profitability. *Human Organization* 48(4):299–312.

Florescano, Enrique, ed.

1969   *Precios del maíz y crisis agrícolas en México (1708–1810): Ensayo sobre el movimiento de los precios y sus consecuencias económicas y sociales.* Mexico, D.F.: El Colegio de México.

1980   *Análisis histórico de las sequías en México.* Mexico, D.F.: Secretaria de Agricultura y Recursos Hidráulicos.

Forrest, T.

1993   Disaster Anniversary: A Social Reconstruction of Time. *Sociological Inquiry* 63(4):444–56.

Freidel, David, Linda Schele, and Joy Parker

1993   *Maya Cosmos.* New York: Morrow.

Freudenberg, William R. and Robert Gramling

1992   Community Impacts of Technological Change: Toward a Longitudinal Perspective. *Social Forces* 70(4):937–55.

Freudenberg, William R. and Timothy R. Jones

1991   Attitudes and Stress in the Presence of Technological Risk: A Test of the Supreme Court Hypothesis. *Social Forces* 4(69):1143–68.

Fried, M.

1967   *The Evolution of Political Society.* New York: Random House.

Friedman, Menachem

1990   Jewish Zealots: Conservative Versus Innovative. In *Religious Radicalism and Politics in the Middle East.* E. Sivan and M. Friedman, eds. Pp. 127–41. Albany: State University of New York Press.

1991   Habad as Messianic Fundamentalism: From Local Participation to Universal Jewish Mission. In *Accounting for Fundamentalisms.* M. E. Martin and R. S. Appelby, eds. Pp. 328–57. Chicago: University of Chicago Press.

Fritz, Charles E.

1961   Disaster. In Contemporary Social Problems. *An Introduction to the Sociology of Deviant Behavior and Social Disorganization.* R. K. Merton and R. A. Nisbet, eds. Pp. 651–94. New York/Chicago: Harcourt, Brace/World Inc.

Gandy, Matthew

1996   Crumbling Land: The Postmodernity Debate and the Analysis of Environmental Problems. *Progress in Human Geography* 20(1):23–40.

Garber, Marjorie

1991   *Vested Interests: Crossdressing and Cultural Anxiety.* New York: Routledge.

García-Acosta, Virginia

1992   Enfoques teóricos para el estudio histórico de los desastres naturales. In *Estudios históricos sobre desastres naturales en México.* V. García-Acosta, ed. Pp. 19–32. Mexico, D.F.: Centro de Investigaciones y Estudios Superiores en Antropología Social.

1993   Sequías históricas de México. *Desastres y Sociedad* (LA RED) 1:83–97.

1994   Las catástrofes agrícolas y sus efectos en la alimentación: Escasez y carestía de maíz, trigo y carne en el México central a fines de la época colonial. In *Sociedad, economía y cultura alimentaria.* S.Doode and.E.P. Pérez, ed. Pp. 347–65. Hermosillo, Mexico: Centro de Investigaciones en Alimentación y Desarrollo/Centro de Investigaciones y Estudios Superiores en Antropología Social.

n.d.   Los sismos en la historia de México: El análisis social. Vol. II. México, D.F.: Fondo de Cultura Económica/Centro de Investigaciones y Estudios Superiores en Antropología Social/Universidad Nacional Autónoma de México.

REFERENCES

García-Acosta, Virginia, ed.
1996   *Historia y desastres en América latina.* Vol. I. Bogotá: LA RED/Centro de Investigaciones y Estudios Superiores en Antropología Social.
1997   *Historia y desastres en América latina.* Vol. II. Lima: LA RED/Centro de Investigaciones y Estudios Superiores en Antropología Social.

García-Acosta, Virginia, Rocío Hernández, Irene Márquez, América Molina, Juan Manuel Pérez, Teresa Rojas, and Cristina Sacristán
1988   Cronología de los sismos en la cuenca del valle de México. *Estudios sobre sismicidad en el valle de México.* Pp. 411–96. Mexico, D.F: Departamento del Distrito Federal/PNUD/HABITAT.

García-Acosta, Virginia, Juan Manuel Pérez, and América Molina
n.d.   *Desastres agrícolas en México: Catálogo histórico.* Vol. I:, *Época prehispánica–1822.* Mexico, D.F.: Centro de Investigaciones y Estudios Superiores en Antropología Social.

García-Acosta, Virginia, and Gerardo Suárez
1996   *Los sismos en la historia de México.* Vol. I. Mexico, D.F.: Fondo de Cultura Económica/Centro de Investigaciones y Estudios Superiores en Antropología Social/Universidad Nacional Autónoma de México.

Geertz, Clifford
1973   Religion as a Cultural System. In *The Interpretations of Cultures.* C. Geertz, ed. Pp. 87–125. New York: Basic Books.

Gibbs, Lois
1982   *Love Canal: My Story.* Albany: State University of New York Press.

Giblin, James L.
1992   *The Politics of Environmental Control in Northeastern Tanzania, 1840–1940.* Philadelphia: University of Pennsylvania Press.

Gibson, Charles
1967   *Los Aztecas bajo el dominio español 1519–1810.* Mexico, D.F.: Siglo XXI Editores.

Giddens, Anthony
1991   *Modernity and Self-Identity.* Stanford: Stanford University Press.

Gitlin, Todd
1980   *The Whole World Is Watching.* Berkeley: University of California Press.

Gladwell, Malcolm
1996   Blowup. *New Yorker* 71:32–36.

Glantz, Michael
1987   Drought and Economic Development in Sub-Saharan Africa. In *Drought and Hunger in Africa: Denying Famine a Future.* M. Glantz, ed. Pp. 37–58. Cambridge: Cambridge University Press.

Goldberg, Carey
1998   The Stresses of Distilling Drama from Life. *New York Times,* Sept. 13.

Goodman, Alan, and Thomas Leatherman
1998   *Building a New Biocultural Synthesis: Political Economic Perspectives in Biological Anthropology.* Ann Arbor: University of Michigan Press.

Gottdiener, M.
1995   *Postmodern Semiotics: Material Culture and the Forms of Post-Modern Life.* Oxford: Blackwell.

Gould, Jay M., and Benjamin A. Goldman
1991   *Deadly Deceit: Low-Level Radiation, High-Level Cover-Up.* New York: Four Walls Eight Windows.

Gould, Peter
1990   *Fire in the Rain: The Democratic Consequences of Chernobyl.* Baltimore: Johns Hopkins University Press.

Graeub, Ralph
1994   *The Petkau Effect: The Devastating Effect of Nuclear Radiation on Human Health and the Environment.* New York: Four Walls Eight Windows.

Greenstein, Edward L.
1985   Jewish Terror—How Did We Get It? An Interview with Uriel Simon. *Oz ve Shalom English Bulletin* 6:15–17.

Greider, William
1997   *One World, Ready or Not: The Manic Logic of Global Capitalism.* New York: Simon and Schuster.

Gusterson, Hugh
1996   *Nuclear Rites: A Weapons Laboratory at the End of the Cold War.* Berkeley: University of California Press.

Haas, J. Eugene, Robert W. Kates, Daniel J. Amaral, Robert A. Olson, Reyes Ramos, and Richard Olson
1973   Early Human Response to the 1972 Earthquake in Managua, Nicaragua of December 23, 1972. *Earthquake Engineering Research Institute Conference Proceedings.* Pp. 929–54, vol. 2.

Halevi, Yossi Klein
1997   Coping, or Not. *Jerusalem Report* (Oct.2):20–22.

Haraway, Donna
1989   *Primate Visions: Gender, Race and Nature in the World of Modern Science.* New York/London: Routledge.

Hareven, Shulamith
1988   The First Forty Years. *Jerusalem Quarterly* 48:3–28.

Harkabi, Yehoshafat
1983   *The Bar Kokhba Syndrome: Risk and Realism in International Politics.* Chappaqua, NY: Rossel Books.

Harr, Jonathan
1997   *A Civil Action*. New York: Random House.

Harries-Jones, Peter
1995   *A Recursive Vision: Ecological Understanding and Gregory Bateson*. Toronto: University of Toronto Press.

Harvey, David
1996   *Justice, Nature and the Geography of Difference*. Cambridge: Blackwell.

Hastorf, Christine A.
1993   *Agriculture and the Onset of Political Inequity before the Inka*. Cambridge: Cambridge University Press.

Haynes, Viktor, and Marko Bojcun
1988   *The Chernobyl Disaster: The True Story of a Catastrophe—An Unanswerable Indictment of Nuclear Power*. London: Hogarth Press.

Hewitt, Kenneth
1983   The Idea of Calamity in a Technocratic Age. In *Interpretations of Calamity*. K. Hewitt, ed. Pp. 3–32. Winchester: Allen and Unwin.
1997   *Regions of Risk. A Geographical Introduction to Disasters*. London: Addison Wesley Longman.

Hewitt, Kenneth, ed.
1983   *Interpretations of Calamity*. Winchester: Allen and Unwin.

Hirsch, William B.
1997   Justice Delayed: Seven Years Later and No End in Sight. In *The Exxon Valdez Disaster: Readings on a Modern Social Problem*. J. S. Picou, D. A. Gill, and M. J. Cohen, eds. Pp. 271–308. Dubuque, Iowa: Kendall/Hunt Publishing Co.

Hirschberg, Peter
1998   Unsettled. *Jerusalem Report* (Jan.8):15–17.

Hoffman, Susanna M.
1998   Eve and Adam among the Ashes: In the Gendered Terrain of Disaster. In *Through Women's Eyes*. E. Enarson and B. Morrow, eds. Pp. 55–61. Westport, CT: Greenwood.
1999a   After Atlas Shrugs. In *The Angry Earth: Disaster in Anthropological Perspective*. A. Oliver-Smith and S. Hoffman, eds. Pp. 302–25. New York: Routledge.
1999b   The Worst of Times, the Best of Times: Toward a Model of Cultural Response to Disaster. In *The Angry Earth*. A. Oliver-Smith and S. Hoffman, eds. Pp. 134–55. New York: Routledge.

Hoffman, Susanna M., and Anthony Oliver-Smith
1999   Anthropology and the Angry Earth: An Overview. In *The Angry Earth: Disaster in Anthropological Perspective*. A. Oliver-Smith and S. Hoffman, eds. Pp. 1–16. New York: Routledge.

Hogg, Richard

1982   Destitution and Development: The Turkana of Northwest Kenya. *Disasters* 6(3):164–68.

Holling, C. S.

1973   Resilience and Stability of Ecological Systems. *Ecol. Syst.* 4:1–23.

1994   An Ecologist's View of the Malthusian Conflict. In *Population, Economic Development and the Environment.* K. Lindahl-Liessling and H. Landberg, eds. New York: Oxford University Press.

Horigan, S.

1988   *Nature and Culture in Western Discourses.* London: Routledge.

Horkheimer, Max, and Theodor W. Adorno

1972   *Dialectic of Enlightenment.* J. Cumming, transl. New York: Seabury.

Horlick-Jones, Tom

1995   Modern Disasters as Outrage and Betrayal. *International Journal of Mass Emergencies and Disasters* 13(3):305–16.

IBC Technical Services, Energy Division

1995   Course Notes. Sixth Residential Summer School on Radiological Protection, Magdalene College, Cambridge, UK.

ICRP

1990   Recommendations of the International Commission on Radiological Protection. Annals of the ICRP 21, publication 60. Pp. 1-3. International Commission on Radiological Protection.

Ilan, Amitzur

1984   The Prophecy of a Jewish State and Its Fulfillment. *Jerusalem Quarterly* 33:125–44.

Impact Assessment, Inc.

1990   Final Report: Economic, Social, and Psychological Impact Assessment of the Exxon Valdez Oil Spill. Anchorage: Oiled Mayors Subcommittee, Alaska Conference of Mayors.

Ingold, Peter

1988   *Hunters and Gatherers.* New York: Random House.

Ingold, Tim

1992   Culture and the Perception of the Environment. In *Bush, Base: Forest Farm.* E. Croll and D. Parkin, eds. Pp. 39–55. London: Routledge.

Iyengar, Shanto

1991   *Is Anyone Responsible?* Chicago: University of Chicago Press.

Jakobson, Roman

1956   Two Aspects of Language and Two Types of Aphasic Disturbances. In *Fundamentals of Language.* Roman Jakobson and Morris Halle, eds. Gravenhage: Mouton.

Jassanoff, Sheila, ed.

1994   *Learning from Disaster: Risk Management after Bhopal:* University of
        Pennsylvania Press.

Johansen, Mayvi

1998   Handtering av Uforutsigbarhet i Fiske og Fangst. *In* Risk and Danger
        Seminar. Tromso University, Institute of Social Sciences (photocopy).

Jones, Robin Russell, and Richard Southwood

1987   *Radiation and Health: The Biological Effects of Low-Level Exposure to Ionizing
        Radiation.* Chichester, UK: John Wiley and Sons.

**Jones, Terry L., Gary M. Brown, L. Mark Raab, Janet L. McVickar, W. Geoffrey
Spaulding, Douglas J. Kennett, Andrew York, and Phillip L. Walker**

1999   Environmental Imperatives Reconsidered: Demographic Crises in Western
        North America During the Medieval Climatic Anomaly. *Current
        Anthropology* 40:137–70.

Jorgensen, Joseph G.

1990   *Oil Age Eskimos.* Berkeley: University of California Press.

Katriel, Tamar

1986   *Talking Straight: Dugri Speech in Israeli Sabra Culture.* Cambridge: Cambridge
        University Press.

Katz, Jacob

1961   *Tradition and Crisis.* New York: Free Press of Glencoe.

Keefer, David K.

1994   The Importance of Earthquake-Induced Landslides to Long-Term Slope
        Erosion and Slope-Failure Hazards in Seismically Active Regions.
        Geomorphology 10:265–84.

Keller, Evelyn Fox

1990a   Critical Silences in Scientific Discourse: Problems of Form and Reform. E.
        F. Keller, ed. Pp. 73–93. New York/London: Routledge.

Kolata, Alan L.

1993   *The Tiwanaku: Portrait of an Andean Civilization.* Cambridge: Blackwell.

Konrad, Herman W.

1985   Fallout of the Wars of the Chacs: The Impact of Hurricanes and
        Implications for Prehispanic Quintana Roo Maya Processes, Status,
        Structure and Stratification: Current Archaeological Reconstructions. The
        Sixteenth Annual Conference of the University of Calgary Archaeological
        Association, Calgary, pp. 321–30.

Kramer, Martin

1997   The Middle East, New and Old. *Daedalus* 126(2):89–112.

Kroll-Smith, J. Stephen

1998   Legislators, Interpreters, and Disasters: The Importance of How as Well as
        What Is Disaster? In *What Is a Disaster? Perspectives on the Question.* E. L.
        Quarantelli, ed. New York: Routledge.

Kroll-Smith, J. Stephen, and Stephen R. Couch

1991   What Is a Disaster? An Ecological Symbolic Approach to Solving the Definitional Debate. International *Journal of Mass Emergencies and Disasters* 9(3):355–66.

Kroll-Smith, J. Stephen, and H. Hugh Floyd

1997   *Bodies in Protest.* New York: New York University Press.

Kruse, John A.

1991   Alaska Inupiat Subsistence and Wage Employment Patterns: Understanding Individual Human Choice. *Human Organization* 50(4):317–26.

Lagos Preisser, Patricia, and Antonio Escobar Ohmstede

1996   La inundación de San Luis Potosí en 1887: Una respuesta organizada. In *Historia y desastres en América latina.* V. García-Acosta, ed. Pp. 325–72, vol. I. Bogota: LA RED/Centro de Investigaciones y Estudios Superiores en Antropología Social.

Lakoff, George, and Mark Johnson

1980   *Metaphors We Live By.* Chicago: University of Chicago Press.

Landau, Yehezkel, ed.

1983   *Religious Zionism: Challenges and Choices.* Jerusalem: Oz ve Shalom.

LA RED

1993   *Red de estudios sociales en prevención de desastres en América latina: Agenda de investigación y constitución orgánica.* Lima: LA RED/Intermediate Technology Development Group.

Laughlin, Charles D.

1995   The Cycle of Meaning: Some Methodological Implications of Biogenetic Structural Theory. In *Anthropology of Religion: A Handbook.* S. Glazier, ed. Pp. 471–88. Ithaca: Cornell University Press.

Lavell, Allan

1993   Ciencias sociales y desastres naturales en América latina: Un encuentro inconcluso. In *Los desastres no son naturales.* A. Maskrey, ed. Pp. 135–54. Bogota: LA RED/Intermediate Technology Development Group.

Lee, Richard B.

1969   Kung! Bushman Subsistence: An Input-Output Analysis. In *Environment and Culture Behavior.* A. P. Vayda, ed. Pp. 47–79. New York: Natural History Press.

Lees, Susan, and Daniel Bates

1990   The Ecology of Cumulative Change. In *The Ecosystem Approach in Anthropology.* Emilio Moran, ed. Pp. 247–78. Ann Arbor: University of Michigan Press.

Lefebvre, Henri

1991   *The Production of Space.* Oxford: Basil Blackwell.

Levine, Adeline
1982   *Love Canal: Science, Politics, and the People.* Lexington, MA: Lexington Books.

LeVine, T.
1992   *Inka Storage Systems.* Norman: University of Oklahoma Press.

Levi-Strauss, Claude
1963a   *Structural Anthropology.* New York: Basic Books.
1963b   The Bear and the Barber. *Journal of the Royal Anthropological Institute* 93.
1966   *The Savage Mind.* Chicago: University of Chicago Press.
1969   *The Raw and the Cooked: Introduction to a Science of Mythology.* J. and D. Weightman, transl. Vol.1. New York: Harper and Row.
1973   *From Honey to Ashes: Introduction to a Science of Mythology.* J. and D. Weightman, transl. Vol. 2. New York: Harper and Row.
1978a   When Myth Becomes History. In *Myth and Meaning.* C. Levi-Strauss, ed. Pp. 34–43. New York: Shocken.
1978b   *The Origin of Table Manners.* J. and D. Weightman, transl. London: Jonathan Cape.
1985   *The View from Afar.* J.Neugnoschel and P. Hoss, transl. New York: Basic Books.
1989   *The Naked Man.* J.and D. Weightman, transl. Chicago: University of Chicago Press.
1995   *The Story of Lynx.* C. Tihanyi, transl. Chicago: University of Chicago Press.

Lewontin, Richard
1982   Organism and Environment. In *Learning, Development and Culture.* H. C. Plotkin, ed. Chichester, UK: Wiley.

Liebman, Charles S., and Eliezer Don-Yehiya
1984   *Religion and Politics in Israel.* Bloomington: Indiana University Press.

Locke, John
1965   *Two Treatises on Government.* New York: New American Library-Mentor.

Lord, Nancy
1991   *Dark Waters.* Homer, AK: Homer Society of Natural History and Pratt Museum.

Lovejoy, Arthur O.
1964   *The Great Chain of Being.* Cambridge: Harvard University Press.

Lovejoy, P. E., and S. Baier
1976   The Desert-Side Economy of the Central Sudan. In *The Politics of Natural Disaster.* M. Glantz, ed. Pp. 145–75. New York: Praeger Publishers.

Lozada, M. C.
1998   The Senorío of Chiribaya: A Bio-Archaeological Study in the Osmore Drainage of Southern Peru. Ph.D. diss., Department of Anthropology, University of Chicago.

Lubbe, Hermann

1993   Security: Risk Perception in the Civilization Process. In *Risk Is a Social Construct: Perceptions of Risk Perception.* B. Ruck, ed. Pp. 23–39. Munich: Knesebeck.

Luhmann, Niklas

1993   *Risk: A Sociological Theory.* Berlin: Walter de Gruyter.

MFC

1985   *The Bhopal Disaster Aftermath: An Epidemiological and Socio-Medical Survey.* Bhopal: Medico Friends Circle (MFC).

MacCormack, Sabine

1988   Pachacuti: Miracles, Punishments, and Last Judgment: Visionary Past and Prophetic Future in Early Colonial Peru. *American Historical Review* 93(4):960–1006.

Marples, David

1988   *The Social Impact of the Chernobyl Disaster.* New York: St. Martin's Press.

Martin, Emily

1994   *Flexible Bodies: Tracking Immunity in America from the Days of Polio to the Age of AIDS.* Boston: Beacon Press.

Maskrey, Andrew

1989   *El manejo popular de los desastres naturales: Estudios de vulnerabilidad y mitigación.* Lima: Intermediate Technology Development Group.

1993   Vulnerabilidad y mitigación de desastres. In *Los desastres no son naturales.* A. Maskrey, ed. Pp. 111–34. Bogotá: LA RED/Intermediate Technology Development Group.

1996   *Terremotos en el trópico húmedo.* Lima: LA RED/Intermediate Technology Development Group.

Maskrey, Andrew, ed.

1993   *Los Desastres No Son Naturales.* Bogotá: LA RED/Intermediate Technology Development Group.

McCabe, J. Terrence

1990   Success and Failure: The Breakdown of Traditional Drought Coping Institutions among the Turkana of Kenya. *Journal of Asian and African Studies* XXV(3–4):146–60.

1997   Risk and Uncertainty among the Maasai of the Ngorongoro Conservation Area in Tanzania: A Case Study in Economic Change. *Nomadic Peoples* (issue unknown).

McCabe, J. Terrence, and J. E. Ellis

1987   Beating the Odds in Arid Africa. *Natural History* 96(1):33–41.

McCabe, J. Terrence, Mollel Naftali, and Tumainai Anna

1997   Food Security and the Role of Cultivation. In *Multiple Land-Use: The Experience of the Ngorongoro Conservation Area, Tanzania.* M. Thompson, ed. Gland, Switzerland: IUCN.

REFERENCES

McCabe, J. Terrence, S. Perkin, and C. Schofield
1992   Can Conservation and Development Be Coupled among Pastoral People? The Maasai of the Ngorongoro Conservation Area, Tanzania. *Human Organization* 51(4):353–66.

Mileti, Dennis
1997   Plenary Address, presented at the Annual Summer Workshop of the Natural Hazards Research and Applications Information Center, University of Colorado, Boulder.

Mintz, Alan
1987   Catastrophe. In *Contemporary Jewish Religious Thought*. A. A. Cohen and P. Mendes-Flohr, eds. Pp. 41–45. New York: Charles Scribner's Sons.

Molina del Villar, América
1990   Junio de 1858: Temblor, iglesia y estado. Hacia una historia social de las catástrofes en la Ciudad de México. Ethnohistory thesis, Escuela Nacional de Antropología e Historia.

1996   Por voluntad divina: Escasez, epidemias y otras calamidades en la Ciudad de México, 1700–1762. Mexico, D.F.: Centro de Investigaciones y Estudios Superiores en Antropología Social.

1998   La propagación del Matlazahuatl: Espacio y sociedad en la Nueva España 1736–1746. Ph.D. diss., Department of History, El Colegio de México.

Molotch, Herbert
1972   Oil Spill in Santa Barbara and Power in America. *Sociological Inquiry* 40(Winter):131–44.

Morehouse, Ward, and M. Arun Subramanian
1986   *The Bhopal Tragedy: What Really Happened and What It Means for American Workers and Communities at Risk*. New York: Council on International and Public Affairs.

Moseley, Michael E.
1992   *The Incas and Their Ancestors*. London: Thames and Hudson.

1997   Catástrofes convergentes: Perspectivas geoarqueológicas sobre desastres naturales colaterales en los Andes centrales. In *Historia y desastres en América latina*. Virginia García-Acosta, ed. Pp. 59–75, vol. II. Lima: LA RED/Centro de Investigaciones y Estudios Superiores en Antropología Social.

Moseley, Michael E., and Alana Cordy-Collins, eds.
1990   *The Northern Dynasties: Kingship and Statecraft in Chimor*. Washington, DC: Dumbarton Oaks.

Moseley, Michael E., and Eric Deeds
1982   The Land in Front of Chan Chan: Agrarian Expansion, Reform, and Collapse in the Moche Valley. In *Chan Chan: Andean Desert City*. M. E. Moseley and K. C. Day, eds. Pp. 25–53. Albuquerque: University of New Mexico Press.

Moseley, Michael E., and R. A. Feldman

1982a   Vivir con crisis: Percepción humana de proceso y tiempo. *Revista del Museo Nacional* 46:267–87.

1982b   Hydrological Dynamics and the Evolution of Field Formeters and Use: Resolving the Knapp-Smith Controversy. *American Antiquity* 49:403–8.

Moseley, Michael E. and J. B. Richardson III

1992   Doomed by Disaster. *Archaeology* 45(6):44–45.

Moseley, Michael E., J. E. Tapia, D. R. Satterlee, and J. B. Richardson III

1992   Flood Events, El Niño Events, and Tectonic Events. In *Paleo-Enso Records, International Symposium, Extended Abstracts*. L. Ortlieb and J. Machare, eds. Pp. 207–12. Lima: OSTROM.

Moseley, Michael E., D. Wagner, and J. B. Richardson III

1991   Space Shuttle Imagery of Recent Catastrophic Change Along the Arid Andean Coast. In *Paleoshorelines and Prehistory: An Investigation of Method*. L. L. Johnson and M. Stright, eds. Pp. 215–35. Boca Raton, FL: CRC Press.

Murphy, Raymond

1994   *Rationality and Nature*. Boulder: Westview Press.

Murra, John V.

1975   The Vertical Control of a Maximum of Ecologic Tiers in the Economies of Andean Societies. In *Formaciones económicas y políticas del mundo andino*. Lima: Instituto de Estudios Peruanos.

Nader, Laura

1996   Anthropological Inquiry into Boundaries, Power, and Knowledge. In *Naked Science*. L. Nader, ed. Pp. 1–25. New York/London: Routledge.

Narayan, Swamy M. R.

1999   Tens of Thousands Still Haunted by 1984 Bhopal Gas Disaster. *Agence France Presse*, December 1.

Neale, R.

1971   Monetization, Commercialization, Market Orientation, and Market Dependence. In *Studies in Economic Anthropology*. G. Dalton, ed. Pp. 25–29. Garden City, NY: Natural History Press.

Nicholson, Irene

1967   *Mexican and Central American Mythology*. London: Paul Hamlyn.

ONERN (Oficina Nacional de Evaluación de Recursos Naturales)

1976   *Inventario, evalucación, y uso racional del recursos naturales de la costa. Vol. II, Informe y anexos*. Lima: ONERN.

1985   *Recursos hidráulicos del sur del Perú*. Lima: ONERN.

Oliver-Smith, Anthony

1979   The Crisis Dyad: Culture and Meaning in Medicine. In *Nourishing the Humanistic: Essays in the Dialogue between the Social Sciences and Medicine*. W. R. Rogers and D. Bernard, eds. Pp. 73–93. Pittsburgh: University of Pittsburgh Press.

REFERENCES

1986a   *The Martyred City: Death and Rebirth in the Peruvian Andes.* Albuquerque: University of New Mexico Press.

1986b   Introduction. Disaster Context and Causation: An Overview of Changing Perspectives in Disaster Research. In *Natural Disasters and Cultural Responses.* A. Oliver-Smith, ed. Pp. 1–34. Studies in Third World Societies, vol. 36. Williamsburg, VA: College of William and Mary.

1994   Perú, 31 De Mayo, 1970: Quinientos años de desastre. *Desastres y Sociedad* (LA RED) 3:9–22.

1995   Perspectivas antropológicas en la investigación de desastres. *Desastres y Sociedad* (LA RED) 5:53–74.

1996   Anthropological Research on Hazards and Disasters. *Annual Review of Anthropology* 25:303–28.

Oliver-Smith, Anthony, and Susanna Hoffman, eds.

1999   *The Angry Earth: Disaster in Anthropological Perspective.* New York: Routledge.

O'Neil, John

1996   Dinosaurs-R-Us: The (Un)Natural History of Jurassic Park. In *Monster Theory.* J. Cohen, ed. Pp. 292–308. Minneapolis: University of Minnesota Press.

Orlove, Benjamin, and David Guillet

1985   Theoretical and Methodological Considerations on the Study of Mountain Peoples: Reflections on the Idea of Subsistence Type and the Role of History in Human Ecology. *Mountain Research and Development* 5:3–18.

Ortloff, C. R., and A. L. Kolata

1993   Climate and Collapse: Agro-Ecological Perspectives on the Decline of the Tiwanaku State. *Journal of Archaeological Sciences* 20:195–221.

Owen, B.

1993a   Early Ceramic Settlement in the Coastal Osmore Valley: Preliminary Report. Paper presented at the Institute of Andean Studies Annual Meeting.

1993b   A Model of Multiethnicity: State Collapse, Competition, and Social Complexity from Tiwanaku to Chiribaya in the Osmore Valley, Peru. Ph.D. diss., Department of Anthropology, University of California–Los Angeles.

Paine, Robert

1989   High-Wire Culture: Comparing Two Agonistic Systems of Self-Esteem. *Man* 24(4):657–72.

1992a   Chernobyl Reaches Norway: The Accident, Science, and the Threat to Cultural Knowledge. *Public Understanding of Science* 1(3):61–280.

1992b   Anthropology Beyond Routine: Cultural Alternatives for the Handling of the Unexpected. *International Journal of Moral and Social Studies* 7(3):183–203.

1992c   Jewish Ontologies of Time and Political Legitimation in Israel. In *The Politics of Time.* H. Rutz, ed. Pp. 150–179, vol. 4. Washington, DC: American Ethnological Society.

1993   Israel: The Making of Self in the "Pioneering" of the Nation. In *Defining the Nation.* Orvar Lofgren and Ulf Hannerz, eds. Ethnos 3–4:222–240.

1995a   Behind the Hebron Massacre, 1994. *Anthropology Today* 11(1):8–15.

1995b   Topophilia, Zionism, and "Certainty": Making a Place out of the Space That Became Israel Again. In *The Pursuit of Certainty.* W. James, ed. Pp. 161–92. London: Routledge.

1996   Signal Values and Politics: The Puzzle of the Israel-Palestinian Prisoner Exchange, May 1985. *Anthropological Forum* 7(2):245–58.

Palerm, Angel

1980   *Antropología y Marxismo.* Mexico, D.F.: Centro de Investigaciones Superiores del Instituto Nacional de Antropología e Historia/Editorial Nueva Imagen.

Palmer, B.

1990   *Descent into Discourse: The Reification of Language and the Writing of Social History,* Philadelphia: Temple University Press

Parasuraman, S., and P. v. Unnikrishnan, eds.

2000   *India Disasters Report.* Delhi: Oxford University Press.

Pastor, Rodolfo

1981   Introducción. In *Fuentes para la historia de la crisis agrícola de 1785–1786.* E. Florescano, ed. Pp. 29–63, vol. I. Mexico, D.F.: Archivo General de la Nación.

Patterson, Thomas

1994   Toward a Properly Historical Ecology. In *Historical Ecology: Cultural Knowledge and Changing Landscapes.* C. Crumley, ed. Pp. 223–38. Santa Fe: School of American Research.

Pehrson, Robert N.

1966   *The Social Organization of the Marri Baluch.* Chicago: Aldine.

Peterson, Scott

1990   *Native American Prophecies.* New York: Paragon House.

Phoenix Journal

1992–94   Oakland, CA.

Picou, J. Steven, and Duane A. Gill

1995   *The Exxon Valdez Oil Spill and Alaska Natives in Cordova: A User's Guide to 1991 and 1992 Survey Data.* Draft report to the Regional Citizens Advisory Council. Social Science Research Center, Mississippi State University.

Picou, J. S., D. A. Gill, and M. J. Cohen, eds.

1997   *The Exxon Valdez Disaster: Readings on a Modern Social Problem.* Dubuque, IA: Kendall/Hunt Publishing Co.

Piper, Ernest

1993   *The Exxon Valdez Oil Spill: Final Report, State of Alaska Response.* Anchorage: Alaska Department of Environmental Conservation.

REFERENCES

Poffenberger, Mark, and Betsy McGean

1998   *Village Voices, Forest Choices: Joint Forest Management in India.* Delhi: Oxford University Press.

Poveda, German, and Oscar J. Mesa

1997   Tropical South America and Large Scale Ocean-Atmospheric Phenomena. *Journal of Climate* 10:2690–2701.

Prattis, J. Ian

1984   Man and Metaphor. *Communication and Cognition* 17(2/3):187–204.

1997   Anthropology at the Edge. Lanham, MD: University Press of America.

Prescott, Anne L.

1996   The Odd Couple: Gargantua and Tom Thumb. In *Monster Theory.* J. Cohen, ed. Pp. 75–91. Minneapolis: University of Minnesota Press.

Pringle, Peter

1981   *The Nuclear Barons.* New York: Holt, Rinehart and Winston.

Quarantelli, E. L.

1985   What Is Disaster? The Need for Clarification in Definition and Conceptualization in Research. In *Disasters and Mental Health: Selected Contemporary Perspectives.* S. Solomon, ed. Washington, DC: U.S. Government Printing Office.

1991   More and Worse Disasters in the Future. Paper presented at the International Conference on the Impact of Natural Disasters: Agenda for Future Action, UCLA, Los Angeles, July 10–12.

Quinn, W. H., V. T. Neal, and S. E. Antunez de Mayolo

1987   El Niño Occurrences over the Past Four and a Half Centuries. *Journal of Geophysical Research* 92:14449–61.

Raab, L. M., and Daniel O. Larson

1997   Medieval Climatic Anomaly and Punctuated Cultural Evolution in Coastal Southern California. *American Antiquity* 62:319–36.

Radder, Hans

1992   Normative Reflections on Constructivist Approaches to Science and Technology. *Social Studies of Science* 22:141–73

Rajan, S. Ravi

1988   Rehabilitation and Volunteerism in Bhopal. *Lokayan Bulletin* 6(1/2):3–32.

1999   Bhopal: Vulnerability, Routinization and the Chronic Disaster. In *The Angry Earth: Disaster in Anthropological Perspective.* A. Oliver-Smith and S. Hoffman, eds. New York: Routledge.

Ram, N.

2001   Scimitars in the Sun. *Frontline* January 19, 2001:4–18.

Rappaport, Roy

1968   *Pigs for the Ancestors.* New Haven: Yale University Press.

1988 Toward Postmodern Risk Analysis. *Risk Analysis* 8(2).

1992 Distinguished Lecture in General Anthropology: The Anthropology of Trouble. *American Anthropologist* 95(2):295–303.

Ravitzky, Aviezer

1985 *The Phenomenon of Kahanism: Consciousness and Political Reality.* Jerusalem: The Institute of Contemporary Jewry.

1987 Peace. In *Contemporary Jewish Religious Thought.* A. A. Cohen and P. Mendes-Flohr, eds. Pp. 685–702. New York: Charles Scribner's Sons.

1997 *Messianism, Zionism, and Jewish Religious Radicalism.* Chicago: University of Chicago Press.

Redmond, Charles L.

1999 *Human Impact on Ancient Environments.* Tucson: University of Arizona Press.

Robben, Antonius C. G. M.

1989 *Sons of the Sea Goddess.* New York: Columbia University Press.

Rodin, Mari, Michael Downs, John Petterson, and John Russell

1997 Community Impacts of the Exxon Valdez Oil Spill. In *The Exxon Valdez Disaster: Readings on a Modern Social Problem.* J. S. Picou, D. A. Gill, and M. J. Cohen, eds. Pp. 193–210. Dubuque, IA: Kendall/Hunt Publishing Co.

Rojas, Teresa, Juan Manuel Pérez, and Virginia García-Acosta, eds.

1987 *"Y volvió a temblar...": Cronología de los sismos en México (de 1 Pedernal a 1821).* Mexico, D.F.: Centro de Investigaciones y Estudios Superiores en Antropología Social.

Rostworowski de Diez Canseco, Maria

1981 *El Litoral Peruana.* Lima: Instituto de Estudios Peruanos.

Roth, Eric

1996 Traditional Pastoral Strategies in a Modern World: An Example from Northern Kenya. *Human Organization* 55(2).

Rowe, J. H.

1946 Inca Culture at the Time of the Spanish Conquest. In *Handbook of South American Indians, vol. 2, the Andean Civilizations.* J. Steward, ed. Pp. 183–330. Washington DC: U.S. Government Printing Office.

Rubinstein, Amnon

1984 *The Zionist Dream Revisited: From Herzl to Gush Emunim and Back.* New York: Schocken Books.

Ruck, Bayerische, ed.

1993 *Risk Is a Construct: Perceptions of Risk Perception.* Munich: Knesebeck.

Ryan, Charlotte

1991 *Prime Time Activism.* Boston: South End Press.

Sathyamala

1988 The Medical Profession and the Bhopal Tragedy. *Lokayan Bulletin* 6(1/2):33–56.

Satterlee, D.

1993   Impact of a Fourteenth-Century El Niño Flood on an Indigenous
        Population near Ilo, Peru. Ph.D. diss., Department of Anthropology,
        University of Florida.

Saussure, Ferdinand de

1966   *A Course in General Linguistics.* C. Gally and A. Sechehaye, transl. New York:
        McGraw Hill.

Sawislak, Karen

1994   *Smoldering City: Chicago and the Great Fire.* Chicago: University of Chicago
        Press.

Saxena, N. C.

1997   *The Saga of Participatory Forest Management in India.* Jakarta: CIFOR.

Schaaf, Crystal B.

1988   Establishment and Demise of Moche V: Assessment of the Climatic
        Impact. MA thesis, Department of Anthropology, Harvard University
        Extension School.

Schneider, David M.

1957   Typhoons on Yap. *Human Organization* 16(2):10–15.

1976   Notes toward a Theory of Culture. In *Meaning in Anthropology.* K. Basso
        and H. Selby, eds. Pp. 197–220. Albuquerque: University of New Mexico
        Press.

Scholem, Gershom

1971   *The Messianic Idea in Judaism and Other Essays.* New York: Schocken Books.

Schudson, Michael

1995   *The Power of News.* Cambridge: Harvard University Press.

Schweid, Eliezer

1985   *The Land of Israel: National Home or Land of Destiny.* London: Associated
        University Presses.

Schwimmer, Eric

1969   *Cultural Consequences of a Volcanic Eruption Experienced by the Mt. Lamington
        Orokaiva.* Salem: University of Oregon Press.

Scott, James C.

1998   *Seeing Like a State: How Certain Schemes to Improve the Human Condition Have
        Failed.* New Haven: Yale University Press.

Segal, Haggai

1988   *Dear Brothers: The West Bank Jewish Underground.* I.B.R.T. Jerusalem, transl.
        Jerusalem: Beit-Shamai Publications Inc.

Segre, Dan V.

1980   *A Crisis in Identity: Israel and Zionism.* Oxford: Oxford University Press.

Seltzer, Geoffrey O.

1991   Glacial History and Climatic Change in the Peruvian-Bolivian Andes.
        Ph.D. diss., Department of Geology, University of Minnesota.

Seltzer, Geoffrey O., and Christine A. Hastorf

1990   Climatic Change and Its Effects on Prehistoric Agriculture in the Peruvian Andes. *Journal of Field Archaeology* 17:397–417.

Sen, Amartya

1999   *Poverty and Famines.* Delhi: Oxford University Press.

Shah, Ahanshyam

1997   *Public Health and Urban Development: The Plague in Surat.* New Delhi: Sage Publications.

Shapiro, D. S.

1985   The Jewish Attitude Towards Peace and War. In *Violence and the Value of Life in Jewish Tradition.* Y. Landau, ed. Pp. 56–103. Jerusalem: Oz Ve Shalom Publications.

Shimada, I., C. B. Schaff, L. G. Thompson, and E. Mosley-Thompson

1991   Cultural Impacts of Severe Droughts in the Prehistoric Andes: Application of a 1,500-Year Ice Core Precipitation Record. *World Archaeology* 22:247–70.

Sjoberg, Gideon

1962   Disasters and Social Change. In *Man and Society in Disaster.* G. Baker and D. Chapman, eds. New York: Basic Books.

Smith, Carl

1995   *Disorder and the Shape of Belief.* Chicago: University of Chicago Press.

Soule, Michael E.

1995   The Social Siege of Nature. In *Reinventing Nature? Responses to Post-Modern Deconstruction.* Michael E. Soule and Gary Lease, eds. Pp.137–70. Washington, DC, and Covelo, CA: Island Press.

Spencer, Robert F.

1959   *The North Alaskan Eskimo: A Study in Ecology and Society.* Washington: U.S. Government Printing Office.

Stine, S.

1994   Extreme and Persistent Drought in California and Patagonia during Mediaeval Times. *Nature* 369:546–49.

Stephens, Sharon

1993   Children and Radiation Conference Reports. Oslo: Norwegian Centre for Child Research.

1994   Children and Environment: Local Worlds and Global Connections. *Childhood* 2(1994):1–22.

1995   Social Consequences of Chernobyl in Norway: An Anthropological Perspective. In *Biomedical and Psychosocial Consequences of Radiation from Man-Made Radionuclides in the Biosphere.* B. Henningsen, ed. Pp. 181–202. Trondheim: Royal Norwegian Social Science Letters.

1996   The "Cultural Fallout" of Chernobyl Radiation in Norwegian Sami Regions: Implications for Children. In *Children and the Politics of Culture.* S. Stephens, ed. Pp. 292–321. Princeton: Princeton University Press.

REFERENCES

Stonich, Susan

1993 *"I Am Destroying the Land!" The Political Ecology of Poverty and Environmental Destruction in Honduras.* Boulder: Westview Press.

Strathern, Marilyn

1980 No Nature, No Culture: The Hagen Case. In *Nature, Culture and Gender.* C. MacCormack and M. Strathern, eds. Pp. 174–219. Cambridge: Cambridge University Press.

Stratton, Lee

1989 *Resource Use in Cordova: A Coastal Community of South Central Alaska.* Technical Paper No. 153. Anchorage: Alaska Department of Fish and Game, Subsistence Division.

Suárez, Gerardo, Virginia García-Acosta, and Roland Gaulon

1994 Active Crustal Deformation in the Jalisco Block, Mexico: Evidence of a Great Historical Earthquake in the 16th Century. *Tectonophysics* (234):117–27.

Tainter, Joseph A.

1988 *The Collapse of Complex Societies.* New York: Cambridge University Press

Talmon, Yonina

1972 *Family and Community in the Kibbutz.* Cambridge, Mass: Harvard University Press.

Taylor, Laurison Sale

1979 *Organization for Radiation Protection: The Operations of the ICRP and NCRP, 1928–1974.* Washington, DC: U.S. Department of Energy.

Tester, K.

1991 *Animals and Society: The Humanity of Animal Rights.* London: Routledge.

Thompson, Edward P.

1994 *Historia social y antropología.* Mexico, D.F.: Instituto Mora.

Thompson, Lonnie G., M. E. Davis, and E. Mosley-Thompson

1994 Glacial Records of Global Climate: A 1500-Year Tropical Ice Core Record of Climate. *Human Ecology* 22:83–95.

Thompson, Lonnie G., E. Mosley-Thompson, J. F. Bolzan, and B. R. Koci

1985 A 1500-Year Record of Tropical Precipitation in Ice Cores from the Quelccaya Ice Cap, Peru. *Science* 229:971–73.

Thompson, Lonnie G., E. Mosley-Thompson, W. Dansgaard, and P. M. Grootes

1986 The Little Ice Age as Recorded in the Stratigraphy of the Tropical Quelccaya Ice Cap. *Science* 234:361–64.

Thompson, Lonnie G., E. Mosley-Thompson, M. E. Davis, P. N. Lin, K. A. Henderson, J. Cole-Dai, J. F. Bolzan, and K. Liu

1995 Late Glacial Stage and Holocene Tropical Ice Core Records from Huascarán, Peru. *Science* 269:46–50.

Thompson, Lonnie G., E. Mosley-Thompson, D. A. Peel, R. Mulvaney, J. Cole-Dai, P. N. Lin, M. E. Davis, and C. F. Raymond

1994   Climate since A.D. 1510 on Dyer Plateau, Antarctic Peninsula: Evidence for Recent Climate Change. *Annals of Glaciology* 20:420–26.

Time Life Books

1982   *Volcanos.* Alexandria, VA: Time Life.

Torry, William I.

1978a   Natural Disasters, Social Structure and Change in Traditional Societies. *Journal of Asian and African Studies* XIII(3–4):167–83.

1978b   Bureaucracy, Community and Natural Disasters. Human Organization 37:302–8.

1979a   Anthropology and Disaster Research. *Disasters* 3(1):43–52.

1979b   Anthropological Studies in Hazardous Environments: Past Trends and New Horizons. *Current Anthropology* 20:517–41.

Tossi, J., and ONERN

1976   Mapa ecológico del Perú: Guía explicativa. Lima: ONERN.

Traweek, Sharon

1988   *Beamtimes and Lifetimes: The World of High Energy Physics.* Cambridge: Harvard University Press.

Tuan, Y-F

1984   In Place, Out of Place. In *Place: Experience and Symbol.* I. M. Richardson, ed. Pp. 3–10. Baton Rouge: Louisiana State University.

Tuchman, Gaye

1978   *Making News: A Study in the Construction of Reality.* New York: Free Press.

Turner, Victor

1974   *Dramas, Fields, and Metaphors.* Ithaca: Cornell University Press.

Varley, Ann, ed.

1994   *Disasters, Development and Environment.* London: Wiley.

Vayda, Andrew P., and Bonnie J. McCay

1975   New Directions in Ecology and Anthropology. *Annual Reviews in Anthropology* 1975:293–306.

Vayk, J. Peter

1978   *Doomsday Has Been Cancelled.* Menlo Park: Peace Publishers.

Verano, John

1987   Cranial Microvariation at Pacatanamu: A Study of Cemetery Population Variability. Ph.D. diss., Department of Anthropology, University of California–Los Angeles.

Visvanathan, Shiv

1988   Reflections on the Transfer of Technology: Notes on the New Panopticon. *Lokayan Bulletin* 6(1/2):147–60.

Vital, David

1975   *The Origins of Zionism.* Oxford: Clarendon Press.

Vorosmarty, Charles J., Berrien Moore III, Annette L. Grace, and Patricia Gildea

1989   Continental Scale Models of Water Balance and Fluvial Transport: An Application to South America. *Journal of Global Biochemical Cycles* 3:241–65.

Waddell, Eric

1975   How the Enga Cope with Frost: Responses to Climatic Perturbations in the Central Highlands of New Guinea. *Human Ecology* 3(4):249–73.

Wagner, Roy

1986   *Symbols That Stand for Themselves.* Chicago: University of Chicago Press.

Wallace, Anthony .F.C.

1956a   Revitalization Movements. *American Anthropologist* 58:204–81.

1956b   Human Behavior in Extreme Situations. Washington, DC: National Academy of Sciences-National Research Council.

1956c   Mazeway Resynthesis: A Bio-Cultural Theory of Religious Inspiration. *Transactions of the New York Academy of Sciences* 18:626–38.

1957   Mazeway Disintegration: The Individual's Perception of Socio-Cultural Disorganization. *Human Organization* 16:23–27.

Wallman, Sandra

1998   Ordinary Women and Shapes of Knowledge: Perspectives on the Context of STD and AIDS. *Public Understanding of Science* 7:169–85.

Warner, W. Lloyd

1947   *The Social System of the Modern Factory.* Oxford: Oxford University Press.

Waterhouse, Ruth

1996   Beowulf as Palimpsest. In *Monster Theory.* J. Cohen, ed. Pp. 26–39. Minneapolis: University of Minnesota Press.

Waters, Frank

1975   *Mexico Mystique.* Chicago: Sage Books.

1977   *Book of the Hopi.* Harmondsworth: Penguin.

Watts, Michael

1983   On the Poverty of Theory: Natural Hazards Research in Context. In *Interpretations of Calamity.* K. Hewitt, ed. Pp. 231–262. Winchester: Allen & Unwin Inc.

Weber, M.

1949   *The Methodology of Social Sciences.* New York: Glencoe.

Weiner, Herbert

1970   *The Wild Goats of Ein Gedi: A Journal of Religious Encounters in the Holy Land.* New York: Atheneum.

Weiskel, Timothy C., and Richard A. Grey

1992   *Environmental Decline and Public Policy.* Ann Arbor: The Pierian Press.

Weissbrod, Lily

1982   Gush Emunim Ideology: From Religious Doctrine to Political Action. *Middle Eastern Studies* 18(3):265-75.

Westgate, K. N. and P. O'Keefe

1976   *Some Definitions of Disaster.* Bradford, UK: Department of Geography, University of Bradford.

Wilches-Chaux, Gustavo

1989   *Desastres, ecologismo, y formación profesional.* Popayan: Servicio Nacional de Aprendizaje (SENA).

1993   La vulnerabilidad global. In *Los desastres no son naturales.* A. Maskrey, ed. Pp. 9–50. Bogotá: LA RED/Intermediate Technology Development Group.

Willey, Gordon

1953   *Prehistoric Settlement Patterns in the Viru Valley, Peru.* Bureau of American Ethnology Bulletin No. 155. Washington, DC: Smithsonian Institution.

Williams, P. R.

1997   Disaster in the Development of Agriculture and the Evolution of Social Complexity in the South-Central Andean Sierra. Ph.D. diss., Department of Anthropology, University of Florida.

Williams, Raymond

1977   *Marxism and Literature.* Oxford: Oxford University Press.

1980   *Problems in Materialism and Culture.* New York: Verso.

Williams, Sloan

1990   The Skeletal Biology of Estuquina: A Late Intermediate Period Site in Southern Peru. Ph.D. diss., Department of Anthropology, Northwestern University.

Willis, Aaron

1992   Redefining Religious Zionism: Shas' Ethno-Politics. *Israel Studies Bulletin* 8(2):3–8.

Wilson, David

1988   *Prehispanic Settlement Patterns in the Lower Santa Valley, Peru.* Washington, DC: Smithsonian Institution Press.

Winchester, Peter

1992   *Power, Choice and Vulnerability.* London: James and James Publications.

Wittfogel, Karl A.

1953   *Oriental Despotism.* New Haven: Yale University Press.

Woolgar, S.

1988   *Science: The Very Idea.* Chichester and London: Ellis Harwood and Tavistock.

REFERENCES

Wybrow, Peter

1986   Comparative Responses and Experiences to Migration Due to Oil Development in Scotland. ISER Conference Papers vol. 1, pp. 53–73. St. John's: Institute of Social and Economic Research, Memorial University of Newfoundland.

Wyckoff, Harold Orville

1980   *From "Quantity of Radiation" and "Dose" to Exposure" and "Absorbed Dose": A Historical Review.* Washington, DC: National Council of Radiation Protection and Measurements.

Zaman, Mohammed Q.

1988   The Socioeconomic and Political Dynamics of Adjustment to Riverbank Erosion Hazard and Population Resettlement in the Bramaputra-Jamuna Floodplain. Ph.D. diss., University of Manitoba.

1991   Social Structure and Process in Char Land Settlement in the Bramaputra-Jamuna Floodplain. *Man* 26(4):549–66.

1994   Ethnography of Disasters: Making Sense of Flood and Erosion in Bangladesh. *Eastern Anthropology* 47:129–55.

Zompolis, Gregory N.

1994   *Operation Pet Rescue: Animal Survivors of the Oakland, California, Firestorm.* Exeter, NH: J. N. Townsend Publishing.

Zulaika, Joseba

1981   *Terranova: The Ethos and Luck of Deep-Sea Fishermen.* St. John's: ISER Books, Memorial University of Newfoundland.

1988   *Basque Violence: Metaphor and Sacrament.* Reno: University of Nevada Press.

Index

A-bomb survivors, 101
absence of information, 61–62, 74
absorbed doses in radiation effects, 99, 100
"acceptable" exposures, 98, 102–3
acceptable risks, 18–19, 94, 98, 248
active agency: vs. ignoring risks, 67; vs. passive victimhood, 147
activist organizations: antinuclear organizations, 93; categorical politics and, 238, 250–54; demonstrations, 252; Oakland, 120
adaptability and responses: adaptation, 21, 65; anthropological theory, 7–9; compromised, 6, 7, 45, 185; coping strategies, 234–35; degrees of disaster and, 8; differential abilities, 62–65; extreme behavior and, 69; flexibility, 9, 13; to hurricanes, 53; linkages, 6; long-standing disasters and, 9; loss of opportunity, 163; on-site research and, 12; punctuated entropy and, 164–66; resistance and resilience, 215; straining limits of, 44; Turkana responses, 220–21; types of, 65; urban dwellers, 64
adaptive entropy and collapse, 20
Adorno, Theodor W., 138, 139
agents of disasters, 3, 57; new forms of, 43; technologies as, 43–44; types of, 25
agriculture: agrarian collapse, 194–95; agricultural crises, 51–52, 64; arable land, 194; differential drought stresses,

198; East African herders and, 233; Mexican colonial era, 54, 64; Peruvian Andes, 188, 200–203, 204–8; relationship to epidemics, 62
agropastoralism in Peruvian Andes, 190
aid and aid agencies. *See* relief efforts
airplane crashes, 137–38
ALARA (as low as reasonably achievable), 97, 105
ALARP (as low as reasonably practical), 105
Alaska Natives Claims Act, 171–72
alliances: "borrowing" in Turkana, 213–14, 226; mobilization of, 10; mutual aid, 227, 228; revealed by disasters, 9, 58
alternative scientists, 94, 101
alternative solutions in Bhopal, 254
altitude, crops and, 205–6
altruism and self-interest, 10
ANCSA (Alaska Natives Claims Act), 171–72
Anderson, Anne, 144, 148–49
Anderson, Jimmy, 148
Angorot, 213–14, 226
animals, 124, 174–76. *See also* herds
anniversaries of disasters, 119, 133, 155
annual cycles in Turkana, 221–23
anthropology: "anthropology of trouble," 46; applied, 14–17; Bhopal disaster and, 254–57; as catalyst for action, 257; disaster focal points for, 45–47; disaster research and, 7–9, 12–14; early disaster studies, 4–5; ethnography of disaster,

School of American Research
Advanced Seminar Series

PUBLISHED BY SAR PRESS

PUBLISHED BY SAR PRESS

-WOMEN & MEN IN THE PREHISPANIC
SOUTHWEST: LABOR, POWER, & PRESTIGE
   Patricia L. Crown, ed.

HISTORY IN PERSON: ENDURING
STRUGGLES, CONTENTIOUS PRACTICE,
INTIMATE IDENTITIES
   Dorothy Holland and Jean Lave, eds.

THE EMPIRE OF THINGS: REGIMES OF
VALUE AND MATERIAL CULTURE
   Fred R. Myers, ed.

URUK MESOPOTAMIA & ITS NEIGHBORS:
CROSS-CULTURAL INTERACTIONS IN THE
ERA OF STATE FORMATION
   Mitchell S. Rothman, ed.

PUBLISHED BY CAMBRIDGE UNIVERSITY PRESS

DREAMING: ANTHROPOLOGICAL AND
PSYCHOLOGICAL INTERPRETATIONS
   Barbara Tedlock, ed.

THE ANASAZI IN A CHANGING
ENVIRONMENT
   George J. Gumerman, ed.

REGIONAL PERSPECTIVES ON THE OLMEC
   Robert J. Sharer & David C. Grove, eds.

THE CHEMISTRY OF PREHISTORIC
HUMAN BONE
   T. Douglas Price, ed.

THE EMERGENCE OF MODERN HUMANS:
BIOCULTURAL ADAPTATIONS IN THE
LATER PLEISTOCENE
   Erik Trinkaus, ed.

THE ANTHROPOLOGY OF WAR
   Jonathan Haas, ed.

THE EVOLUTION OF POLITICAL SYSTEMS
   Steadman Upham, ed.

CLASSIC MAYA POLITICAL HISTORY:
HIEROGLYPHIC AND ARCHAEOLOGICAL
EVIDENCE
   T. Patrick Culbert, ed.

TURKO-PERSIA IN HISTORICAL
PERSPECTIVE
   Robert L. Canfield, ed.

CHIEFDOMS: POWER, ECONOMY, AND
IDEOLOGY
   Timothy Earle, ed.

PUBLISHED BY UNIVERSITY OF CALIFORNIA PRESS

WRITING CULTURE: THE POETICS
AND POLITICS OF ETHNOGRAPHY
   James Clifford &
   George E. Marcus, eds.

PUBLISHED BY UNIVERSITY OF ARIZONA PRESS

THE COLLAPSE OF ANCIENT STATES AND
CIVILIZATIONS
   Norman Yoffee &
   George L. Cowgill, eds.

PUBLISHED BY UNIVERSITY OF NEW MEXICO PRESS

Photo by Katrina Lasko

Participants in the School of American Research advanced seminar "Catastrophe and Culture: The Anthropology of Disaster," Santa Fe, New Mexico, October 1997. From left: Virginia García-Acosta, J. Terrence McCabe, Susanna M. Hoffman, Michael Moseley, Gregory V. Button, Rajan Ravi, Anthony Oliver-Smith, Christopher L. Dyer, Robert Paine. Seated: Sharon Stephens.